GCSE
BUSINESS STUDIES

Pat Bond with Jill Martin

Heinemann Educational Publishers,
Halley Court, Jordan Hill, Oxford OX2 8EJ
a division of Reed Educational & Professional Publishing Ltd

Heinemann is a registered trademark of Reed Educational & Professional Publishing Limited

OXFORD MELBOURNE AUCKLAND JOHANNESBURG BLANTYRE GABORONE
IBADAN PORTSMOUTH (NH) USA CHICAGO

© NDTEF/Learning Solutuions Partnership Ltd 1998

First published 1998
2002 2001 2000 99 98
10 9 8 7 6 5 4 3 2 1

A catalogue record for this book is available from the British Library on request.

ISBN 0 435 011 5

All rights reserved.

Apart from any fair dealing for the purpose of research or private study, or criticism or review as permitted under the terms of the UK Copyright, Designs and Patents Act, 1988, this publication may not be reproduced, stored or transmitted, in any form or by any means, without the prior permission in writing of the publishers, or in the case of reprographic reproduction only in accordance with the terms of the licences issued by the Copyright Licensing Agency in the UK, or in accordance with the terms of licenses issued by the appropriate Reproduction Rights Organization outside the UK. Enquiries concerning reproduction outside the terms stated here should be sent to the publishers at the United Kingdom address printed on this page.

All rights reserved. No part of this publication may be reproduced in any material form (including photocopying or storing it in any medium by electronic means and whether or not transiently or incidentally to some other use of this publication) without the prior written permission of the copyright owner, except in accordance with the provisions of the Copyright, Designs and Patents Act 1988 or under the terms of a licence issued by the Copyright Licensing Agency, 90 Tottenham Court Road, London W1P 0LP. Applications for the copyright of this publication should be addressed in the first instance to the publisher.

Designed by Wendi Watson
Cover designed by Red Giraffe
Typeset by Techset
Printed and bound in Spain by Eldelvives
Illustrations by Keith Richmond, Phil Garner, Pat Murray and Samantha Rugan

Contents

UNIT 1 PURPOSES AND TYPES OF BUSINESS ORGANISATION

Section		Page
1	Business activity	1
2	Types of business ownership	17
3	Management, structure and organisation of business	47
4	Objectives of business	75
5	Influences on business	91
6	New technology	103

UNIT 2 UNDERSTANDING HUMAN RESOURCES

Section		Page
1	People in business	113
2	Role of human resources	131
3	Employer/employee relations	149

UNIT 3 SALES AND MARKETING

Section		Page
1	Marketing	159
2	Market research	175
3	The product	183
4	The price	193
5	The place	201
6	Promotion	211

UNIT 4 ACCOUNTING AND FINANCE

Section		Page
1	Financial planning	223
2	Sources of finance	239
3	Accounting	253

UNIT 5 PRODUCTION

Section		Page
1	Production objectives	269
2	Methods of production	275
3	Calculating the costs of production	283
4	Stock control systems	289
5	Business location	295
6	Quality control and quality assurance	303

INDEX   310

How to use this book

This book has been designed to help you work towards your GCSE Business Studies exam. It will also be helpful for other business courses such as GNVQ. IT tasks have been included so you can show your IT skills in the presentation of your work.

Each unit of work is divided into sections. These sections use businesses to illustrate the new topics you are learning about. In each section there are explanations of different business theories and concepts. These will help you understand how business works and some of the decisions that business people have to make.

The following elements are also included within the units to provide you with practice and extra information.

LEARNING OBJECTIVES
A list of what you will learn in that section.

COURSEWORK ACTIVITIES
A range of tasks for you to do. These vary from research to presentations and from note-taking to IT tasks. All these activities will contribute to the coursework part of your studies.

CASE STUDY
An example of a business situation or problem, usually based on real companies. This will help you understand the new ideas you are studying. At the end of each case study there are questions for you to answer.

REVIEW QUESTIONS
Throughout each unit of work there are review questions, to check that you understand what you have learnt. Some of these questions will take only a few minutes to answer, others, called super review questions, will take a little longer. You should keep all your answers to these questions to help you when revising for the exam.

KEY POINTS
At the end of each topic there is a list of key points that you should have learnt. These points will be useful when you are revising for your examinations.

QUESTION TIME
At the end of each unit there is a series of exam-type questions, including extension questions. These are based on all that you have learnt in the unit.

Sam and Harri are friends and go to the same school. They are both interested in Business Studies.

Sam lives near a craft workshop. Local craftspeople rent the site from the council. They have different skills, from jewellery-making to pottery and from landscape painting to toy-making. They each have a workshop where they make their products. On the ground floor there is a showroom where they sell the products.

Sam is very artistic and when she leaves school she wants to set up her own business. She wants to make hand-painted silk scarves and ties and sell them in the craft shop.

Sam

Harri is not sure what he wants to do yet. He does know that he wants to go on to further education and study Business Studies and Information Technology.

Harri

Both Sam and Harri want to find out more about Business Studies. They want to find out how real businesses work. All through this book they will be discovering more about Business Studies. They will look at why businesses exist, how they are formed, the different departments needed to run a business and how the outside world influences the day-to-day running of a business.

This book will provide them with all the answers they need for their GCSE and help them understand business much more.

Acknowledgements

The Author would like to thank her husband and son who kept her going throughout the writing process and without whose help she would not have been able to complete the book. She would also like to thank Hamble School, Southampton – where she is a Business Studies teacher and Head of Technology and Information Technology – for their continuing support.

Alton Towers – logo, rides
Amazon Internet Bookshop
Bank of England
BBC
Birds Eye
Boden, Gareth – Assorted bags
British Aerospace
British Standards
BSM
Burger King
Cash Photo Library, J Allan – Police, supermarket
Co-op
Department of Transport – Drink driving advertisement
Earls Court & Olympia Ltd – Motor show
Eddie Stobart Ltd – Lorry
Environmental Images, Steve Morgan – Greenpeace photo, Friends of the Earth protest
Ford Motor Company – Escort cars, production line
Frank Lane Images of Nature, H Clark – Puppy
IKEA
KFC
Lectra Systems – Cad system
London Stock Exchange – Stock Exchange building
Marks & Spencer plc
Morgan Car Company
Nissan
NORWEB
Princess Cruises
Raleigh Industries Ltd – Bicycles
Robert Harding Picture Library, Geoff Williamson – Fork lift truck
Robert Harding Picture Library, Premium Stock – Harvesting, industrial photo
Sainsbury's
Shell Internationl Ltd
Sony
SWEB
Tesco
Thames Water Company
The Body Shop International plc
Umbro
Virgin Atlantic Airways Ltd – Aircraft
Virgin Management – Virgin photos and logos
Volkswagen
Walker Snack Foods
Walls
Walmsley, John – Doctors and nurses, classroom, doctors' surgery sign, postman

Purposes and Types of Business Organisation

Section 1 Business activity

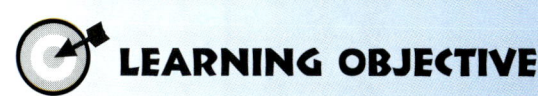

By the end of this section you should have learnt:
- the difference between consumer needs and wants
- how opportunity costs apply to a particular business problem
- the difference between goods and services
- how demand and supply factors apply in a market economy
- how the market price is worked out
- the three main types of economy
- the three different types of business activity (types of production)
- the different groups of people involved in business activity
- the roles and responsibilities of these different groups of people.

UNIT 1 — PURPOSES AND TYPES OF BUSINESS ORGANISATION

TOPIC 1: Consumers, suppliers, goods and services

CONSUMER NEEDS AND WANTS

Businesses exist to make a profit by providing things that people **need** and **want**. From the day we are born we all need food, drink, shelter, warmth and clothes, if we are to survive, so there are businesses that provide us with food, drink, houses and clothes. Some companies make the things and others sell them, for instance, Kellogg's makes corn flakes and Sainsbury's sells them.

There are other businesses that exist to support these companies, for example, transport companies to deliver the raw materials to the factory and finished goods to the customer, banks and insurance companies to provide services to the businesses.

There are other things we would like to make our lives more enjoyable but they are not essential, such as a holiday, a computer, going to the cinema. How we decide to buy what we need and want depends on the amount of money we have to spend. We have to make choices about which are the most important.

OPPORTUNITY COST

Businesses and governments also have to make similar choices. The government has to choose its priorities when spending its income each year. Which is more important: education or social services? A business may have to decide which is more important: a new piece of machinery or an extra member of staff? From the list of things we need and want, the choices we make are always at the cost of something else. This is known as **opportunity cost.**

Sam and Harri need to know what business is and why we need it

BUSINESS ACTIVITY **SECTION 1**

GOODS AND SERVICES

We saw earlier that Kellogg's makes corn flakes for its customers and Sainsbury's sells food to its customers. The corn flakes that Kellogg's makes are **goods**. When Sainsbury's sells the corn flakes it is providing a **service**.

Goods are physical things that can be bought, such as a mountain bike or a CD. Services are non-physical items that can be bought such as having a driving lesson or going to the dentist.

Anyone who buys goods or services is called a consumer. We are all consumers.

The consumer goods that we buy can be:

◆ **consumer durables** which means they can be used over and over again, e.g. a computer or a pair of trainers

◆ **single use** which means they can be used only once, e.g. a packet of crisps or a disposable camera.

Goods and services

KEY POINTS

- **Needs** – what we need to survive, e.g.
  – food
  – drink
  – shelter.

- **Wants** – what we would like but do not need for survival, e.g.
  – a holiday
  – a computer.

- **Business activity** – providing goods and services to satisfy consumer needs and wants.

- **Opportunity cost** – the cost of rejecting the alternatives when choosing between different needs and wants.

- **Goods** – physical objects that can be bought.

- **Services** – non-physical things that can be bought.

- **Consumer durables** – goods that can be used over and over again, e.g.
  – a television
  – a coat.

- **Single use** – goods that can be used only once, e.g.
  – a bottle of milk
  – a chocolate bar.

REVIEW QUESTIONS

1. Draw up a table with three headings: Durable goods   Single use goods   Services
Sort the pictures above into goods and services. List them under the correct headings in the table that you have just drawn up.
2. Explain the difference between needs and wants. Give examples of each of these in your answer.

SUPER REVIEW QUESTION

3. Explain how opportunity cost might apply to you when spending your pocket money.

UNIT 1 — PURPOSES AND TYPES OF BUSINESS ORGANISATION

TOPIC 2 Demand and supply

DEMAND

Before providing goods or services, a business needs to know if there is a high **demand** for them – in other words how many people are likely to buy them. The quantity of goods that a company can sell to the consumer is called the **supply**. If a lot of people want to buy the same goods or services, businesses know that demand will be high, as long as the price is right. Knowing the likely demand helps businesses to decide what to make, how many to make and gives them some idea of the price to charge to meet that demand. For example, when Sony makes televisions:

- if it charged £1 000 for every television not many people would buy them
- if it sold them at £500 more people would buy them
- if it sold them for £250 a lot more people would buy them
- or each person may buy more than one television.

The **demand curve**, as shown opposite, is a simple diagram to show the general rule that if the price is lower the quantity demanded of the goods or service will normally go up and vice versa: if the price goes up the quantity of the goods that are demanded will normally go down.

This rule does not always apply, however, because if people want particular goods badly enough, they will still buy the goods even if the price is increased. Equally, even a small increase in the price of some goods can lead to a big fall in the quantity demanded.

Sam and Harri need to understand how businesses know what goods and services to provide and how many

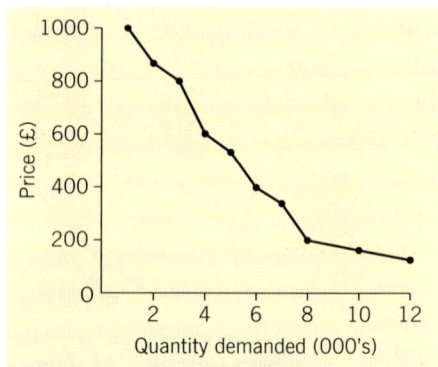

Demand curve for a television at various prices

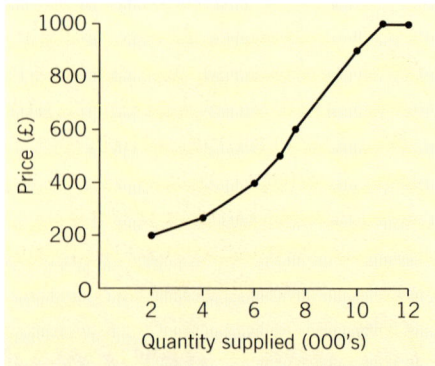

Supply curve for a television at various prices

SUPPLY

As well as the consumer reacting to changes in price, so does the business. For example, if the price of televisions goes up, Sony may produce more in order to make more profit. If the price goes down Sony may produce fewer because they will not make enough profit. This is known as a **supply curve**, as shown on page 4.

MARKET PRICE

The **market** is made up of consumers buying and suppliers selling goods or services. We have seen the effect price has on supply and demand. By placing the supply and demand curves on the same diagram, you can find the **market price** at the point where the two curves cross. This is the point where consumers and suppliers are both satisfied with the price and amount of goods to be put on the market, and is called an **equilibrium point**.

The graph below shows that if the price goes up above this equilibrium point the demand could go down and the suppliers would have goods left over, so they would reduce the amount they supply in future.

If the price goes below the equilibrium point the demand could go up and the supplier could run out of goods, so they would have to increase supply.

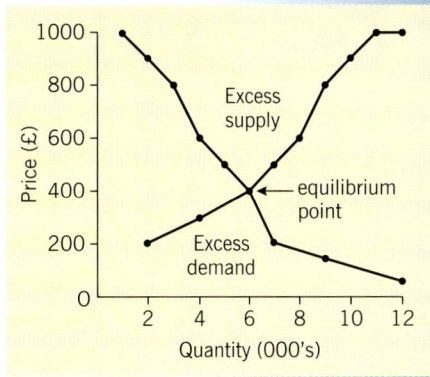

Market price for a television

REVIEW QUESTION

1 Explain why the quantity demanded may go down if the price goes up.

SUPER REVIEW QUESTIONS

2 Explain what may have to happen to the supply of goods if price goes up above the equilibrium point.
3 Explain what might happen to the supplier's goods if the price rises too high.

KEY POINTS

- **Demand** – the quantity of a product that consumers need or want.
- **Supply** – the quantity of the product that the supplier puts out on the market.
- **Excess supply** – the supplier is left with goods.
- **Excess demand** – the supplier runs out of goods.
- **Price** – the supplier should set the price at the equilibrium point to avoid excess supply or excess demand.

UNIT 1 — PURPOSES AND TYPES OF BUSINESS ORGANISATION

TOPIC 3 — Types of economy

Different countries have different ways of deciding which goods and services are provided for the people (consumers). There are now three main types of economy around the world:
- market economy
- planned or command economy
- mixed economy.

Sam and Harri need to understand how different countries run their economies

MARKET ECONOMY

In a **market economy**, such as the USA, consumers decide which goods and services they want and businesses provide them. Almost all businesses in a market economy are privately owned. The main features of a market economy are:
- consumer demands dictate which goods and services the businesses will supply
- the businesses are there to make a profit
- the number of goods and services provided is decided through the price system (the market price)
- most of the factors of production – land, labour, capital – are privately owned.

Advantages of a market economy

- Any entrepreneur (business person) with an idea for a product or service can start up a business if they have the necessary finance.
- There is competition between businesses which encourages greater efficiency and the development of new products.
- There is the opportunity to make large profits.
- The price system helps to match demand and supply so that consumers do not have shortages of goods or services.
- It reduces wastage by preventing surpluses.

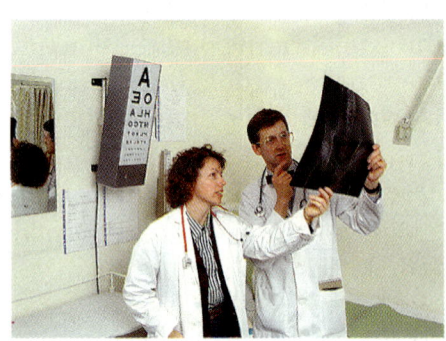

In the UK, the National Health Service is run by the government

Most education in the UK is also run by the government

BUSINESS ACTIVITY SECTION 1

Disadvantages of a market economy
- Businesses will not provide goods or services if they cannot make a profit from them.
- Monopolies can be created and they can then control how much is made and the prices to be charged.
- Too much competition can be wasteful as more goods may be made than the consumers want.

PLANNED ECONOMY

In a **planned (or command) economy** the government or state owns most of the businesses and control the country's resources. The government decides what, and how much will be produced; and then businesses have to meet these targets. The consumer has no say in decisions about goods or services. Many countries, such as Russia, China, Cuba and most East European countries used to have planned economies but now most of these have changed and have become mixed economies.

MIXED ECONOMY

A **mixed economy** is a combination of the market economy and the planned economy. Some decisions are made between the consumer and businesses. Others are made by the government. In the UK we have a mixed economy. The majority of businesses are owned by private individuals, called **entrepreneurs**. Some businesses, such as the Post Office, the National Health Service and most education, are owned and run by the government.

KEY POINTS
- The three main types of economy are:
  - market
  - planned/command
  - mixed.
- A market economy is controlled by:
  - consumer demand
  - business.
- A planned/command economy is controlled by:
  - government.
- A mixed economy is controlled by:
  - government
  - consumer demand
  - business.

REVIEW QUESTION
1. Find out what kind of economy there is in the USA. Explain how the goods and services are provided in this type of economy.

SUPER REVIEW QUESTIONS
2. Explain each of the three main types of economies and the differences between them.
3. Explain why, in this country, the National Health Service and education are provided mainly by the government and not by private businesses.

7

UNIT 1
PURPOSES AND TYPES OF BUSINESS ORGANISATION

TOPIC 4: Production types and factors

PRODUCTION TYPES

Whatever kind of economy a country has, all business activity can be organised into three categories:
- primary production
- secondary production
- tertiary production.

Below is a chart giving examples of the types of work carried out in each of these types of production.

Sam and Harri need to understand the three categories of the production process

Primary	Secondary	Tertiary
Mining	Construction	Retail
Farming	Manufacturing	Wholesale
Fishing	Water supply	Banking
Quarrying	Energy supply	Insurance
Forestry		Communications
		Tourism and leisure
		Direct services, e.g. teachers police driving instructors

extraction of raw materials

turning raw materials into finished goods

providing goods or services

PRIMARY PRODUCTION

The first stage of the production process is where raw materials and natural resources are farmed or extracted from the land or sea. People who work in the primary sector are:
- farmers growing crops or rearing livestock
- miners extracting such things as coal, gold, or diamonds
- foresters planting and growing trees.

SECONDARY PRODUCTION

The second stage of the production process turns these raw materials and natural resources into finished products. Examples of secondary production are:

- bicycle manufacturers
- house builders
- road construction companies
- CD manufacturers.

TERTIARY PRODUCTION

Businesses involved in the third stage of the production process provide services instead of producing goods. Examples of tertiary production are:

- businesses that provide services to industry and individuals, such as banking or insurance
- businesses that provide services to the consumer, such as hairdressing, travel agencies or football clubs
- services to the state such as education (provided by teachers), law and order (provided by the police force) or the National Health Service (provided by doctors and nurses).

REVIEW QUESTION

1 Below is a list of jobs. Draw a chart using the headings:
   Primary   Secondary   Tertiary
   and sort the following jobs into the correct types of production:

   shop assistant   veterinary surgeon
   midwife   disc jockey
   coal miner   car production line worker
   bus driver   teacher
   farm worker   paramedic
   furniture maker   baker

2 British Petroleum (BP) is involved in all three types of business activity. Explain in what ways BP is involved in primary, secondary and tertiary production. You may wish to use illustrations in your answer.

COURSEWORK ACTIVITY

1 Carry out a survey of the businesses in the area near your school or college. Make a list of the company names and the type of business they are, e.g. garage, florist, bank. Make a rough sketch of the site whilst you are there.

2 Sort out the businesses into primary, secondary and tertiary production. Draw a graph showing the numbers of each type of production in your area.

3 Draw a plan of the local area showing the businesses.

4 Using the information you have collected, draw conclusions as to why there are these types of production in your area.

KEY POINTS

- The three types of business activity are:
  - **primary production** – extracting raw materials and natural resources from the land or sea
  - **secondary production** – turning the raw materials and natural resources into finished goods
  - **tertiary production** – providing services.

UNIT 1 PURPOSES AND TYPES OF BUSINESS ORGANISATION

TOPIC 5 — Production factors

For businesses to provide the consumer with the goods and services they want, they need four important resources:
- land
- labour
- capital
- enterprise

These are known as the **factors of production** and are needed to run the business.

Land is needed for the factories, shops or offices to stand on. Land also includes all the natural resources extracted from the land or sea.

Labour is needed to produce the goods or provide the service, but it also includes all the people working in the business, such as office workers, managers, sales assistants.

Capital (or money) is needed to start up and run the business, to buy such things as the buildings, machinery and equipment and pay staff.

Enterprise is needed to bring together the other three factors of production to make a successful business that makes a profit. The people who demonstrate this enterprise are known as **entrepreneurs**.

Sam and Harri need to understand the four factors of production

A number of years ago, crisps were unflavoured. They came with some salt in a twist of blue paper. Then an entrepreneur had the idea of producing crisps ready salted. For these crisps to be manufactured, the entrepreneur needed first of all to find capital to start up the business, then land to grow the potatoes and to build the factory on and finally people to harvest the potatoes and to work in the factory.

BUSINESS ACTIVITY **SECTION 1**

Factors of production

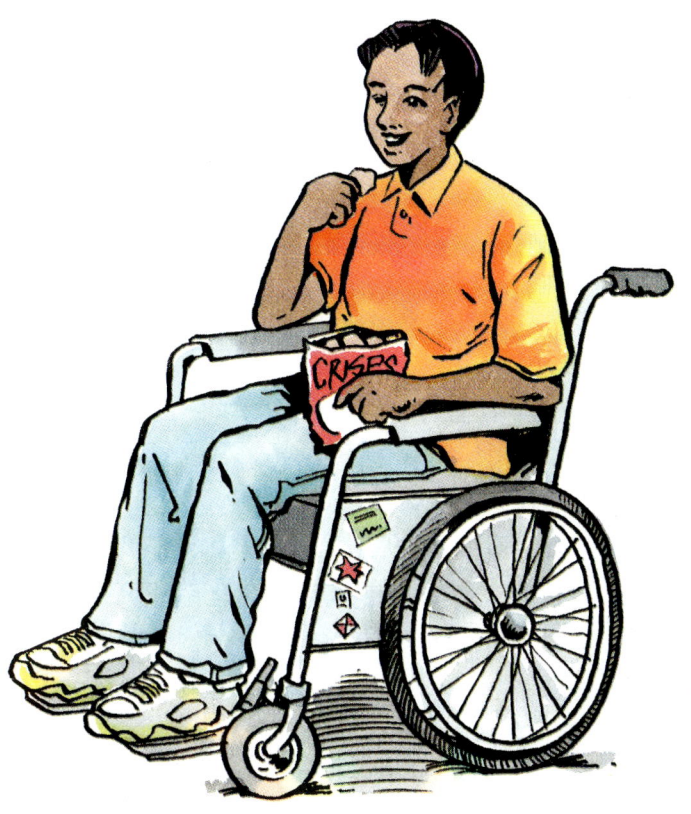

KEY POINTS

The four factors of production are:

- **land**
  – to site premises
- **labour**
  – to produce goods
  – provide services
- **capital**
  – to start up
  – for day-to-day running
- **enterprise**
  – to develop the business
  – to bring together the other factors of production.

COURSEWORK ACTIVITY

1. Draw a chart showing the factors of production for the production of a tin of baked beans.
2. Explain the chart and how the factors of production apply to the tin of baked beans.

UNIT 1

PURPOSES AND TYPES OF BUSINESS ORGANISATION

TOPIC 6 — People involved in business

There are four main groups of people involved in running a business, they are the:
- owners
- shareholders
- managers
- employees

OWNERS

Owners put their own money into a business, e.g. a sole trader or partnership. They have a say in the decision-making in the business and a share of the profits.

Sam and Harri need to know about the different people involved in running a business

SHAREHOLDERS

Shareholders also put money into a business which is either a **private limited company** – owned by employees, family or friends – or a **public limited company** – owned by members of the general public or corporate investors – but they have less say in the running of the business.

Fiona

Deborah and David

There are different people involved in running businesses. For example, Fiona is a small business owner, she runs her own flower shop. Deborah, the Receptionist, is an employee of the doctor's surgery and David is the Practice Manager.

BUSINESS ACTIVITY SECTION 1

MANAGERS

Managers (often called **directors**) are people who are employed by the owners and shareholders. They oversee the day-to-day running of the business for the owners and shareholders and put the owners' decisions into practice.

In small businesses such as **sole traders** the owner is often also the manager and makes all decisions. In larger businesses such as **partnerships** or **limited companies** managers may be employed to look after the business. These managers can be experts in specific areas such as **marketing** or **finance**. You can learn more about the different types of businesses in Section 2 (see pages 17–46).

EMPLOYEES

Employees are paid to work for the business doing a specific and limited job.

STAKEHOLDER SYSTEM

Today some businesses try to promote a **stakeholder** system. This means that when decisions are made the needs of owners and shareholders are balanced against those of all the employees as well as others outside the business – e.g. suppliers and the local community in general. The idea is that if everyone feels they have a **stake** in the business, the business will benefit. For example, suppliers will deliver quality products on time because they feel that this will benefit them as well. You can read more about the external influences on businesses in Section 5 (see pages 91–102).

KEY POINTS

- The four main groups of people involved in business activity are:
  - **owners** – people who start a company with their own money
  - **shareholders** – people who put money into a company if it is a limited company
  - **managers** – people employed to control the general running of a company
  - **employees** – people who perform a specific, limited role within a company.
- **Private limited company** – shares can be owned only by those who set up the company and others whom they allow to own shares.
- **Public limited company** – shares can be owned by anyone.

UNIT 1 PURPOSES AND TYPES OF BUSINESS ORGANISATION

TOPIC 7 Roles of different people

ROLES

In all types of business the main role of the owners and shareholders is to provide the **capital** for the business. In return these groups receive profits from the business. For a small business this will often just be an increase in salary. Whereas, for larger companies the owners and shareholders will receive bonuses and dividends.

Making the important decisions within the business is also part of the role of the owner. For smaller businesses this will mean making the decisions on the future of the business as well as on the day-to-day decision-making. For larger companies the owners leave the day-to-day running to managers and make only important decisions about the future of the business. Shareholders have an opportunity to **vote** on proposals and have some influence on general policy decisions related to the running of the company, at the company's **Annual General Meeting (AGM)**.

The managers of large companies have different roles depending on their level of responsibility. The role of the Managing Director is to set the company objectives and make the important decisions about the future of the whole business. The role of the Department Managers is to make decisions within their specific departments. Line Managers plan and organise the day-to-day running of different parts of the business.

The employees' role is to carry out all the work identified in their job descriptions.

Sam and Harri need to know about the roles of different people in business

Sandra works for Fiona in her flower shop. She is responsible for making up bunches of flowers. Karen is a Manager in a large company. She is responsible for a considerable number of staff and needs to keep track of them all. Douglas works for a train company. He is responsible for driving a train. They are all responsible for following the health and safety guidelines.

RESPONSIBILITIES

The owners and shareholders are responsible for their employees. They must make sure that they have a fair rate of pay and their working conditions are safe and appropriate for the work they do.

Managers have a responsibility to try to achieve the highest profit for the business. They also have a responsibility to the community, e.g., to make sure that the business does not damage the environment by causing pollution or wasting valuable resources.

Managers and employees are all obliged to work to their contract of employment.

Managers are also responsible for putting into action the policies decided by the owners. This will involve:

- motivating workers to try to improve productivity
- ensuring machinery, equipment and materials are used efficiently and waste is kept to a minimum
- putting in place quality control checks to ensure products meet standards set by the business
- ensuring that all employees have equal rights at work whether male, female, disabled or from ethnic minority groups
- monitoring spending in the business and setting budgets and financial targets.

Everyone working in an organisation must make sure that they keep a healthy and safe environment for everyone else to work in. They must also make sure that they do not endanger any colleagues by any action of theirs at work. (See Unit 2 Section 1, pages 113–130.)

Safety at work

KEY POINTS

The different groups of people involved in business activity have different duties and responsibilities.

- **Duties**
  - owners and shareholders – they must provide capital for a business
  - managers – they must make decisions on the general running of the company
  - employees – they must perform their job efficiently and safely.

- **Responsibilities**
  - owners and shareholders – they must make important decisions and are responsible for the employees and for the effect the company has on the environment.
  - managers – they are responsible for following the policy directives of the owners and shareholders, for getting maximum efficiency, and for protecting the rights and safety of the employees.
  - employees – they are responsible for fulfilling their contract and for the health and safety of others.

Section 2 Types of business ownership

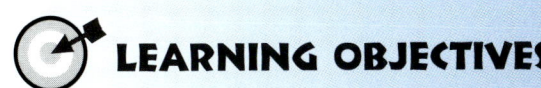
LEARNING OBJECTIVES

By the end of this section you should have learnt:
- the different types of business ownership
- how the different types of business are formed
- the advantages of each type of business
- the disadvantages of each type of business.

UNIT 1 — PURPOSES AND TYPES OF BUSINESS ORGANISATION

TOPIC 1: Sole traders

There are six main types of business organisations:
- sole traders
- partnerships
- private limited companies
- public limited companies
- franchises
- cooperatives

The way a business is organised and run depends upon the type of business.

Sam and Harri need to know about sole traders

WHAT IS A SOLE TRADER?

The craftspeople in the workshop near to where Sam lives are sole traders. The sole trader type of business is owned by one person. The sole trader can employ people but these employees are unlikely to be involved in the control, financing, or decision-making of the business. In your area, people such as electricians, taxi drivers, hairdressers, and guest house owners are probably sole traders.

Sole traders

TYPES OF BUSINESS OWNERSHIP **SECTION 2**

In the UK, the sole trader is the most common form of business ownership, with over three million people in business as sole traders. Many young people today are setting up their own businesses, helped by start-up grants from central government or charities such as the Prince's Trust.

The sole trader has to make all the decisions about running the business. He or she keeps all of the profits. It is more difficult to raise large amounts of money from loans, as sole traders are seen to be more of a risk than large companies. Sole traders often have to use their own money or borrow from family and friends to start up the business. As a result most sole traders are small businesses.

This type of organisation has **unlimited liability**. This means there is no limit to the amount of the business's debts that the owner is responsible for. If the business should fail, the sole trader may have to sell personal possessions – e.g. house and car – to pay off the business's debts.

SETTING UP AS A SOLE TRADER

If you want to set up your own business, first of all you need a good **idea**. You need to think of a product or service that you think people need or want. It could be something completely new, or something that already exists. If you plan to provide goods or services that already exist, you will be in competition with other businesses.

You will need to decide on a **name** for your business. You may need to find business **premises**. You will have to raise the **capital** necessary to start the business. You will have to decide whether or not you want to **employ** any people to help you run the business. You need to be able to **keep the accounts** accurately yourself or find an accountant who will do them for you.

Some business ideas are more appropriate than others for a sole trader, such as offering a service, for example, dog grooming, or window cleaning. A good idea and sufficient expertise and capital can provide the starting point. Business **growth** for a sole trader is often achieved by **word of mouth**, that is, one satisfied customer telling another.

Sam is producing an example of her work

Sam is thinking up names for her business

Sam is looking at a possible site for her business

Sam is going to the bank to ask about a loan to start up her business

UNIT 1 PURPOSES AND TYPES OF BUSINESS ORGANISATION

ADVANTAGES

- It is easy to set up a business as a sole trader as there are no complicated forms or procedures to follow before you can start.
- Sole traders can make decisions quickly as they do not have to get agreement from anyone else.
- Sole traders usually need less capital to set up.
- They are taxed differently from any other type of business. In particular National Insurance contributions are paid at a lower rate (but because of this they receive fewer benefits).
- All the profits can be kept by sole traders, which motivates them to work harder – the harder they work, the more successful the business, and the more opportunity there is for profits to be made.
- The sole trader can offer the personal attention and service to customers that a large company is unable to provide.
- The sole trader does not have to make public any information about the state of the business.
- Sole traders are their own bosses.

DISADVANTAGES

- Sole traders have unlimited liability which means they can lose their personal possessions to pay off any debts the business might run up.
- Small businesses are seen as more of a risk by financial institutions, so it can sometimes be difficult to raise money to help start up a business or to expand later on.
- Sole traders do not have the advantages of economies of scale that a large business has (see Unit 1 Section 4, pages 78–79) which means they cannot easily compete on prices.
- Ill-health and holidays may affect the business as there is no one to take over the running of the business if the sole trader is taken ill or wants to go on holiday. It will often mean the business closing for this period of time.

TYPES OF BUSINESS OWNERSHIP **SECTION 2**

COURSEWORK ACTIVITY

Find a sole trader in your local area who will help you to discover what it is like to be a sole trader. Draw up an interview sheet like the one below and keep a record of the sole trader's answers.

SAMPLE INTERVIEW SHEET

Name of business _____

Name of owner _____

Type of business _____

Why did you choose this type of business?
_____
_____

How did you decide on the name for the business?
_____
_____

Do you employ any staff? _____

If so, how many? _____

How did you decide on the premises for the business?
_____
_____

What are the advantages of being a sole trader?
_____
_____

What are the disadvantages of being a sole trader?
_____
_____

Is there any advice you would give to anyone starting a business as a sole trader?
_____
_____

KEY POINTS

- A business is called a sole trader when:
  - there is only one owner
  - the owner has to make all the decisions
  - the owner has unlimited liability.
- **Unlimited liability** – the owner is responsible for all the debts of the business.
- A sole trader business needs:
  - a desirable product or service
  - a name for the company
  - business premises
  - starting capital
  - accurate financial records
  - satisfied customers to tell other potential customers
  - possibly to employ other staff.
- Advantages:
  - easy to set up
  - small amount of capital needed
  - can make all the decisions
  - can keep all the profits
  - can provide a more personal service
  - is own boss.
- Disadvantages:
  - unlimited liability
  - difficult to raise capital
  - difficult to compete with large companies in terms of price
  - business cannot be run if owner is on holiday or is ill.

UNIT 1 — PURPOSES AND TYPES OF BUSINESS ORGANISATION

CASE STUDY

Limi Janata is married and has two children. She wants to work but does not want set hours, as she wants to be able to take her children to school and be at home for the school holidays. A friend suggests she finds out about starting up her own business. She is very artistic and has been making hand-painted silk scarves, hair bands and ties for her family and friends as birthday and Christmas present for some time, and everyone loves them.

She goes to the library and takes out a book on starting and running a small business. After reading it, she realises that there are lots of questions she needs answered before she can set up her own business, such as:

- why do I want to set up my own business?
- what type of business ownership should I consider?
- how will I raise the money to start the business?
- do I need premises, or can I work from home?

Limi likes the idea of starting up her own business but now needs some more advice on how to go about it. Her local bank has a small-business adviser, so she makes an appointment to see him. The meeting helps her make some of the decisions. She now knows that if she goes ahead with the idea:

- she will be a sole trader
- she will work from home
- she will begin by selling her silk products at craft fairs.

There are other things she needs to go away and think about before making up her mind, such as:

- how to raise the capital to start the business
- how to present her case for raising capital
- whether to advertise the business and if so, how?
- what financial records need to be kept.

1. Carry out research into the different ways of raising finance for a small business, and into ways of presenting the case for raising capital to other people.
2. Carry out research into the different ways that small businesses advertise.
3. Produce a word processed summary on 'Starting up a small business'. Include all the points that Limi has had to consider for starting up her business.

TYPES OF BUSINESS OWNERSHIP **SECTION 2**

REVIEW QUESTIONS

1. List four different types of sole traders in your local area, e.g. hairdresser.
2. Explain what is meant by unlimited liability.
3. Explain what is meant by a sole trader being an entrepreneur.

SUPER REVIEW QUESTIONS

4. Discuss the advantages of being a sole trader.
5. Discuss the disadvantages of being a sole trader.
6. Consider the objectives of Lesley Jerome in setting up her own business.

UNIT 1 PURPOSES AND TYPES OF BUSINESS ORGANISATION

TOPIC 2 Partnerships

WHAT IS A PARTNERSHIP?

A partnership involves more than one person. It is normal for a partnership to include between 2 and 20 people, but they may be larger for some professions. Partnerships are common with businesses involving professionals such as doctors, dentists, accountants, solicitors, as most professions do not allow their members to form limited companies.

The partners are the joint owners of the business. They may be involved in the decision-making themselves or they may employ a manager. For example, a doctor's surgery may employ a Practice Manager to manage the day-to-day running of the surgery, leaving the doctors more time to concentrate on treating their patients.

Like the sole trader they have unlimited liability, which means that if the business fails, they are all liable for the debts of the business. If one partner incurs the debt, all the partners are liable for its payment, even if it means selling personal possessions to pay off the debt of the business. The profits of the business are shared among the partners according to the amount of capital each one invested to start up the business, unless stated otherwise in the Deed of Partnership. For example if three partners each invested £10 000 they would each take equal shares from the profits, but if one partner had invested £20 000 and the two others had invested £10 000 the first partner would receive 50 per cent of the profits and the other two partners would each receive 25 per cent.

Sam and Harri need to know about partnerships

SETTING UP A PARTNERSHIP

The law states that when setting up an ordinary partnership there should be between 2 and 20 partners for most professions. The partners should draw up a **Deed of Partnership** and most partnerships find a solicitor to do this for them. The Deed of Partnership should include details of:

- the names of all the partners
- how much capital each is putting into the partnership
- how the profits and losses will be shared among the partners
- the duties of each partner
- the procedures for adding new partners
- the procedures for partners leaving the partnership.

The **Partnership Act of 1890** lays out the rules for setting up and running partnerships if a Deed of Partnership is not drawn up.

Some partners may want to invest in the business but not be involved in the running of it. They are known as **limited** or **sleeping partners** and they can register with the Registrar of Companies as a limited partner. They have **limited liability**, which means they are not personally responsible for any debts incurred by the partnership and will not have to sell personal possessions in order to pay off any business debts. However, any partnership must have at least one **ordinary** partner who will have unlimited liability for any debts.

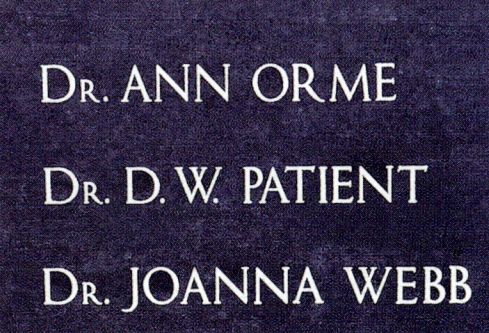

UNIT 1 — PURPOSES AND TYPES OF BUSINESS ORGANISATION

ADVANTAGES

Many of the advantages of being a sole trader also apply to a partnership.

- It is easy to set up.
- The amount of capital needed to start up the partnership is often small.
- Forming a partnership can mean it is easier to raise extra capital when needed as all the partners can contribute.
- All the profits go to the partners and usually the partners work in the business, which motivates them to work harder in order to make higher profits.
- Partnerships are often small businesses employing a few workers, so there are usually good working relationships among all those working in the business.
- The partnership does not have to make public any information about the state of the business.
- Partners can contribute a range of skills and experiences to the business, such as accounting skills, marketing skills.
- With partners, there is someone to share problems with and talk things over.

DISADVANTAGES

- The partners have unlimited liability for the debts of the business, unless they are limited partners.
- Partners can have disagreements about the running of the business, which is why the Deed of Partnership is so important. Disagreements over control of the business, sharing of the profits, withdrawal from the partnership or inviting new partners to the business can all be covered in the Deed of Partnership.
- If a partner dies or becomes bankrupt the partnership must be dissolved.

REVIEW QUESTIONS

1. List four different types of partnership businesses in your local area, e.g. doctors.
2. List the details that should be included in a Deed of Partnership.

SUPER REVIEW QUESTIONS

3. Explain the purpose of the Deed of Partnership.
4. Discuss the advantages of being a partnership.
5. Discuss the disadvantages of being a partnership.
6. Explain why a partnership may decide to take on further partners in the future.

TYPES OF BUSINESS OWNERSHIP **SECTION 2**

COURSEWORK ACTIVITY

Imagine you and a friend are setting up a partnership. Decide on the type of business you will set up. You could consider businesses such as a video games shop, a fish and chip shop or window cleaning.

Decide on the amount of capital each of you will invest. On the word processor, draw up a Deed of Partnership for the business.

DEED OF PARTNERSHIP

This Deed of Partnership is made, on

_____ 20X0 between

1. _____
2. _____

Name and type of business:

_____
_____

Capital: _____

Starting date: _____

Division of profits: _____

Voting rights: _____

Signatures of partners:

_____
_____

KEY POINTS

- A partnership is when:
  - more than one person owns the business
  - the partners have unlimited liability.

- A partnership:
  - is usually a professional service e.g. medicine or law
  - needs a Deed of Partnership.

- A Deed of Partnership details:
  - who is part of the partnership
  - how much capital each member put into the partnership
  - how profits will be shared
  - the duties of each partner
  - how members can join or leave the partnership.

- Advantages:
  - easy to set up
  - small amount of capital needed
  - easier to raise capital
  - can keep all the profits
  - can have a range of abilities.

- Disadvantages:
  - unlimited liability
  - possible disagreement between partners
  - partnership dissolved if partner becomes bankrupt or dies.

27

UNIT 1 — PURPOSES AND TYPES OF BUSINESS ORGANISATION

TOPIC 3: Private limited companies

WHAT IS A PRIVATE LIMITED COMPANY?

A private limited company is made up of people who know each other, such as family, friends or work associates. They buy shares in the company and become part owners of the company. Shares cannot be bought by the public, but only by this small group of people – in other words, the owners can control who can buy shares. That is why it is called a **private** limited company. Examples of private limited companies are Raleigh and Eddie Stobart.

There must be a minimum of two people to start the business, but there is no upper limit on how many owners there are. A private limited company has Limited or Ltd at the end of its name to distinguish it from a public limited company. The company can expand by selling more shares to gain more capital, but is limited in this as shares cannot be sold on the Stock Market. Private limited companies are normally medium-sized companies.

The shareholders have **limited liability** which means that if the company goes bankrupt the shareholders can be held responsible only for payments up to the value of their shares – they do not run the risk of having to sell their personal possessions to pay off debts. This is because the company has its own legal identity, separate from the shareholders. This also means that the company can

Sam and Harri need to know about private limited companies

Often private limited companies are owned by larger public limited companies (see page 32). Raleigh is an example of this, they are owned by Derby International Corporation

sue and be sued. To show that the business has a separate identity it is normally called a company. The owners and shareholders can run the company themselves or they can appoint managers to run the company for them.

Each year the company must hold an **Annual General Meeting** of the shareholders. They also have to send an independently audited copy of the company accounts to the Registrar of Companies where they are available to the public. The shareholders cannot sell their shares to the general public on the Stock Exchange and or transfer them to anyone else without permission from the other shareholders.

One of the most high-profile private limited companies in the UK is Eddie Stobart Ltd. You can see Eddie Stobart lorries on roads throughout Britain.

UNIT 1 — PURPOSES AND TYPES OF BUSINESS ORGANISATION

SETTING UP A PRIVATE LIMITED COMPANY

Anyone wishing to set up a limited company must comply with the Companies Acts and register the company with the Registrar of Companies. To do this, two documents have to be completed:

- the Memorandum of Association
- the Articles of Association

The **Memorandum of Association** gives the following details:

- the company's name
- the address of its registered office
- it states that the shareholders will have limited liability
- the amount of share capital to be raised
- the purpose of the company, i.e. the main activity of the business. For example, Sam and Harri could set up a private limited company and the purpose of the company could be to design and make casual clothes such as T-shirts and sweaters.

The **Articles of Association** give details of:

- the names of the directors in the company and their role
- how the profits will be distributed
- the internal rules for running the business, such as rules about meetings and the voting rights of the shareholders
- the procedures to be followed at the Annual General Meeting.

The shareholders can vote to change the Articles of Association at a later date.

Once the Memorandum of Association and Articles of Association have been drawn up they are sent to the Registrar of Companies. When the Registrar is satisfied with all the details given in the two documents he or she will issue a **Certificate of Incorporation** and the private limited company can then begin trading.

COURSEWORK ACTIVITY

With three other members of your class, discuss the type of business you could set up together as a private limited company.

Now draw up the Memorandum of Association and Articles of Association for your business. Issue a share certificate to each shareholder once you have received approval from your teacher (representing the Registrar of Companies issuing the Certificate of Incorporation).

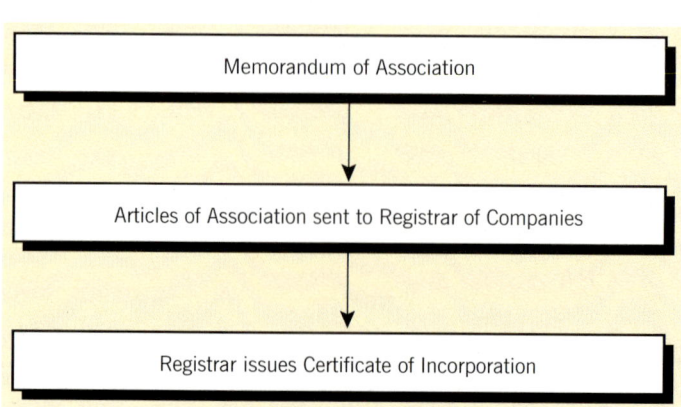

Memorandum of Association
↓
Articles of Association sent to Registrar of Companies
↓
Registrar issues Certificate of Incorporation

TYPES OF BUSINESS OWNERSHIP — SECTION 2

ADVANTAGES

- The owners of a private limited company (the shareholders) have limited liability which means that if the company fails, they are liable for debts only up to the value of the amount they invested in shares. Their personal possessions are not at risk.
- The company can raise extra capital by selling more shares in the company and thus giving it more of an opportunity to expand.
- The shareholders can employ managers to run the business if they do not want to run it themselves.
- The company can continue trading even if a shareholder dies – it does not have to be dissolved as it does in a partnership.
- The private limited company has its own legal status, separate from the shareholders. This means that, like people, it can sue and be sued and it can own property.

DISADVANTAGES

- The accounts of the company cannot be kept private. They have to be audited each year and a copy must be sent to the Registrar of Companies where it is available to the public.
- It is more difficult and more expensive to set up a limited company than a partnership or sole trader business, as there is much more administrative work to do.
- The limited company cannot sell its shares on the Stock Market.
- The company is limited by its Articles of Association as to the type of business it can undertake.

KEY POINTS

- A business is a private limited company when:
  - at least two people set it up
  - the owners have shares in the company
  - only people the owners want to sell shares to can buy shares, such as family, friends or employees
  - the owners have limited liability.

- **Limited liability** – shareholders are responsible for debts equal to the value of their shares.

- A private limited company needs:
  - a Memorandum of Association and Articles of Association, to register the company with the Registrar of Companies
  - an Annual General Meeting (AGM) of shareholders
  - an **audited** set of accounts available to the public.

- **Audit** – accounts must be audited (checked) by independent accountants to ensure that the accounts are honest and truthful.

- Advantages:
  - limited liability
  - can raise capital by selling shares
  - does not need to be dissolved if one owner dies
  - legal status is separate from owners.

- Disadvantages:
  - needs audited accounts to be made public
  - more expensive to set up
  - cannot sell shares on Stock Market
  - limited in what types of business it can compete in.

TOPIC 4 — Public limited companies

WHAT IS A PUBLIC LIMITED COMPANY?

Only two people are needed to set up a public limited company and there is no upper limit. It has **plc** at the end of its name, which stands for public limited company. This distinguishes it from a private limited company.

Sam and Harri need to find out about public limited companies

Members of the general public, as well as other businesses and financial institutions, can buy shares in a public limited company. Most shares in public limited companies are owned by organisations rather than individuals. The shares of most UK public limited companies are bought and sold through the Stock Exchange. Share prices are printed in some of the national newspapers each day so the public can check on the current status of their shares. The company can expand by selling more shares on the Stock Market. Public limited companies are generally larger than private limited companies.

The shareholders, as in the private limited company, have limited liability – if the company goes bankrupt the shareholders can be held responsible only for payments up to the value of their shares. The company has its own legal status separate from the shareholders. This also means that the company can sue and be sued.

Public limited companies often start as private limited companies. The private limited company may want to grow but it cannot offer its shares to the general public, so it decides to 'go public'.

SETTING UP A PUBLIC LIMITED COMPANY

There are far more rules and regulations about the starting and running of a public limited company than there are for a private limited company. The procedures for starting a public limited company are similar to a private limited company. The company has to draw up a Memorandum of Association and Articles of Association and send these to the Registrar

TYPES OF BUSINESS OWNERSHIP — SECTION 2

of Companies to apply for a Certificate of Incorporation to show the company has registered.

Before the Certificate of Incorporation is issued, a public limited company needs to convince the Registrar of Companies that it has raised enough capital, at least £50 000, and if the company is going to sell shares on the Stock Exchange it must be approved by the Stock Exchange Council. Once the Certificate of Incorporation has been received the company can issue a prospectus. This is an advertisement inviting the public to buy shares in the company. Once the shares have been issued the Registrar of Companies will draw up a **Certificate of Trading**. The company can start trading.

A merchant bank may underwrite the share issue. The company pays a fee and the bank undertakes to buy any unsold shares.

Another way of starting up a public limited company instead of inviting the public to buy shares through the prospectus would be for the merchant bank to buy all the shares. The merchant bank advertises an **offer for sale** and the public buys the shares from the bank. This method allows the merchant bank to keep the unsold shares and also to retain an interest in the company.

The public limited company must appoint a Board of Directors to manage the company. They have to hold an Annual General Meeting for the shareholders. They must have their accounts audited annually and a copy must be sent to the Registrar of Companies where it is available to the public.

The Stock Exchange

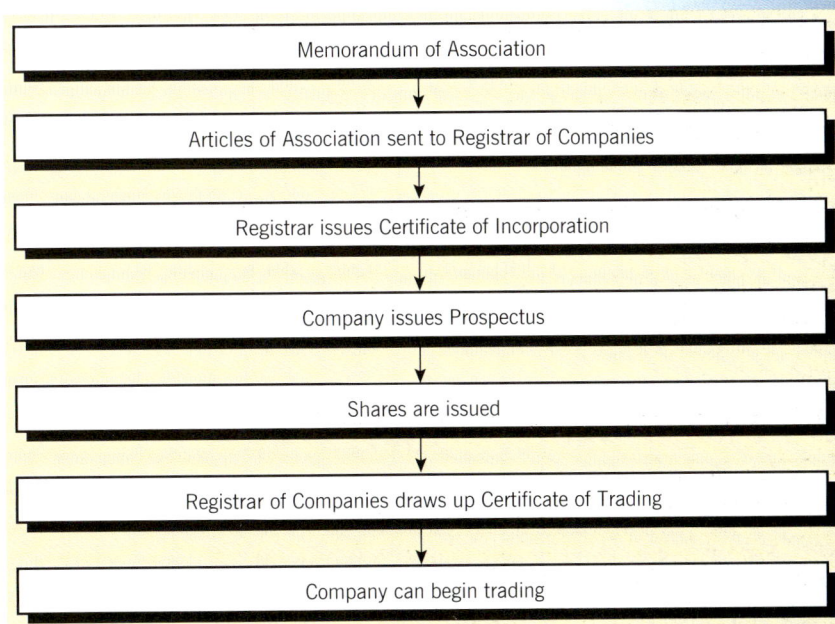

Memorandum of Association
↓
Articles of Association sent to Registrar of Companies
↓
Registrar issues Certificate of Incorporation
↓
Company issues Prospectus
↓
Shares are issued
↓
Registrar of Companies draws up Certificate of Trading
↓
Company can begin trading

UNIT 1 PURPOSES AND TYPES OF BUSINESS ORGANISATION

ADVANTAGES

- The shareholders have limited liability.
- It is easy to raise capital by issuing more shares.
- It is much easier to raise finance because the banks are much more willing to lend money to a large, well-established company, as they see it as much less of a risk.
- This all makes it easier for the public limited company to grow and expand.
- The shareholders will appoint specialists to manage and run the company for them.

DISADVANTAGES OF BEING A PUBLIC LIMITED COMPANY

- Setting up a public limited company is expensive. There is a lot of administrative work involved and at least £50 000 has to be raised before a public limited company can be set up.
- The public limited company has to issue much more information about itself and this again is very expensive to produce. It has to prepare an Annual Report as well as Annual Accounts and these have to be printed and sent to all the shareholders. They are also available to the general public and competitors to see.

VIRGIN GROUP

MARKS & SPENCER

PEARSON

STAGECOACH

BRITISH AIRWAYS

HOUSE OF FRASER

BARCLAYS

POWER GEN

CADBURY-SCHWEPPES

BSKYB

BRISTOL LTD

TATE & LYLE

REVIEW QUESTIONS

1. Name the two kinds of limited companies.
2. Who owns a limited company?
3. Explain the term **limited liability**.

SUPER REVIEW QUESTIONS

4. Explain the purpose of the Memorandum of Association and Articles of Association.
5. Discuss the advantages to a family of starting a business as a private limited company rather than a partnership.

TYPES OF BUSINESS OWNERSHIP **SECTION 2**

CASE STUDY - ALTON TOWERS

The site where Alton Towers stands today was originally a fortress, built over 1000 years ago. A castle was built on the site in the 12th century, and destroyed in the Civil War around 1650.

In the 1700s a farmhouse stood on the site which was later improved and named Alton Abbey. It started to be an attraction to the public in the 1800s when people came to see the beautiful gardens and watch acts such as acrobats and firework displays.

The 'Towers' was closed in 1939 with the outbreak of war and requisitioned by the army for Officer Cadet Training. It was returned to the owners in 1951.

The gardens were opened again in 1952 by a private limited company headed by Dennis Bagshaw. By then there were a few small rides, rowing boats and a cable car system.

Alton Towers was then gradually developed. In 1973 the owners obtained the first ride franchise and installed the double loop rollercoaster – the Corkscrew. After this many rides followed and themed areas were developed, e.g. Adventureland. More and more exciting rides were added and in 1986 Towers Street was created. This was an entrance system capable of handling thousands of visitors a day.

In 1990 the Tussaud's Group, part of Pearson plc acquired the park. The Tussaud's Group owns many of Britain's leading tourist attractions e.g. Madame Tussaud's and Warwick Castle.

In 1992 development began of three new sites at a cost of £10 million. The Nemesis and Toyland Tours rides were a £12 million investment.

More rides were added in 1995 and in 1996 the Alton Towers Hotel was built.

1. Give reasons why you think it was necessary for Alton Towers to change from being a private limited company to part of a public limited company.
2. Carry out research to find the names of some of the other companies that form Pearson plc.

KEY POINTS

- A business is a public limited company when:
  – at least two people set it up
  – it is owned by shareholders
  – shares can be bought on the Stock Market
  – shareholders have limited liability.

- A public limited company needs:
  – a Memorandum of Association and Articles of Association to register the company with the Registrar of Companies
  – a prospectus to get investors to buy shares
  – an Annual General Meeting (AGM) of shareholders
  – an audited set of accounts available to the public.

- Advantages:
  – limited liability
  – can raise capital by selling shares
  – easier to raise finance as seen as less of a risk
  – large company, so can compete on economies of scale.

- Disadvantages:
  – needs annual accounts and reports to be made public
  – more expensive to set up
  – needs at least £50 000 in capital
  – size of company can affect speed of decision-making
  – little contact between shareholders and employees.

UNIT 1 — PURPOSES AND TYPES OF BUSINESS ORGANISATION

TOPIC 5: Franchises

WHAT IS A FRANCHISE?

In a franchise, a small-business owner buys the right to sell the goods or services of a large, well-established company, e.g. The Body Shop, British School of Motoring (BSM), KFC. The small business buying the rights is the **franchisee**. The large business selling the rights is the **franchisor**. The large company can use franchising as a method of expanding its business, without having to invest more money.

SETTING UP A FRANCHISE

The franchisor sets out the rules for the running of the business, to make sure that quality and standards are maintained. In return, the franchisor will:

- give a well-known name to the new business
- provide advice on the running of the business
- provide training to start the business
- organise the advertising campaigns
- supply the materials used for the goods or service
- provide equipment, e.g. shop fittings in Burger King, so that all the businesses look the same and can perform to the same standard.

The small business has to pay for the privilege of a stake in the large owner's business. It has to pay a **start-up fee** for a licence from the franchisor to run the business and a **royalty** in the form of a percentage of annual profits to the franchisor.

Sam and Harri need to find out about franchises

ADVANTAGES

- The franchisor chooses the franchisees carefully. The franchisor knows the characteristics that will make a successful franchisee.
- The franchisor decides how much money the franchisee must invest in the business. Many small businesses fail because the owners do not realise the amount of capital needed to start up and run a business.
- The franchisor provides support with management advice and training and can help the franchisee solve problems.

36

DISADVANTAGES

◆ Franchisees do not have the freedom of running their own business. They are bound by rules set out by the franchisor. For example, they cannot vary the product or the price.
◆ The franchisee cannot sell the business without the permission of the franchisor.
◆ In some cases, the franchisor can end the franchise without consulting the franchisee and the franchisee may not receive compensation for the loss of the business.
◆ The franchisee always has to pay a percentage of the profits to the franchisor in royalties.
◆ The franchisee will never own the business outright.

REVIEW QUESTIONS

1. Explain the difference between a franchisor and a franchisee.
2. Explain the terms **start-up fee** and **royalty**.

SUPER REVIEW QUESTIONS

3. Explain how a franchisor makes a profit from the business.
4. State and explain the disadvantages of a small-business owner being a franchisee.

KEY POINTS

■ **Franchise** – large business sells rights to produce goods or services to small business.

■ **Franchisee** – owner of the small business.

■ **Franchisor** – the large business.

■ A franchise needs:
 – a well-known brand
 – a one-off fee paid by franchisee to franchisor
 – to pay royalties to franchisor.

■ Advantages:
 – safer way of starting a business
 – franchisor must provided training, help with management and materials.

■ Disadvantages:
 – franchisee must follow rules set by franchisor
 – franchisee cannot sell business without permission
 – franchisee has to pay percentage of profit to franchisor
 – franchisee will never own their business.

UNIT 1 — PURPOSES AND TYPES OF BUSINESS ORGANISATION

TOPIC 6 Cooperatives

WHAT IS A COOPERATIVE?

There are many kinds of cooperatives, but most people think of the Co-op stores or worker cooperatives when talking about cooperatives.

WORKER COOPERATIVES

Worker cooperatives are different from the Co-operative Society (see case study). These are businesses owned by all the workers in the business. Each worker has shares based on how much he or she has invested in the business. Cooperative businesses include some fruit growers and playgroups. All the workers are involved in making the decisions. Each worker has one vote when making decisions – the number of votes are not related to the number of shares they own in the business, unless it is a limited company and then the worker has one vote for every share. They all share in the profits and must all contribute to the running of the business. There is no limit to the number of members in a cooperative.

Sam and Harri need to know about worker cooperatives

TYPES OF BUSINESS OWNERSHIP — SECTION 2

ADVANTAGES

- Because the workers are the owners, there are likely to be fewer disagreements about how to run the business.
- All the workers have an interest in making the business successful, improving morale and productivity.
- Increases in profits are shared equally among all the workers.

DISADVANTAGES

- New workers have to buy shares and become part-owners in the business – new employees may find it difficult to raise the money to buy the shares when they first start work.
- Successful worker cooperatives are often pressured to sell the business, meaning they lose all the freedoms they have. An example of this was the Triumph motorcycle company. When the company was threatened with closure because of new technology and Japanese competition in the 1970s, the workers bought out the company and it became a workers' cooperative. Later it was sold on by the workers, to new owners.
- If the business wants to expand it will have to find new workers willing to invest in the business. If the business does not need more workers, it will find it difficult to expand.
- With worker cooperatives all the workers are paid the same. In other businesses the managers are paid more. It may therefore be difficult to recruit the best managers for the job because of these pay limitations.

REVIEW QUESTION

1. State who makes the decisions in a worker cooperative. Explain why this should be an advantage to the company.

SUPER REVIEW QUESTIONS

2. Explain how a worker cooperative is run.
3. Explain why it may be difficult for a worker cooperative to expand.

KEY POINTS

- A business is a cooperative when:
  - it is owned by the workers
  - the workers own the shares
  - decisions are made by workers voting
  - all the workers are responsible for the business
  - all the workers are paid the same and have receive the same share of profits.

- Advantages:
  - less disagreement as workers are owners
  - workers receive profits and so have more incentive.

- Disadvantages:
  - new workers need to capital to invest in the business before they can begin work
  - often pressure to sell successful cooperatives
  - expansion needs new workers who can invest in the business
  - difficult to get good managers if all workers are paid the same.

UNIT 1 — PURPOSES AND TYPES OF BUSINESS ORGANISATION

CASE STUDY – THE CO-OPERATIVE

The Co-operative Society was set up in 1844 in Rochdale in Lancashire. A group of workers (known as the Rochdale Pioneers) decided to buy food and other goods at wholesale prices and sell them cheaply to the members of the group. The profits from sales were then shared by the members in the form of a dividend. This was worked out from the amount of money the members spent (the more they spent the more they received back). This was the start of the Co-operative Retail Society (CRS).

The Society then decided it would be cheaper to provide its own goods as far as possible instead of buying them from someone else. Farms were bought and the Co-operative Wholesale Society (CWS) was set up to provide up to 60% of the goods for the Retail Societies. This now includes the 'Co-op own brand' goods.

The Co-operative Society today owns the Leo supermarkets and hypermarkets. It owns the furniture retailers Home World. The Co-operative Funeral Undertakers is the largest in the UK. The travel business United Norwest, based in the north west of England, is one of the larger tour operators. The Co-operative Wholesale Society is the largest farmer and wholesaler in the UK. It also owns the Co-operative Insurance Society and the Co-operative Bank. The Co-operative Retail Society is the part of the business that is struggling the most, because it is finding it hard to compete with the large supermarket chains such as Asda and Tesco.

TYPES OF BUSINESS OWNERSHIP — SECTION 2

THE PURPOSES OF BUSINESS

The purpose or objectives of a business will probably depend on its size. The sole trader's first objective is to make enough money to live on, and then to make sure the business survives. Once the business is secure the owner can concentrate on expanding the business.

COURSEWORK ACTIVITY

Look at share prices in a national newspaper or other relevant source (e.g. Internet, Teletext). Choose three well-known public limited companies. One should be involved in primary production, one in secondary production, and one in tertiary production.

For a period of four weeks, regularly check the price that their shares are selling for on the Stock Market.

Use these figures to produce a graph showing the fluctuations in share price.

Try to suggest why the share price of each company might have changed.

Objectives, control, sources of finance, and distribution of profits of various types of business

Type of ownership	Control	Sources of finance	Distribution of profits
Sole trader	Sole trader has total control	Owner, family and friends	Owner keeps all profits
Worker cooperative	Run by members by regular meetings and voting on decisions	Members provide finance, can sometimes get financial assistance from local authority	Profits distributed to members in 'fair' way, not always directly related to the amount of money invested
Franchise	Franchisor makes most of decisions, franchisee has limited control	Franchisees provide start-up fee and banks usually willing to lend money as working with well-established company	Franchisee keeps profit after paying royalty to franchisor
Private limited company	Shareholders have final say. Directors decide company objectives and policy	Shareholders buy shares in the company and other financial institutions lend money	Some as dividends to shareholders as stated in the Articles of Associated, some reinvested in company
Public limited company	Shareholders have control (usually financial organisations and businesses rather than individuals)	Selling shares in the company. Financial institutions more willing to lend money to large companies	Some profit retained to reinvest in company expansion. Distributed profit used to pay dividends to shareholders

UNIT 1 — PURPOSES AND TYPES OF BUSINESS ORGANISATION

TOPIC 7 The public sector

The UK is a mixed economy, which means that most businesses are privately owned, but some organisations providing goods and services are run and owned by the government (see Section 1). The three main groups in the public sector are:
- central government
- local government
- public corporations and nationalised industries.

Sam and Harri need to find out about central and local government

CENTRAL GOVERNMENT

Central government provides services to the public either free or by charging a fee. We can all go to a doctor when we feel ill – the National Health Service provides doctors and we, the public, pay for them by paying taxes such as income tax, VAT (Value Added Tax) and National Insurance contributions. Additional fees such as dental charges and prescription charges are added to help to pay for the National Health Service. Other public services include such things as defence, and the provision of main roads around the country.

LOCAL GOVERNMENT

Local government is run by local councils and they provide such services as education, police, fire services, social services, council housing, planning, libraries and local roads. A large percentage of the money for providing these services comes from central government, the rest comes from local government councils raising money from householders with the Council Tax, from taxes on local businesses (Uniform Business Rates), and from additional charges, such as library fines. In the past, local government employed staff themselves to provide these services to the public, but recent governments have insisted that the work should be carried out by the business that puts in the lowest tender (bid) for the work, so services such as refuse collection or road works, can be contracted out for private businesses to carry out for local government.

The Bank of England

TYPES OF BUSINESS OWNERSHIP SECTION 2

PUBLIC CORPORATIONS

The government is responsible for a number of industries and businesses such as the British Broadcasting Corporation (BBC), the Bank of England and the Post Office. A public corporation is set up by an Act of Parliament and the government appoints a chairperson to be responsible for the day-to-day running of the corporation.

MAIN FEATURES OF THE PUBLIC SECTOR

The main objectives of the public sector are:
- to provide the public with essential services that could not always be run profitably
- to prevent the public from being exploited by private ownership
- to protect jobs and key industries needed by the UK economy.

The public sector is controlled by central and local government. The public corporations are required to appoint a chairperson, Board or Council to take charge of the day-to-day running of the organisation.

Finance can be obtained from annual grants from central government, subsidies, loans from other institutions and charges such as the BBC's licence fee or postage stamps.

KEY POINTS

- The public sector is made up of three areas:
  - central government
  - local government
  - public corporations and nationalised industries.

- The public sector is run to:
  - provide essential services that private business would often not consider profitable
  - prevent exploitation of essential services by private businesses
  - to provide employment and protect industries seen as vital to the country's interests.

- Central government provides services to the whole country paid for by taxes or a fee, e.g.
  - National Health Service
  - national road network.

- Local government provides services to specific parts of the country paid for by taxes, e.g.
  - education
  - police
  - fire services.

- Public corporations and nationalised industries are businesses run by the government which charge fees and are subsidised by the government, e.g.
  - the BBC
  - the Post Office.

UNIT 1 — PURPOSES AND TYPES OF BUSINESS ORGANISATION

TOPIC 8 — Privatisation

NATIONALISED INDUSTRIES

Until the 1980s some industries were considered so important to the nation that they were directly controlled by the government. Such industries included energy, water, railways, buses, steel and telecommunications.

It was felt that these would benefit from economies of scale, and the government could prevent the public being exploited by private owners since these industries had monopolies on their products – only one organisation provided electricity for example. It was also thought that running these industries for profit might not be in the interests of the country. Many nationalised industries needed state subsidies to keep them running as they were not profitable organisations. Nationalised industries were set up by an Act of Parliament. The government appointed a Board (or Council) to run the business and this was directly responsible to a Minister or Secretary of State in central government, e.g. British Airways, British Rail and the National Bus Company were all responsible to the Minister of Transport.

Sam and Harri need to know about privatisation

1980S PRIVATISATION

In the 1980s the majority of these nationalised industries were sold back into the private sector as the Conservative government of the time believed that only the private sector could provide the necessary entrepreneurship to make them profitable and that subsidising them was a drain on the nation's funds. This was done by selling off the organisations to financial institutions such as pension funds, insurance companies and private individuals.

TYPES OF BUSINESS OWNERSHIP **SECTION 2**

REVIEW QUESTION
1 List the industries that you think are still nationalised. Check with your teacher to see if you are correct.

SUPER REVIEW QUESTIONS
2 Give reasons for and against privatising national industries.
3 Discuss your reasons with your classmates and take a vote for or against privatisation.

KEY POINTS
- Many nationalised industries were privatised in the 1980s.

UNIT 1 — PURPOSES AND TYPES OF BUSINESS ORGANISATION

TOPIC 9 — Differences between public and private sectors

Public corporation	Private sector companies
Started by an Act of Parliament	Started by issuing a prospectus inviting the general public and financial institutions to buy shares in the company
Owned by the government	Owned by the shareholders
The objectives of the organisation are to provide essential services to the public, to set annual commercial targets and to consider the social costs and benefits provided by the organisation	The objectives are to maximise profits and to promote company growth
The day-to-day running is by the chairperson and managers appointed by the government	The day-to-day running is by the Board of Directors and managers appointed by the shareholders
The sources of finance are grants and loans from government and the charging of fees	Finance is raised by selling shares to the public and financial institutions. Financial institutions also willing to lend money to large well-established companies

COURSEWORK ACTIVITY

1. Conduct a survey of your local area. By observation, note down the names and addresses of businesses and their main activity, e.g. farming, providing goods and services. If you are looking at a wider geographical area, e.g. a trading estate, it may be better to use other methods, e.g. maps and information from the local Chamber of Commerce. When you return to your classroom look up their telephone numbers and add these to the details you have already collected.
2. Now discuss with your teacher the type of business activity each business is involved in – i.e. primary, secondary or tertiary – and who has control of the business, – i.e. sole trader, partners etc. Add these details to the research you have already carried out.
3. Set up a database file of all these details about businesses in your local area.

Section 3 Management, structure and organisation of business

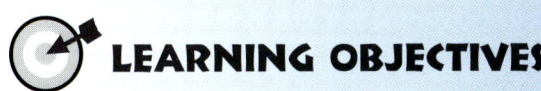# LEARNING OBJECTIVES

By the end of this section you should have learnt:
- the range of management structures found in different types of companies
- the different organisational structures – i.e. functional, regional, product
- to draw an organisation chart for a large company
- the terminology – hierarchy, span of control, chain of command, delegation, line and staff relationships
- the meaning of centralisation and decentralisation
- the effects different leadership styles can have on the business
- the methods of internal and external communication used within a business
- the different channels of communication
- methods of communication used by business – verbal, written, visual and electronic
- to produce a range of documents to illustrate different methods of communication within a business.

UNIT 1 — PURPOSES AND TYPES OF BUSINESS ORGANISATION

TOPIC 1: Management structures and organisation charts

Any small business, such as a sole trader or a partnership, will have a very simple management structure that will enable decisions to be passed down quickly from the owners to the employees.

Sam and Harri need to find out about management structure

CASE STUDY

Judy is a young entrepreneur. She has worked as a manager in a large travel agent's office, but has decided to start her own travel business.

Her father is prepared to lend her some of the capital to start up, so they both become part owners and form a private limited company, but her father lets Judy run the business. She opens one travel agent's office called Rapid Travel and employs two people to work for her.

In Judy's company, the **hierarchical structure**, which shows the levels of responsibility within the company, has just two levels, as shown in the organisation chart below. Judy, who is in charge, is at the top, and on the next level down, are the two employees.

```
         Judy (Director)
         _____|_____
        |                 |
       Sara             Rashid
```

Three years later, Judy has met Robert and they have married. Robert becomes one of the owners in the business, with Judy and her father, and as the first office has done so well, they decide to open a second office at the other side of town. In the new office they employ three staff. At the top of page 49 is an organisation chart showing the change in the management structure in the company.

MANAGEMENT, STRUCTURE AND ORGANISATION OF BUSINESS

SECTION 3

KEY POINTS

Every company has a management structure that can be shown on a chart.

- **Hierarchy** – the levels of responsibility in a company.
- **Chain of command** – the route by which decisions are passed between the different levels of a company.
- **Span of control** – how many other people a manager is responsible for.

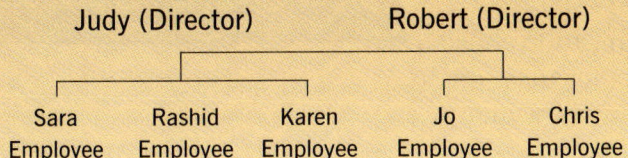

After another two years, Judy and Robert look for a suitable location for a third office. Judy and Robert decide to employ an office manager in the first office and increase the number of employees there to four. They will concentrate their time on setting up the new office and employ three people to work for them there.

The new organisation chart will have three levels to the hierarchy. The organisation chart shows the **span of control** for each director and the manager. The span of control is the number of employees one person has responsibility for. For example, the office manager's span of control is of the four employees working in his office.

The chart also shows the **chain of command**. This is the way decisions are passed down, or up, from one level to the next; e.g. the senior management team will pass decisions down to middle managers, who will pass decisions down to junior managers and so on.

COURSEWORK ACTIVITY

Draw a new organisation chart for Rapid Travel Ltd, from the information above, showing the three levels of the hierarchy and the revised management structure.

UNIT 1 — PURPOSES AND TYPES OF BUSINESS ORGANISATION

TOPIC 2: Tall organisation

The organisation chart below shows that the management structure is based on a **hierarchy**, which is like a pyramid, with the people with the most responsibility at the top. The management structure has several clear levels of responsibility. People on the same line of the chart have equal responsibility. The people they are responsible for are on the next line down on the chart.

Equally, decisions and suggestions can be passed **up** to the management from the workers; for example, with a company that uses Total Quality Management the workers might pass up suggestions to their supervisors on methods of improving quality standards in the business. (See Unit 5 Section 6, pages 303–307 for further details.) Each person on the organisation chart is responsible for a number of staff, except for those on the bottom level. The span of control shows how many people one person is responsible for.

Sam and Harri need to understand tall organisations

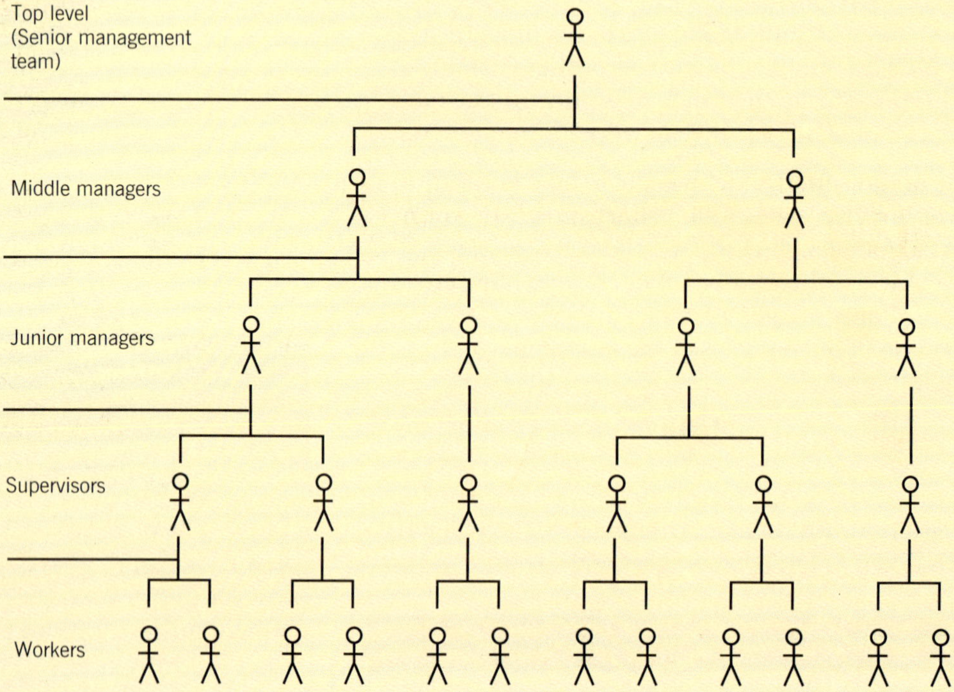

- Top level (Senior management team)
- Middle managers
- Junior managers
- Supervisors
- Workers

MANAGEMENT, STRUCTURE AND ORGANISATION OF BUSINESS SECTION 3

The organisation chart on page 50 shows a **tall organisation**. This means the company has a narrow span of control.

ADVANTAGES

- Each employee has only one manager to whom he or she is responsible.
- It is easier to check everyone's work because there are managers and supervisors at all levels of the hierarchy.
- Communication should be better because the chain of command shows a clear line for messages from the top to the bottom of the hierarchy.

DISADVANTAGES

- The hierarchical system is rigid and inflexible.
- People's position in the management structure shows their level of responsibility and authority and it is often seen as a status symbol with clear divisions between the managers and the workers.
- There can be too many layers of management and this will then create a long chain of command.
- A long chain of command will mean it takes decisions a long time to reach the workers at the bottom of the hierarchy.

KEY POINTS

- A tall organisation is:
  - one which has many levels of management
  - where managers have a narrow span of control.
- Advantages:
  - easier to control workers
  - easier to check work
  - clear structure for communicating between different levels.
- Disadvantages:
  - can be rigid and inflexible
  - can cause friction between different levels
  - long chain of command can affect communication.

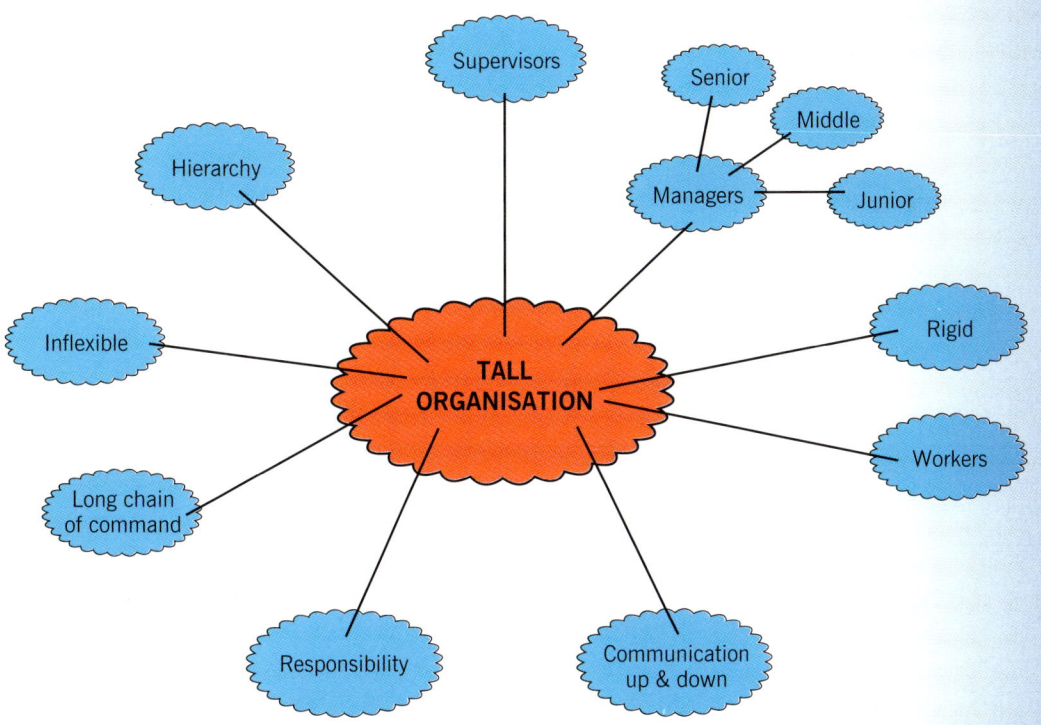

UNIT 1 — PURPOSES AND TYPES OF BUSINESS ORGANISATION

TOPIC 3: Flat organisation

In a **flat organisation** each manager has a wider span of control.

There are less levels of management and therefore the chain of command is much shorter. People on the lower levels tend to have more responsibility than in a tall organisation. Managers therefore need to be confident in their staff. They also need to be happy delegating work to their subordinates.

Sam and Harri need to understand flat organisations

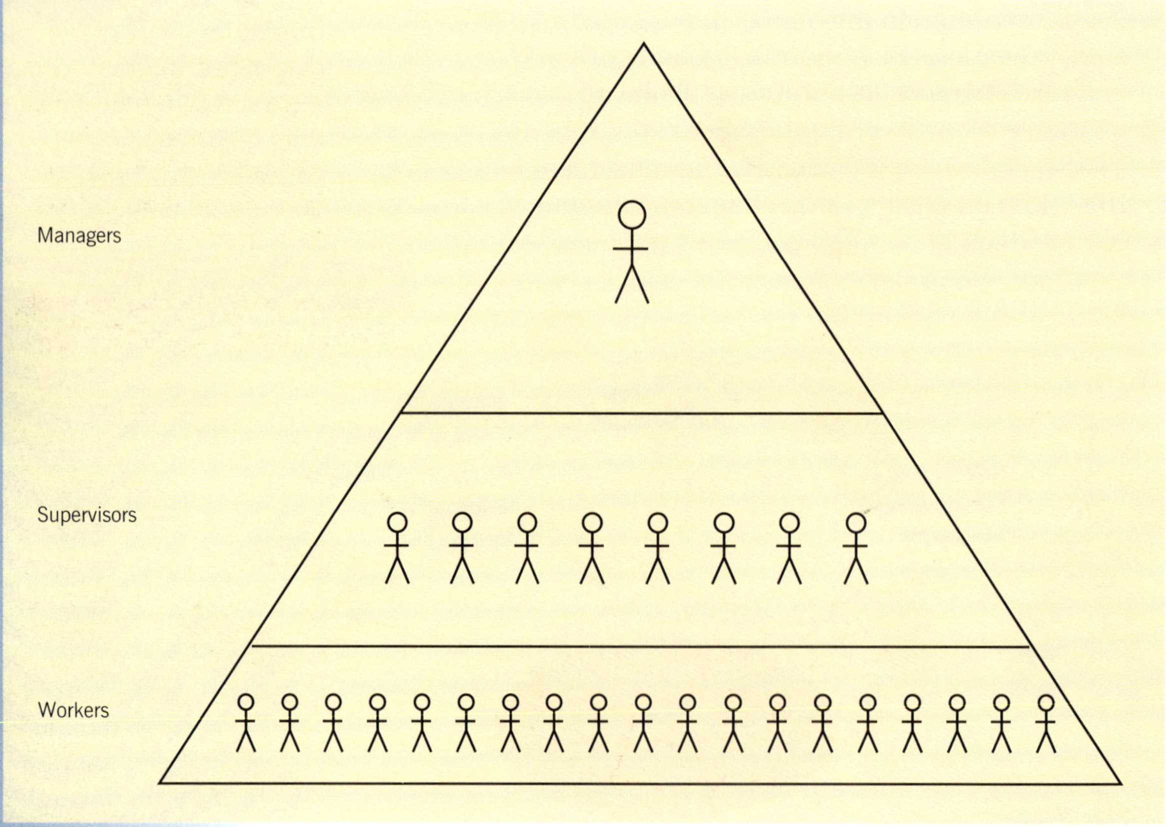

- Managers
- Supervisors
- Workers

ADVANTAGES

- Fewer managers are needed.
- Managers give more responsibility to the workers.
- More responsibility leads to more job satisfaction for the workers.
- Much shorter chain of command leads to faster, more efficient communication between management and staff.

DISADVANTAGES

- Each manager is responsible for more people.
- Managers have to rely on their subordinate staff much more to work efficiently and safely.
- Managers may lose control of subordinates as there is too wide a span of control for each manager.

KEY POINTS

- A flat organisation is:
  - one which has few levels of management
  - where managers have a wider span of control.
- Advantages:
  - fewer managers needed
  - workers given more responsibility
  - shorter chain of command means better communication.
- Disadvantages:
  - managers responsible for more people
  - more responsibility lies with workers
  - cannot check the work of each worker and so lose control.

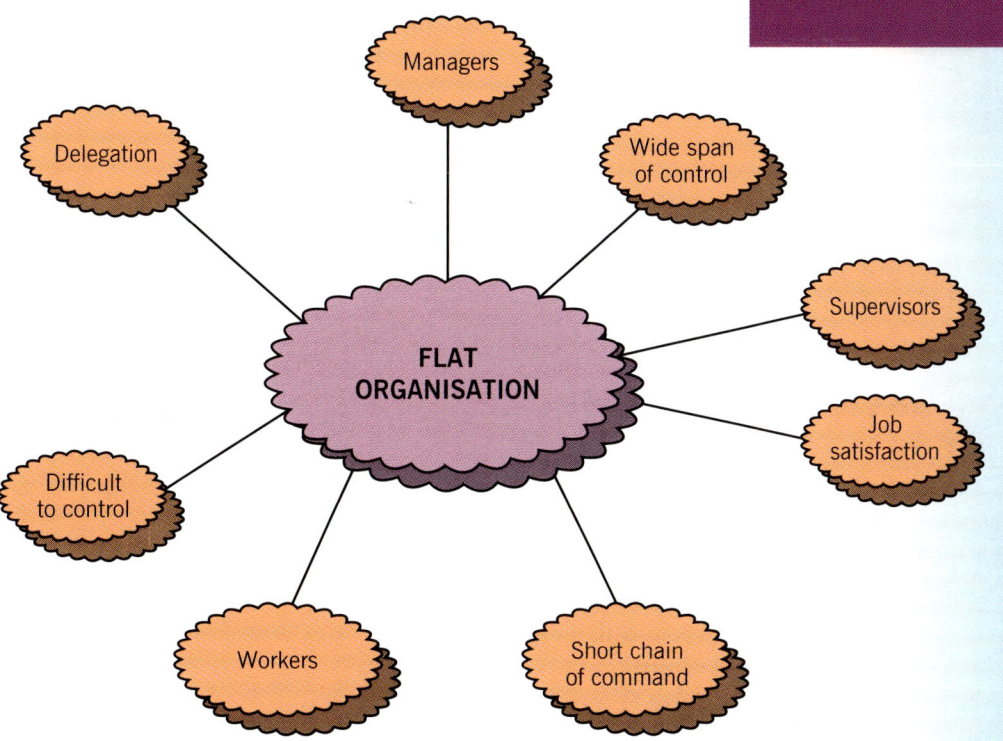

UNIT 1 — PURPOSES AND TYPES OF BUSINESS ORGANISATION

TOPIC 4 — Retail organisation

In large companies the structure is likely to change according to the type of business activity. For example, the management structure of a retail organisation would be very different from that of a manufacturing company. Below is a diagram showing the top levels of the organisation chart in a retail company. This company has also been structured according to the business functions – that is Marketing, Retail, Purchasing, Finance and Human Resources. This is known as a **functional** organisation chart.

Sam and Harri need to know how a retail organisation might be structured

```
                    Managing Director
   ┌──────────┬──────────┬──────────┬──────────┐
Marketing   Retail    Purchasing  Sales     Human
Director   Director   Director   Director  Resources
                                           Director
```

REVIEW QUESTIONS

1. From the organisation chart above, state the span of control of the Managing Director.
2. State the number of levels in the hierarchy shown on this organisation chart.

SUPER REVIEW QUESTIONS

3. Explain the difference between a tall organisation and a flat organisation.
4. State the advantages and disadvantages of a highly hierarchical structure in a company.
5. In the organisation chart for a tall organisation, explain the chain of command from the Managing Director to the workers.

MANAGEMENT, STRUCTURE AND ORGANISATION OF BUSINESS

RESPONSIBILITIES OF DIRECTORS AND DEPARTMENTS

The Marketing Director is responsible for market research to identify the current consumer needs and wants. He or she also tries to predict future buying trends. The Marketing department is also responsible for advertising, packaging and sales promotion for the company.

The Purchasing Director is responsible for buying all the goods for sale to the consumer. He or she is also responsible for buying supplies and equipment for the company – e.g. office equipment and stationery. The Purchasing department also chooses the suppliers and makes sure that only good-quality goods are bought at the right price.

The Sales Director is responsible for making sure that the company provides an efficient service to the consumer. The Sales department deals with consumer complaints and is often in charge of distribution (transport) – unless this work is contracted out to a specialist haulage contractor.

The Finance Director is responsible for keeping accurate records of all business transactions and keeping the company's finances in order.

The Human Resources Director is responsible for the employees – recruiting, training and dismissing staff.

KEY POINTS

- A retail organisation will probably have a functional structure
- **Functional structure** – departments organised according to what they do

UNIT 1 PURPOSES AND TYPES OF BUSINESS ORGANISATION

TOPIC 5 — Manufacturing organisation

In a manufacturing company the management structure might be like the one below.

The Marketing, Finance and Human Resources Directors will have similar roles to those in the retail organisation. The additional director – the Production (or Operations) Director – is responsible for manufacturing the company products. The Purchasing Director in a manufacturing company is also responsible for the purchasing of raw materials and semi-finished products.

These are examples of functional directors – directors who are in charge of one of the company's specific functions. Depending on the type of business the company is in there will be different titles – for example, Medical Research (drugs company), Editorial (publishing company), Logistics (distribution company).

Sam and Harri need to know how a manufacturing company might be organised

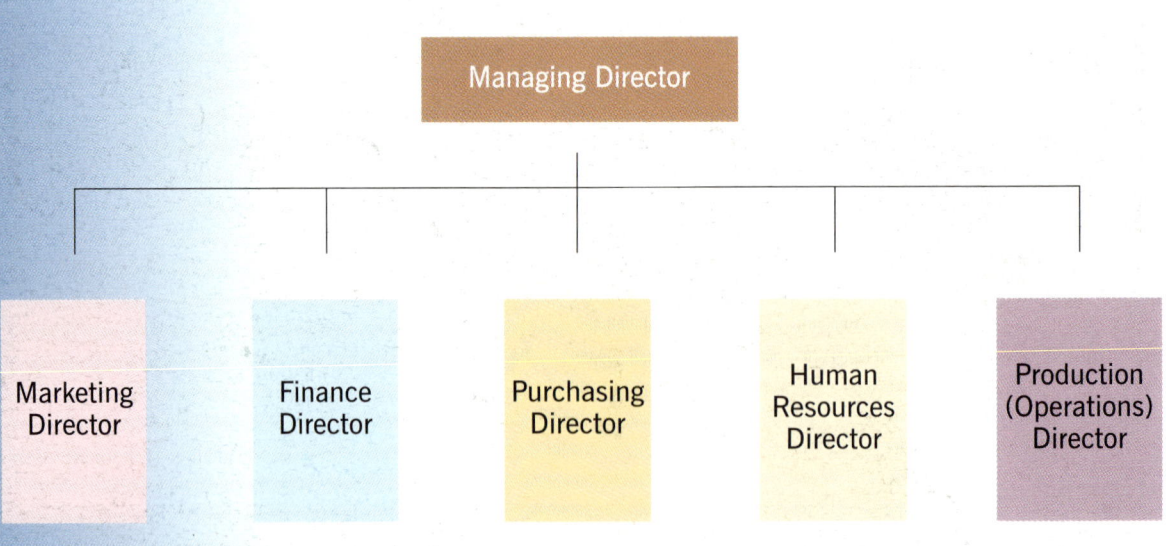

56

MANAGEMENT, STRUCTURE AND ORGANISATION OF BUSINESS SECTION 3

COURSEWORK ACTIVITY

Ask some of your friends and family what different directors' titles they know of. Discuss with your classmates what titles they can think of. Write down all the titles you come up with then write a brief description of what this part of the company does.

KEY POINTS

- A manufacturing organisation will probably have a functional structure with functional directors

- **Functional directors** – directors whose responsibilities are organised according to the job they do

UNIT 1 PURPOSES AND TYPES OF BUSINESS ORGANISATION

TOPIC 6 — Functional, regional and product organisational structures

Very large multinational companies are too large to organise just on a **functional** basis, that is by departments such as Finance, Human Resources, Marketing and Sales, so large companies are often organised in several different ways.

Many are organised **functionally** across the whole business for some activities of the business, such as marketing. For example, the Burger King fast food chain is run so that each fast food restaurant is responsible for its own day-to-day running, but all marketing such as advertising and promotional campaigns are run centrally.

Sam and Harri need to know how very large organisations are structured

Companies can be organised **regionally** if the company has bases all over the world. For example, they could be organised according to the continents **in which they trade**, so a company such as McDonalds could have a headquarters in the USA, another one in the UK for Europe, another one in Russia for Asia, and another one in Australia. Smaller companies within the UK could organise according to region, i.e. into northern and southern divisions.

They could also be organised according to the **product**. For example, News Corporation has television, film, newspaper and also computer game divisions; Unilever has detergent companies (Lever Bros), frozen food companies (Birds Eye), ice cream divisions (Walls).

MANAGEMENT, STRUCTURE AND ORGANISATION OF BUSINESS — SECTION 3

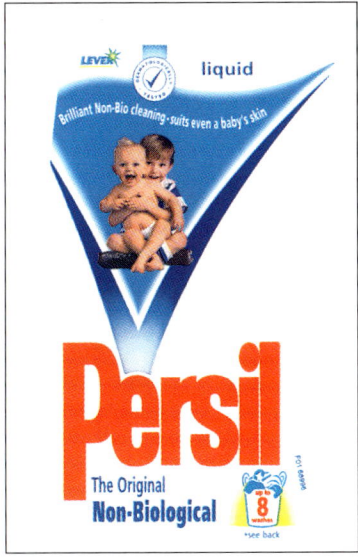

REVIEW QUESTION

1. List the departments that you think would be necessary in a large company like Marks and Spencer.

SUPER REVIEW QUESTION

2. Explain the functions of these departments and the responsibilities of the directors within each department.

KEY POINTS

Very large companies, often multinationals, are too large to be organised in a simple way.

They can be organised by:

- **function** – some business activities cover the entire company, others are covered by individual parts of the business

- **region** – the same business activities are performed by different teams in different countries or regions

- **product** – the same business activities are performed by different teams working on different products.

UNIT 1 — PURPOSES AND TYPES OF BUSINESS ORGANISATION

TOPIC 7: Centralisation and decentralisation

CENTRALISED

The organisation of many large companies is **centralised** which means all the major decisions are made by the directors, often at the Head Office. In a manufacturing company these decisions are then passed down to the various departments in the company. In the case of retail organisations the decisions can be made centrally and then passed down to the managers in the individual stores and superstores around the country. The managers have very little say in the running of their own store.

This centralised type of decision-making has its advantages as it means everyone is working to the same orders and decisions. It provides a common format for running the whole company and there is tight central control of the decision-making.

The biggest disadvantage is that the managers do not feel in control, and the decisions made by the Directors at the Head Office may not take into account regional differences. Companies with centralised decision-making can be slow putting the decisions in place because it takes time for the decisions to pass down from the Head Office to the regional offices or stores.

Sam and Harri need to understand centralised and decentralised structure

MANAGEMENT, STRUCTURE AND ORGANISATION OF BUSINESS SECTION 3

DECENTRALISED

Decentralised organisations **delegate** most of the decisions to the managers of the departments in the manufacturing organisation or to the store managers in the retail organisations. The directors will make the major decisions and then allow the managers in different departments or stores more freedom to make decisions on day-to-day running.

The advantages of this type of organisation are that it motivates managers and encourages competition and new initiatives to be developed between the different sections of the company. The managers are more in contact with what is happening in their area and are able to act more quickly than if they had to wait for decisions to come down from the Head Office.

The disadvantages are that managers can sometimes lack the expertise for the responsibilities they have, or they may not understand the way that individual decisions could affect the whole company. Departments or stores working totally independently will not have the advantages of economies of scale.

KEY POINTS

Decision-making can be:

- **centralised** – all major decisions are made by the directors, often based in a Head Office
- **decentralised** – most decisions are made by managers in individual branches or departments.

COURSEWORK ACTIVITY

Draw an organisation chart for a large company in your local area. Label the main levels of responsibility. Describe the type of management structure used by the company. Explain the terms: hierarchy, chain of command, span of control. Show how each of these terms applies to the company you have researched.

UNIT 1: PURPOSES AND TYPES OF BUSINESS ORGANISATION

TOPIC 8: Leadership styles

Directors and managers are **leaders** in their companies. They set targets for their workers, organise their work and monitor their progress. The ways that managers lead workers is important for the business, because if the workers do not respond to the leader the business can fail. There are three main leadership styles.

Sam and Harri need to learn about different leadership styles

AUTOCRATIC LEADERS

This type of leader makes all the decisions and then gives orders to the workers. There is very little communication with the workers because they are told everything they have to do from above. If the leader is giving the right orders it can work well, but it can also be very demotivating for the workers who have no say in what they are doing. An example of an autocratic leader is a ship's captain, whose orders must be obeyed by the crew under his command.

LAISSEZ-FAIRE

This loosely means 'do your own thing'. This type of leader allows the workers to make most of the decisions themselves. It can encourage the workers to think more and try to help solve problems because they are involved, but it can also make the workers feel there is no one in charge and no sense of direction in the company.

DEMOCRATIC LEADERS

This type of leader shares some of the decision-making with the workers. The leader still makes most of the decisions but then **persuades** the workers it is the right decison instead of giving direct orders. For example, the manager may have decided to change the workers' starting time in the morning. He or she wants the workers to believe it is a good idea, so the matter is discussed with them and all the advantages pointed out. This way it is hoped the workers feel they have made the decision, not the manager. Alternatively, the leader can genuinely **consult** with the workers before making the decisions. This will motivate the workers more, as they really are involved in decision-making, but it takes much longer to reach decisions using this type of leadership. Richard Branson is viewed to be a democratic leader, as he regularly meets and consults with his managers and workers.

REVIEW QUESTIONS

1. State what type of leader the manager is if he or she always tells the workers what to do and never consults them before making decisions.
2. Explain the following terms:
   - a regional organisation structure
   - centralisation
   - a democratic leader.

KEY POINTS

There are three main leadership styles:

- **autocratic** – decisions are made by the manager and workers are ordered to follow them
- **democratic** – decisions are made by the manager in consultation with workers and the managers persuade the workers to follow them
- **laissez-faire** – the manager encourages workers to make most of the decisions for themselves.

UNIT 1 — PURPOSES AND TYPES OF BUSINESS ORGANISATION

TOPIC 9 — Communication

IMPORTANCE OF COMMUNICATION

Effective and efficient forms of communication are essential if a business is to succeed. Businesses need to communicate to gather information, to give information to others, to give orders or to discuss issues. For example, Rapid Travel uses **booking forms** to gather information from its clients, **memos** via **electronic mail** to send information to staff in its other offices, such as details of an invitation to a promotion event, and **letters** to clients confirming their bookings. Managers would **telephone** members of staff to tell them about a training course that is available, or hold a **meeting** with staff to discuss changes to uniform.

Sam and Harri need know about different methods of comminication

COMMUNICATION IN THE CHAIN OF COMMAND

We saw that, in some management structures, the chain of command can be quite long from the managing director to the workers, making it even more important for a business to have good forms of communication if decisions and orders are to get through to the workers accurately and quickly. Today, businesses use a wide range of methods of communication. Some examples are: the telephone, fax, electronic mail, face-to-face meetings, letters, notices for the noticeboard or reports.

All businesses communicate both internally and externally.

MANAGEMENT, STRUCTURE AND ORGANISATION OF BUSINESS

INTERNAL COMMUNICATION

Internal communication takes place between people **inside** the business and a variety of different methods can be used to pass information from one person to another, such as verbal messages, face-to-face meetings, a memorandum, a report, a notice, the internal telephone system and electronic mail. For example, a Managing Director could send a memorandum to line managers to remind them of an important meeting.

EXTERNAL COMMUNICATION

External communication takes place between the company and outside organisations and people. Methods such as letters, telephone calls, electronic mail, fax machines, and the Internet are all used to communicate information outside the business.

KEY POINTS
- Successful businesses need good communication.
- Communication can be:
  - **internal** – communication between people inside the business
  - **external** – communication between the business and people outside the business, such as consumers or other businesses.

UNIT 1 — PURPOSES AND TYPES OF BUSINESS ORGANISATION

TOPIC 10 Channels of communication

When information passes from one person to another it travels along **channels of communication**.

FORMAL

The **formal** channels of communication are agreed by the management and workers. Information can pass **vertically** through the business down the chain of command, for instance the Managing Director would pass on information to the Production Director that needed to reach the production line workers. The Production Director would pass this information on to the supervisor who would pass it on to the workers. Information can also pass in the opposite direction, from the worker to the Production Director.

Sam and Harri need to understand channels of communication

When information is passed from one worker to another on the same level, this is known as **horizontal** communication. For example, an assistant in a fast food restaurant telling a colleague just coming on duty that a till is not working.

INFORMAL

Not all communication within the business is **formal**. There is always chat and gossip between workers that is often nothing to do with work and this kind of information also passes around the business. This is called **informal** communication. This sort of communication does not follow any set route – it can be passed around to anyone who is listening.

Informal conversation

Formal conversation

MANAGEMENT, STRUCTURE AND ORGANISATION OF BUSINESS   SECTION 3

The manager, Gail, passes on information about training courses for the new sewing machines (vertical communication). Bernadette passes information up about the safety hazards of some cotton waste (vertical communication). Bernadette tells Jana that the canteen now has decafinated coffee (horizontal communication). Bernadette knows Depak because their children are in the same class at school. Depak tells Bernadette that George, the Production Director, is going to the factory in Manchester for six months to sort out the production problems (informal communication).

KEY POINTS

- **Channels of communication** – the ways in which internal communication takes place:
  - **vertical** – formal passing of information through the chain of command
  - **horizontal** – formal passing of information between people working at the same hierarchical level.
- Information can be passed between people through informal conversation such as rumours.

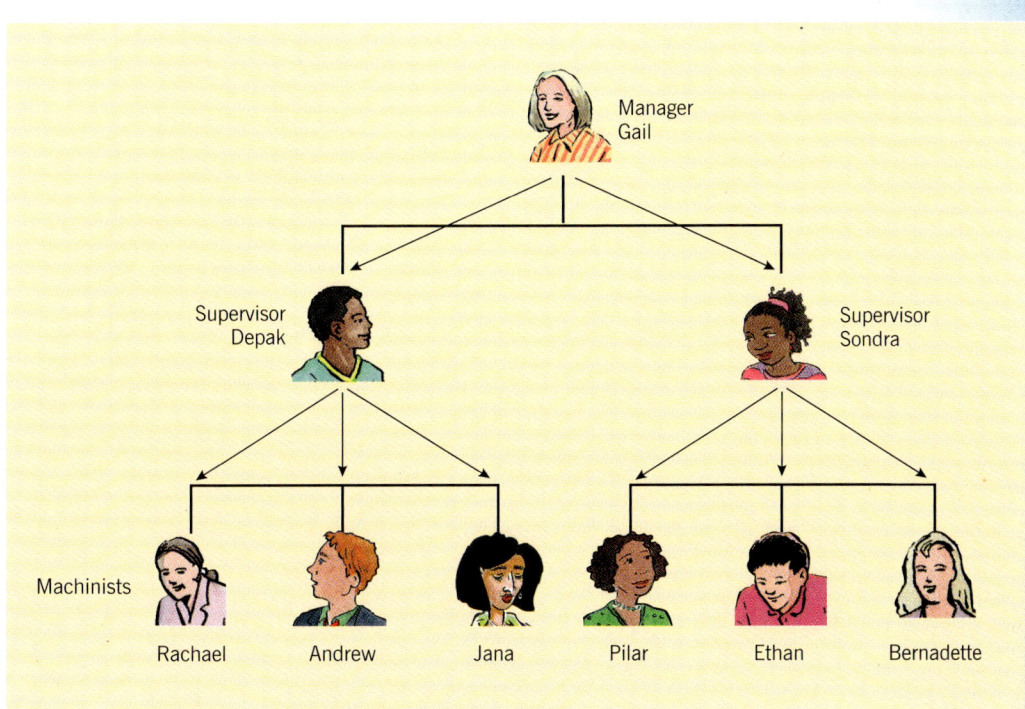

UNIT 1 PURPOSES AND TYPES OF BUSINESS ORGANISATION

TOPIC 11 Methods of communication

The main methods of communication used by businesses are listed in the chart below. They all have their advantages and disadvantages. The method you choose will depend on the situation and the money and time available. For example, you might fax a contract to someone so they can have a chance to read through it, but send the original to them by post so that they can sign it.

Sam and Harri need to know about different methods of communication

Method	Advantages	Disadvantages
Post	traditional, everyone knows it	slow
Courier	quick	can be expensive
Fax	quick and efficient	does not always look clear
Video-conferencing	face-to-face instant exchange of views among many people, saves transport costs	equipment is expensive
Telephone	instant	no written record, can't see the other person
Interview	face-to-face	time-consuming
Meeting	face-to-face exchange of views among many people	time-consuming, have to pay for transport and sometimes accommodation

MANAGEMENT, STRUCTURE AND ORGANISATION OF BUSINESS
SECTION 3

KEY POINTS
- The main methods of external communication are:
  - written – letters, memoranda, reports
  - electronic – faxes, electronic mail, web sites
  - verbal – telephones, interviews, meetings
  - visual – videos, graphs, posters.

REVIEW QUESTION

1 State the most appropriate method of communication in the following circumstances:
   ◆ Hospital receptionist needs to talk to a consultant who is doing the rounds on the wards.
   ◆ A manager wants to tell staff about a company outing that is being organised to London, to go to the theatre.
   ◆ A Finance Director has to give a presentation to the Board on the last quarter's accounts.
   ◆ The Managing Director's Personal Assistant needs to send an urgent document to clients which must reach them today.

UNIT 1 — PURPOSES AND TYPES OF BUSINESS ORGANISATION

TOPIC 12 Examples of business document formats

MEMORANDUM

A memorandum (usually called **memo**) is a short note sent from one person to another within the company. It is used when it is necessary to have a record of the information being sent. The example below shows the headings generally used.

```
              MEMORANDUM

To:    Judy         Date    10/4/20X1

From:  Rachida

Subject:  Vision Car Hire

Mr and Mrs Collinson came into the
shop today and complained about the
extra charges Vision Car Hire put on
their bill – despite their thinking
everything was pre-paid. I have asked
them to put their complaint in
writing.
This is the third complaint about
Vision Car Hire this month and I am
concerned our tailor-made packages
will be getting a bad name.
```

Sam and Harri need to know about different business documents

ELECTRONIC MAIL

As electronic communication becomes more popular the paper memo is becoming a thing of the past. Now employees within an organisation are more likely to send an electronic mail message to each other.

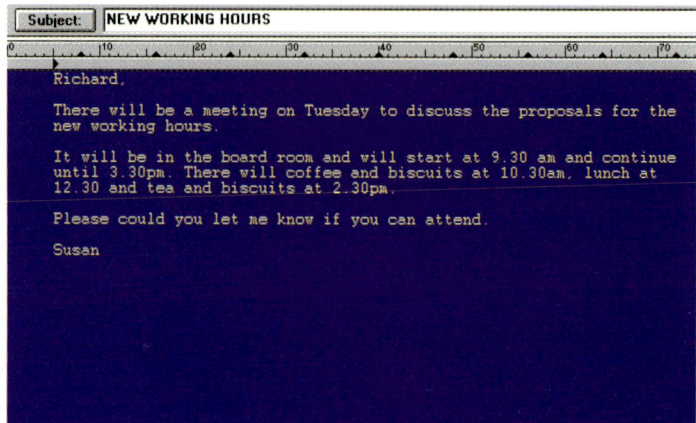

70

REPORTS

Reports need a clear structure – a beginning, a middle and an end.

The beginning should:
- set the scene
- make clear the topic for discussion
- set out the objectives and purpose of the report.

The middle should:
- put over the detail/content of the report
- ensure clarity and style appropriate to readers.

The end should:
- reach and present a conclusion
- pull together and summarise the content
- end positively.

The format of the report

The report should begin with **a title page**. This should include: the company name, a clear title for the report, the terms of reference. It could also include a date and circulation slip of the recipients.

The beginning of the report should include:

To:

From:

Date:

Terms of reference:
(The objectives and purpose of the report)

The middle of the report could be titled:
Findings or Content

The end of the report should include:
Conclusions:
Recommendations:

RAPID TRAVEL

REPORT ON VISION CAR HIRE

16/4/20X1

Terms of reference
To investigate the complaints that have been received about extra charges from Vision Car Hire and to conclude whether it is in the company's best interests to continue using the car hire firm.

Introduction

There have now been ten complaints about extra charges being levied by Vision Car Hire. We state in our tailor-made package brochure that the car-hire is pre-paid.

The complaints

Three couples were charged £25 for 'post-trip maintenance', two couples have been charged £30 for 'fuel missing' and five people have been charged £20 for 'post-trip cleaning'.

Response from Vision Car Hire

The 'fuel missing' charge is, apparently, standard if a car is brought back without a full tank of petrol. However, Vision have admitted that the 'post-trip maintenance' and 'post-trip cleaning' should not have been charged as they are included in the price we pay them as part of the deal. They have agreed to refund the money they have received for those charges and assure us that it will not happen again.

Figures

The tailor-made packages form a large part of our business – 20% – and the inclusion of car-hire in the deal is particularly popular (75% of customers say it is important for them). The deal with Vision is a good one and they also market our business as part of the deal by distributing leaflets to their customers.

Conclusion

I propose that we continue with Vision for the time being and monitor their service carefully. We should, at the same time, make some investigations into alternative car hire companies should we need to change in the future.

We should put a statement in the letter that is sent to customers with their tickets informing them that they are required to return the car with a full tank of petrol otherwise a charge of £30 will be levied by the hire company.

Providing we monitor them carefully, I believe that we should be able to continue our relationship with Vision satisfactorily.

UNIT 1 PURPOSES AND TYPES OF BUSINESS ORGANISATION

BUSINESS LETTERS

A business letter is probably still the most common type of external communication between two companies. It is fast being replaced by electronic mail and faxes, but it still has an important place in the business world. However the letter is sent it is important that it is written in good, polite English and that its contents are clear. The person who receives the letter should be able to understand it easily and have a good opinion of the sender.

J & J Clothing

2 Newtown Industrial Estate, Newtown NI6 5AB

Tel: 01112 222111
Fax: 01112 112211

1 May 20X2

Mr P Rayner
Customer Services Manager
Material Supplies
22 Park Road
OLDTOWN
OP2 5AB

Dear Mr Rayner

Denim delivery – Order no: 32789

It has been brought to my attention that the above order has not yet been delivered. The order was placed on 15 January 20X2. My assistant has telephoned your department on four different occasions and has been told each time that the order is on its way.

I regret that this amount of delay is unacceptable. If we do not receive the order by 7 May then I will be forced to cancel it. We will also find another supplier for any future orders.

I would be grateful if you could let me know as soon as possible when the order will arrive and also provide me with an explanation for the extreme delay of this order.

Yours sincerely

Ms H Aitcheson
Production Director

REVIEW QUESTIONS

1. List the four main methods of communication used by businesses.
2. Explain the difference between internal and external communication.

SUPER REVIEW QUESTIONS

3. Explain the importance of effective communication to any business.
4. Explain how the channels of communication work.
5. Explain how informal communication differs from formal communication.

MANAGEMENT, STRUCTURE AND ORGANISATION OF BUSINESS **SECTION 3**

KEY POINTS

Forms of written communication include:
- Memoranda
- Electronic mail
- Reports
- Business letters

COURSEWORK ACTIVITY

1. Draw a table with four column headings:
   Verbal   Written
   Visual   Electronic
2. Look at each of the drawings above and place them under the correct heading.
3. Give an example of different jobs in Rapid Travel Ltd, where it would be appropriate to use each of these methods of communication.

UNIT 1 — PURPOSES AND TYPES OF BUSINESS ORGANISATION

CASE STUDY – RAPID TRAVEL LTD

Rapid Travel Ltd is doing so well that Judy and Robert decide to open a fourth office. As the company is getting very much bigger they decide they can no longer look after the day-to-day running of the business, except with the long-established clients who still want their personal service. They employ four full-time staff and an office manager in each of the four branches.

David, Judy's father, now begins working for the business and sets up a Cruise Line section but he does this himself from home. He does not have any help with this work. Judy and Robert will be responsible for the decision-making, monitoring of each office, hiring and dismissing staff and the company finances. The office managers will be in charge of the day-to-day running of each branch.

The offices have the latest technology with personal computers in each office. Electronic mail is used to link the offices and pass information between them. A network has been installed to link the offices with the tour operators for booking holidays.

Below is a picture showing some of the work going on in one of the offices. A wide range of methods of communication is being used. One member of staff is with a client booking a holiday. Another member of staff is word processing a letter to a client confirming that their holiday has been booked. Another member of staff is sending a fax message to their printing company ordering some more headed notepaper. One member of staff is putting a poster in the window advertising a special offer.

1. Draw an organisation chart for Rapid Travel Ltd after this latest expansion. Label the chart with the job titles of each member of staff.
2. Explain the chain of command if Judy wants to pass information to an assistant in Office 1.
3. Judy and Robert, as directors, take joint responsibility for the running of the company. David is responsible only for the Cruise Line section. State the span of control of Judy and Robert in the business now it has expanded again.
4. Read through the Case Study and then carry out the tasks listed below:
   ◆ Produce a booking form for the travel agency to use.
   ◆ Write a letter to some clients confirming the details of the holiday they have just booked.
   ◆ Send a fax to the office stationery supplier ordering 1000 copies of their headed paper.
   ◆ Design a poster to put in the window advertising a big reduction for a last-minute booking for a particular holiday.
   ◆ Make a list of all the information you need for each task before you begin. State on each document the method of communication being used, i.e. verbal, written, visual, or electronic.

Use the information in the Case Study to help you produce each of these business documents.

Section 4 Objectives of business

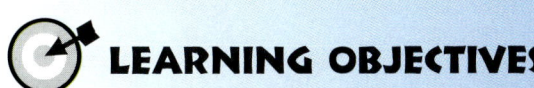
LEARNING OBJECTIVES

By the end of this section you should have learnt:
- the main business objectives
- the motives and benefits of company growth
- how to measure business success
- the methods of internal expansion
- how a company grows through a merger or a takeover
- the controls on mergers and takeovers
- the drawbacks of growth.

UNIT 1
PURPOSES AND TYPES OF BUSINESS ORGANISATION

TOPIC 1 — Main business objectives

Any entrepreneur starting up a business has a number of goals that he or she wants to achieve. These are called **objectives**.

One of the major objectives of any business owner is to make a profit, but this is not the only one. A person can start up a business for a variety of reasons:

- To begin with, the new owner will just want the business to survive.
- Soon he or she will hope the business will begin to make a profit, by increasing the sales and increasing the market share.
- He or she may want to be independent, and is tired of working for someone else.
- Later the owner may wish the business to grow.
- He or she will want to give customer satisfaction, by providing a good product or service.
- The owner may get satisfaction from providing employment for other people.

These are the main business objectives, but there are many others that motivate an entrepreneur to want to start up in business.

Sam and Harri need to understand business objectives

MOTIVES AND BENEFITS OF COMPANY GROWTH

Most businesses want to grow and be more successful. Many large companies are motivated to make their business grow because they want to be more powerful in the business world. Most large companies, even the multinationals, can often be traced back to a single owner starting up a small business with a good idea: Richard Branson is such a person. His first business venture started in January 1968, with the first issue of his Student Magazine. Two years later he started the Virgin Mail-order operation, and in 1971 he opened his first record shop in Oxford Street. Since then the Virgin Group of companies has grown and grown.

OBJECTIVES OF BUSINESS **SECTION 4**

Type of ownership	Objectives
Sole trader	After survival and profit, most sole traders want independence and job satisfaction
Partnership	Often prefer to share the responsibility of the business with others, job satisfaction
Worker cooperative	Want to work instead of being unemployed. Believe in an ideal world this is how all businesses should be run, with worker participation
Franchise	Franchisees want to run their own business but do not want the risk of starting it up themselves
Private limited company	Steady growth in profits, growth in turnover and increase in market share. Objectives are laid down for each individual company in their Memorandum of Association
Public limited company	Shareholders want to maximise profits. Directors and managers want business growth. All employees want good pay and working conditions

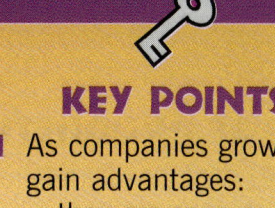

KEY POINTS

- As companies grow they gain advantages:
  - they are seen as less of a risk and so find it easier to borrow capital
  - as they get larger their influence on other businesses and even governments increases
  - they can spend more time and money on developing new ideas
  - they can use economies of scale.

There are definite advantages from being a large company when it comes to expansion and growth:

◆ It is easier to borrow money for growth, as the large company is not seen as such a risk, as it is not likely to go bankrupt.
◆ Large companies, because of their size, have a lot of influence around the world, both with other businesses and with governments.
◆ It is easier for them to develop new ideas as they have more money to spend on research and development.
◆ Large companies can take advantage of **economies of scale**.

UNIT 1 — PURPOSES AND TYPES OF BUSINESS ORGANISATION

TOPIC 2: Economies of scale

SCALE OF PRODUCTION

Economies of scale means that as the company grows and produces more goods the average costs of production should fall. As the company grows it will employ more staff, buy more equipment to make more goods. This is called increasing the **scale of production**. With the increase in the scale of production the average costs should reduce. An example of how economies of scale works could be the cost of making a bicycle.

OVERHEADS

If a company makes 100 bicycles per week, it will still have to pay the same amount of rent or mortgage, business rates, administration fees, heating and lighting bills, each week, as it would if it were making 10 000 bicycles. These costs are called **overheads** and always have to be paid no matter how many bicycles are being made. But when these costs are divided by the number of products made, the cost to the company for making each bicycle is very much less. For example:

Sam and Harri need to understand economies of scale

The labour and materials for one bicycle costs £50. The overheads for the company are £100 000 per week.

If only 100 bicycles were made per week this would make the final cost of one bicycle £50 plus the overhead costs split among 100 bicycles.

i.e. $\dfrac{£100\,000\,(\text{overheads})}{100\,(\text{number of bicycles})} = £1000$ per bicycle

If 10 000 bicycles were made per week this would make the final cost of one bicycle £60 per bicycle.

i.e. $\dfrac{£100\,000}{10\,000} + £50 = £60$

Also, as the bicycle company can buy its raw materials and component parts in large quantities, that is buy in **bulk**, it can often get discounts on the price it pays.

OBJECTIVES OF BUSINESS SECTION 4

There are other economies of scale to be gained from being a large company:

- **Technical economies** – such as the **division of labour**, which means workers can specialise in one job and become expert at it; or being able to use larger plant and equipment, which can do the job more quickly.
- **Labour economies** – such as a company being able to afford to employ their own specialists, such as a Marketing department instead of using outside agencies. Also, large-scale production usually involves some form of automation which means a reduction in the number of staff the company need to employ and, therefore, also leads to lower wage bills.
- **Administrative economies** – costs for management or computers can be reduced in a large company.
- **Financial economies** – such as borrowing money. The financial institutions see the large company as a much safer investment. They are less likely to go bankrupt and so the financial institution is much happier to lend money to a large company rather than a small one. The large company may even be offered lower interest rates when borrowing money as the financial institution wants the company to come back again to use their services.
- **Risk-bearing economies** – the large company often has a range of goods or services they provide and sell in a variety of countries around the world.

CASE STUDY – VIRGIN

Richard Branson and the Virgin Group are an example of economies of scale. The company uses risk-bearing economies. This means that the company's risks are spread, because if one section of the business fails, the others are still there to carry on. If a drop in sales of a certain product or a natural disaster in a certain company should affect one part of the group's operations, other sections can keep the group going.

Not all companies want to grow. Some want to stay small because they feel the small business can offer a higher quality individual product or service, give personal attention and they like the direct contact with their customers. Some people like working on their own and some want to stay in charge of their own business and not lose control to shareholders.

UNIT 1
PURPOSES AND TYPES OF BUSINESS ORGANISATION

TOPIC 3: Diseconomies of scale

If companies become too large they can become too big to manage efficiently and this can then lead to costs rising and **diseconomies of scale**. Some of the main reasons for diseconomies of scale are:

- There are too many layers of management. As the company grows they employ more and more managers and this can cause problems.
- The costs increase because of having to pay the managers.
- It takes longer for decisions to be made, which slows down business operation.
- The company loses sight of its original business objectives. Because it is so big, it loses touch with consumer demands and also with the purpose of the company.
- The managers in a large company may begin to feel complacent and set in their ways. They resist change and can become very inflexible in their attitudes towards the company and its workers.
- In large companies the directors can very easily lose all contact with the other employees. Passing orders and decisions down the chain of command is slow because there are so many levels of managers in the company structure.
- Because of this lack of contact with the senior management, employees can become demotivated as they feel no one has their interests at heart or listens to their ideas.

Sam and Harri need to understand diseconomies of scale

TOO MANY LAYERS OF MANAGEMENT

OBJECTIVES OF BUSINESS **SECTION 4**

KEY POINTS

- **Economies of scale** – the more goods the company produces the less it costs to produce one unit.
- **Overheads** – the costs of a business that do not depend on the amount of production.
- Economies of scale can be:
  - **technical** – better equipment or worker specialisation
  - **labour** – having functions performed in the company or increased automation
  - **administrative** – cutting costs in management
  - **financial** – borrowing money
  - **risk-bearing** – having a wide range of goods and markets.

KEY POINTS

- Management costs are too high
  - the company is not focused on its main objectives
  - managers become less willing to change
  - too many layers of management reduce communication and increase tension between managers and workers.

81

UNIT 1 PURPOSES AND TYPES OF BUSINESS ORGANISATION

TOPIC 4 — Measuring success

SUCCESS

As a company grows, how does it know that it is being successful? Is the fact that the company is growing enough? There are different ways of measuring a business's success:

- Look at the amount of profit made by the company each year. For example, if the company makes a pre-tax profit of £500 000 in year one and a pre-tax profit of £550 000 the next it has made an increase in profit of 10% on the first year.
- Look at the company's **turnover**, that is the total number of sales they make each year.
- The number of employees the company has working for it is another indicator of success.
- Finally, the company's **assets** – that is, what they own, such as land, buildings, equipment and the capital it can employ.

The company's turnover, the number of employees and the assets they own are also used to calculate the company's **size**.

Sam and Harri need to learn about measuring success

EFFICIENCY

Although all these measures are used to work out the success and size of the company, they cannot be used to work out if the company is working **efficiently**. Profit gives some guidance but the **profitability** of the company is a better indicator. The profitability is worked out by calculating the relationship of profits to the assets of the company (see Unit 4 Section 3, pages 253–265).

MARKET SHARE

Another way is to measure the company's **market share** for their product. The market share can be worked out by volume or price.

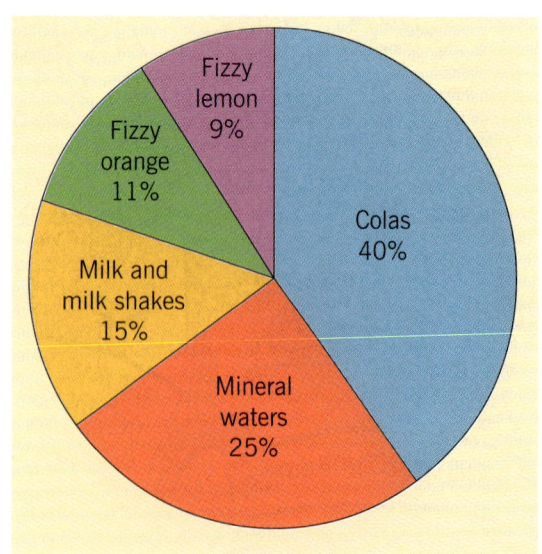

OBJECTIVES OF BUSINESS SECTION 4

VOLUME

Volume is when the number of products sold by all the different companies who make the same, or similar, products are added together and then the number of sales made by each individual company is worked out as a percentage of the whole.

For example, Virgin Cola could look at the number of sales of Cola type drinks, such as Pepsi, Coke, brand name Coca-Cola drinks. From the number of their own sales they can then work out their share of the market.

Market share can also be based on **price**, where a company look at the total value of sales. For example, Rolls-Royce sells fewer cars than Lada but the value of its sales is far higher because a Rolls-Royce costs far more than a Lada.

The directors of the company must also make sure it is run in the most cost-efficient way. The day-to-day running costs of the company must be kept to the minimum possible without compromising the quality of the product.

The final test of a company's success and efficiency is whether the customer is happy. If the customer is happy with the quality of the product and the price being charged, and the customer returns again and again, the company can consider itself successful.

KEY POINTS

- Success can be measured by:
  – increase in profits
  – increase in sales
  – the number of workers
  – the amount and types of assets.
- **Assets** – things that the company owns, e.g.
  – land
  – buildings
  – equipment.
- Efficiency can be measured by:
  – **profitability** – the relation between profits and assets
  – **market share** – what percentage of the total market does a product have, either by volume or price.

REVIEW QUESTION

The Kemp Trading Company plc has made the following net profit in each of the last four years.

1999	1998	1997	1996
£2 000 000	£1 500 000	£1 250 000	£1 000 000

1 Calculate the rate of growth each year.

SUPER REVIEW QUESTION

2 Comment on the company's success over this four-year period.

UNIT 1 PURPOSES AND TYPES OF BUSINESS ORGANISATION

TOPIC 5 Methods of expansion

Most businesses start off small and, as they make a profit and succeed, want to grow in size. Other terms sometimes used to describe types of business expansion include **company growth** and **integration** (vertical, horizontal or lateral). By taking advantage of the economies of scale, companies can put the profits back into the business and grow by increasing the number of products they make. This is known as **internal expansion**. This method is often slow and, if a company wants to grow and expand more quickly, **external expansion** may be considered by either a **merger** or **takeover**.

Sam and Harri need to understand methods of business expansion

INTERNAL EXPANSION

Internal expansion can come about in one of four ways:

1 **Natural growth**, sometimes called organic growth, is when the company is being run efficiently and the demand for the product just keeps growing and growing **naturally**. Some of the profits will be paid to the shareholders and some will be reinvested into the company which will help it to keep growing. The Body Shop started in this way. Anita Roddick started with just one shop in Brighton selling only a very small range of skin and hair care products. As demand grew she expanded to more and more shops around the country. As the demand has grown so quickly many branches of The Body Shop outlets are now franchised.

2 **Planned growth** is linked to market share, as when a company **plans** to try to increase its market share, for example, from 10% to 12% of the whole market. The Body Shop planned a move into men's skin and hair care products in 1986 in order to increase their market share of the toiletries business.

OBJECTIVES OF BUSINESS — SECTION 4

3 **Geographical growth** is when the company grows by looking to sell its products in new locations, either new parts of the country where they do not normally trade, or moving into exports and beginning to sell in foreign countries. From one shop in Brighton The Body Shop now trades in 47 countries around the world.

4 **Diversification** is when a company starts to develop new products or services for its customers either in its present market or by finding new markets to sell to. Richard Branson has diversified over the years moving from the Virgin recording studios to Virgin Atlantic (the airline section) to Virgin Direct (the financial services section). These are just a few of the different sections of the group.

REVIEW QUESTION

1 List the four main ways of internal expansion for a company.

SUPER REVIEW QUESTION

2 Look through the business sections of some national newspapers to find examples of four companies, each of which has been involved in one of these types of internal expansion. Explain how each of them has expanded.

EXTERNAL EXPANSION

External expansion comes about by:
- the company merging with another company,
- or by another company putting in a takeover bid for the company.

KEY POINTS

- Companies can grow by internal expansion, mergers, or takeovers.
- Internal expansion can be:
  - **natural growth** – consumer demand for the goods or services increases naturally
  - **planned growth** – the company plans to increase market share in the products it sells
  - **geographical growth** – the company plans to sell its products in new areas
  - **diversification** – the company develops new products similar to existing products, sells existing products to new markets, or produces new products with no connection with existing products.

UNIT 1 PURPOSES AND TYPES OF BUSINESS ORGANISATION

TOPIC 6 — Mergers and takeovers

MERGERS

Mergers are another method of growth. This growth involves other companies, as two or more companies agree to **merge** to make one new company, such as Citibank's recent merger with Travelers Group to form Citigroup, the worlds largest bank.

TAKEOVERS

A **takeover** is when one company wants to take over another company and make it part of its existing business, usually against the other company's will. The takeover company will try to persuade shareholders of the other company to sell their shares to them. It does this by offering a higher price for their shares than the current market value. Alternatively, it may offer shares in the takeover company, or a combination of shares and money. Most takeovers are large companies taking over smaller companies. Sometimes the takeovers are **aggressive** or **hostile**, for example, when a company is trying to eliminate a rival and reduce overheads. These takeovers are often fought by the Board of Directors. Most takeovers are friendly, such as a public limited company taking over a smaller private limited company.

Sam and Harri need to find out about mergers and takeovers

Benefits of mergers and takeovers

Company growth is much quicker by external expansion as the size of the company can virtually double immediately. Internal expansion is slower, because it means increasing demand or moving into new markets and this takes time, building a reputation and proving to the consumer that the company provides a quality product. When companies join together they will also both be able to reach a wider market segment. For example, if an insurance company and a bank merge then the bank can recommend the insurance company's services to its existing clients.

CONGLOMERATES

Conglomerates are a number of companies that have no common product or market areas which are brought together either through merger or takeover. For example, a conglomerate could be made up of a clothing manufacturer, an oil exploration company and an insurance company. There are no links between the different goods or services they provide. The companies usually join together to spread the risks across a wide range of products and services. This type of merger is not so popular in the current market and many large companies are selling off some of the smaller more diverse sections of their business to concentrate on core activities.

DE-MERGING

De-merging happens when large conglomerates or previously merged companies decide to sell off parts of their business. This might be to raise capital, concentrate efforts on a narrower range of activities or to float off one that has grown and become profitable.

TYPES OF INTEGRATION

There are three main types of integration – horizontal, lateral and vertical.

- **Horizontal** – when companies that make the same product integrate, for example, two manufacturers of aircraft.
- **Lateral** – when companies that make similar or related products integrate, for example, when an aircraft manufacturer merges with an aircraft engine manufacturer.
- **Vertical** – when two companies in the same industry that are involved at different stages of the production process integrate. In takeovers, when one company is more dominant than the other, these can be:
- **forward** – when the dominant company takes over a company at a **later** stage in the production process, for example an aircraft manufacturing company (secondary) taking over an airline (tertiary).
- **backward** – when the dominant company takes over a company at an **earlier** stage in the production process, for example, an aircraft manufacturing company (secondary) taking over a company that refines aluminium for aircraft panels (primary).

REVIEW QUESTION

1. Using a pair of trainers as an example, draw a diagram, showing how a trainer manufacturer could be involved in the three different types of integration. Put the pair of trainers in the middle of the diagram.

UNIT 1 — PURPOSES AND TYPES OF BUSINESS ORGANISATION

CONTROLS ON MERGERS AND TAKEOVERS

If only one company made and sold all the bicycles in this country it would have a **monopoly**. It could make as many as it wanted, control the supply and demand to the consumer and put the price up whenever it felt like it because it would have no competition. Governments have passed legislation to stop this happening, and any company that has at least 25 per cent of the whole market for a particular product may be referred to the Monopolies and Mergers Commission in order to protect the public interest.

The Daily Business

Microsoft in Monopoly Wrangle

The Government's lawyers are engaged in the third major phase of an enormously important investigation. Its target is a young company with a mere 18,000 employees – a fraction of the size of IBM and AT&T, the last great subjects of antitrust action. Microsoft does not control a manufacturing industry (as IBM did), a natural resource (as Standard Oil did) or a regulated public utility (as AT&T did). Microsoft's strategic monopolies – for it does possess and covet monopolies, despite vehement denials from its lawyers – are in a peculiarly subtle and abstract commodity: the standards and architectures that control the design of modern software.

In a historical eye blink, as the technologies of computing have come to pervade the world's economic life, Microsoft has turned 20 years old. When Ronald Reagan became President, Bill Gates's new company was an unincorporated partnership with accounts kept in handwritten ledgers. Apple was a big new personal-computer company, worth $3 billion; I.B.M., the mainframe giant, was cobbling together its first personal computer out of parts from outside suppliers. By 1990, just a decade later, Microsoft had become the world's richest software company, though it had no leading product in any important category but operating systems. Today nearly half of the world's total P.C. software revenue goes directly to Microsoft.

"I personally believe that Microsoft is the most powerful economic force in the United States in the second half of the 20th century," says Eric Schmidt, chief technology officer of Sun Microsystems -- a minicomputer and networking company whose business used to be remote from Microsoft's but now finds itself under direct competitive pressure. Some of Microsoft's control over computing, at all levels, is obvious. Much, however, is invisible. Even longtime insiders are just beginning to understand the nature of that power: how Microsoft acquired it, preserves it and exercises it.

"The question of what to do about Microsoft is going to be a central public policy issue for the next 20 years," says Mitchell Kapor, the founder and former C.E.O. of Lotus Development Corporation -- once the leading P.C. software company. "Policy makers don't understand the real character of Microsoft yet -- the sheer will-to-power that Microsoft has."

The vast majority of the world's personal computers -- estimates range from 80 percent to more than 90 percent -- run on Microsoft software from the instant they are turned on. Yet, pervasive as P.C.'s are now, Microsoft has made clear that they are only the beginning. The company is working toward wallet computers that carry digital signatures, money and theater or airplane tickets; toward new generations of fax machines, telephones with screens, and car navigation systems; toward Microsoft-run interactive television boxes, office networks and wireless networks,

Ctd on page 5 col.3

OBJECTIVES OF BUSINESS **SECTION 4**

If a company is seen to be
- taking advantage of its percentage of the market
- trying to join with another company that could possibly create a monopoly
- or trying to take over another company with assets of over £30 000 000

the Monopolies and Mergers Commission or the Office of Fair Trading will investigate the position. They then take their findings to the President of the Board of Trade who can block any mergers or takeovers. They can also investigate price-fixing between companies. This is where the companies making the same products make an agreement to keep prices at a certain level. For example, there have been investigations into the prices of CDs. They also investigate cartels, which are illegal. This is when two or more companies agree to either fix the price of their goods or slow down or stop production for a period of time to keep prices artificially high.

The Monopolies and Restrictive Trade Practices Act (1965), the Monopolies and Mergers Act (1965) and the Competition Act (1980) all allow companies to be investigated by the Monopolies and Mergers Commission or the Office of Fair Trading.

REVIEW QUESTIONS

1. State what is meant by an aggressive takeover bid.
2. Explain the terms takeover, conglomerate, and monopoly.

SUPER REVIEW QUESTIONS

3. Explain the difference between a merger and a takeover bid.
4. Discuss how the Monopolies and Mergers Commission can protect consumers' interests.

KEY POINTS

- A merger is when two or more companies voluntarily join together as equal partners.
- A takeover is when one company takes control of another by buying shares, often at a higher price than market value.
- Takeovers can be:
  - **friendly** – a large company takes over a small company to increase growth
  - **aggressive** – a company takes over another company to remove a rival or to sell its assets and make a quick profit.
- **Conglomerate** – a group of companies which sell different products.
- **De-merger** – selling an individual component of a company or conglomerate.
- When only one company controls the market for a particular product they have a monopoly.
- The Monopolies and Mergers commission protects the public from monopolies.
- The government can prevent mergers or takeovers from going ahead if this might result in a monopoly.
- Companies working together can also gain the benefits of a monopoly by:
  - **price-fixing** – agreeing to keep the price of a product higher than the market price would be
  - **cartels** – deals between companies to reduce production of a product in order to keep the price high. These are illegal.

Section 5 Influences on business

 **LEARNING OBJECTIVES**

By the end of this section you should have learnt:
- how business affects the local environment – e.g. by creating jobs
- the influences local government has on business – e.g. planning permission and local environmental issues
- the influence pressure groups have on business activity
- how business fits into the national environment
- the effects central government has on business – e.g. through inflation, taxes, interest rates, legislation, economic policy or regional aid
- how business fits into the international environment – e.g. how business makes decisions on importing and exporting goods.

UNIT 1 — PURPOSES AND TYPES OF BUSINESS ORGANISATION

TOPIC 1: Local environment

LOCAL ENVIRONMENT

When a large company starts up in a new area it can have a number of influences on the local people and environment:

- It creates jobs.
- It may create work for other local businesses such as local shops near to the new business.
- It puts money into the local economy by paying business rates to the local council.
- It may contribute to the local infrastructure by building new roads or a school near the business.
- It will train new employees.
- It can provide a more skilled workforce for the local community.
- It can create pollution.
- it can put strains on local amenities.

Sam and Harri need to know about the influences of the local environment

LOCAL GOVERNMENT

The local government can also influence the environment if it tries to attract businesses to its area. When large companies move into an area they can be a strain on the infrastructure of that area, that is the roads, schools, houses, police, medical services and gas, water and electricity supplies. The local government can try to help this situation by offering advice and information to these businesses, on such matters as:

- how to obtain grants from the European Union and central government
- planning permission for new premises
- planning permission for existing premises where it will involve a change of business
- many local authorities keep registers of land and premises for sale and rent locally, to help prospective businesses find a suitable location.

Planning permission is given by the local council for companies to start up in business only if it felt that the business will benefit the community. They may be asked to contribute towards improving the local amenities before planning permission is given. For example, if a large out-of-town shopping centre is to be built, the retailers may be asked to contribute towards upgrading the roads in the immediate area to cope with the increase in traffic that will occur. For many areas with high unemployment the local government will be mainly concerned with attracting new companies to provide jobs.

KEY POINTS

- When they move into a new location large companies can affect an area by:
  – providing jobs for local people
  – putting more money into the local economy, meaning more work for local businesses
  – funding local amenities, either directly or through taxes
  – creating pollution
  – putting strain on local amenities such as road systems.

- Local government has responsibilities when a business wants to move into an area:
  – giving planning permission for new or existing premises
  – obtaining grants from central government to help attract the business
  – helping to find a suitable site
  – making sure local amenities will not be overstretched, possibly by asking the business to help.

UNIT 1 — PURPOSES AND TYPES OF BUSINESS ORGANISATION

TOPIC 2: Pressure groups

INFLUENCE OF PRESSURE GROUPS

Pressure groups can have a great influence on companies in trying to protect the consumer and the environment. For example, if local residents feel that the building of an out-of-town shopping centre near to their homes will affect their quality of life through added noise levels or traffic pollution, they could form a pressure group and try to influence the council's decision about giving planning permission for the site. These types of groups normally exist to protest only against one particular development.

Sam and Harri need to know about pressure groups

There are many other well-known pressure groups such as Green Peace and Friends of the Earth that exist to fight over a wide range of issues throughout the world. They can carry a great deal of influence over companies and governments, and often have support from the general public. For example, when Shell tried to dump the Brent Spa oil platform at sea, Green Peace launched a high-profile publicity campaign to stop them, claiming it would damage the environment. Brent Spa is currently in a Norwegian fiord and is now likely to be disposed of by being dismantled and recycled, at a cost of around £16 million. Shell obviously think this worthwhile in order to preserve their image as a caring company.

The Consumers' Association is another well-known pressure group that tests products on the consumer's behalf and publishes the results in their magazine called *Which?*

Television programmes such as *Watchdog* are now also very popular and they have been set up to campaign for consumer rights against companies that they feel are not serving the consumers' best interests.

INFLUENCES ON BUSINESS **SECTION 5**

COURSEWORK ACTIVITY

Carry out research in your local area. Choose a location that has recently been developed. It could be that a leisure centre or sports facility has been built, a new shopping centre, a new road, a new school, a new factory.

1 Draw a map of the area showing the new development.

2 Discuss the impact it has had on the local community. Draw up a chart to show the good points and bad points the new development has brought to the local community. Answer such questions as:

- Has it improved the quality of life for people nearby?
- What has the new development replaced – what was on the site before?
- How much employment has it brought to the area?
- How has it affected other local businesses and amenities?

KEY POINTS

- Pressure groups can be:
  - local groups formed for one specific cause
  - large international groups that have a range of interests and influence with governments and businesses.

- Well-known pressure groups are
  - Green Peace
  - Friends of the Earth
  - the Consumers' Association.

UNIT 1 PURPOSES AND TYPES OF BUSINESS ORGANISATION

TOPIC 3 Influence of central government

Central government has a large amount of influence on business.

FISCAL

Each government, whichever political party it might be, has an economic policy that it will try to achieve. This is the government's objectives relating to unemployment, **inflation**, the **Balance of Payments** (see page 100 for more on this) and **public borrowing**. There are several ways in which central government tries to meet these objectives, all of which have an influence on businesses:

- It can increase or reduce taxes.
- It can increase or reduce public spending (i.e. the amount of money the government spends).
- It can increase or reduce the amount of money it borrows.
- It can influence interest rates by setting inflation targets.
- It has some influence over exchange rates.

Sam and Harri need to know about central government

When the government meets its objectives the economy does well and this means that the consumer will spend more and unemployment will fall. This is good for businesses as it means the consumer is buying lots of goods and services and providing work for more people. If the economy is doing badly it means the consumer is spending less and unemployment is rising, because when the consumer buys less, companies make less, which means they need fewer workers, which leads to higher unemployment. When the economy is doing badly it is called a **recession**. When it is doing well it is called a **boom**.

INFLUENCES ON BUSINESS SECTION 5

INFLATION

The government always tries to keep the rate of **inflation** low. Inflation is when prices rise. The rate of inflation is the rate at which the general price level is rising. If the rate of inflation rises it has a direct influence on business because the cost of raw materials will rise, transport costs go up, and this all means the company will have to increase the price of its goods to pay for all these increases. The workers then want a pay rise to keep up with the increase in their cost of living and the higher prices they now have to pay. Businesses can gain when inflation rises, because if prices rise it means they have more money coming into the business which could help to pay off debts more quickly, but they can lose as the consumer may not be able to buy so much because of this increase in prices. When inflation is high, money can lose its value if interest rates do not match inflation.

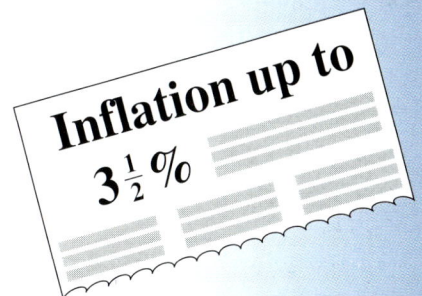

An MP looking at inflation rates

UNIT 1 — PURPOSES AND TYPES OF BUSINESS ORGANISATION

TAXES

Another way in which central government influences businesses is in the taxes and duties it levies. The main taxes levied by the government are:

- **Income tax**: charged at different rates on people's income from their work, their pension or the interest on their bank/building society account.
- **Corporation tax**: paid by companies on their profits.
- **Value Added Tax (VAT)**: paid on most goods and services bought, except essential items such as food and children's clothing.
- **Customs duties**: charged on some goods imported into this country.
- **Excise duties**: charged on some goods such as petrol, beer, wine, spirits and cigarettes.

If the government lowers the rate of tax the consumer will have more money to spend, which means there will be a greater demand for goods and services, which in turn will mean there will have to be an increase in supply and as a result companies should see an increase in profits. However, cutting taxes often means cutting public spending and this can affect the country's economy.

INTEREST RATES

Interest rates are the rates charged for borrowing money over a set period of time. Most businesses have to borrow money at some time from financial institutions. There are lots of different rates of interest from different institutions but all of these are influenced by the UK Interest Rate set by the Bank of England. If the rate of interest is increased it means the company will have to pay more money back for borrowing the money than it had originally expected. If the interest rate falls it means that the loan is now cheaper and this will reduce the business's total costs. Consumers are also affected by changes in interest rates: if they go up consumers have to spend more on mortgages, loans or hire purchase, which means less

INFLUENCES ON BUSINESS **SECTION 5**

to spend on other items. High interest rates can also encourage people to save their money rather than spend it. This has a knock-on effect on business, as demand for goods and services falls.

LEGAL

The government has introduced a range of legislation in recent years that directly influences business. The Sex and Race Discrimination Acts were introduced to provide equal opportunities, and other legislation covers health and safety at work and contracts of employment. See Unit 2 Section 1 on employment laws for more detail.

RACE RELATIONS ACT (1976)

DISABLED PERSONS ACTS (1944, 1958, 1981)

HEALTH AND SAFETY AT WORK ACT (1974)

EQUAL PAY ACT (1970)

EMPLOYMENT PROTECTION ACT (1974)

EMPLOYMENT ACTS (1980, 1982)

SEX DISCRIMINATION ACTS (1975, 1986)

KEY POINTS

- Central government can influence business by:
  - changing taxation
  - changing public spending
  - changing public borrowing
  - influencing changes in interest rates
  - influencing exchange rates.
- **Rate of inflation** – the rate at which prices rise.
- **Boom** – consumers spend lots of money on products, in turn creating more jobs.
- **Recession** – consumers do not spend money, leading to cuts in jobs.
- Central government also influences business legislation concerning:
  - equal opportunities to protect against discrimination
  - conditions of employment
  - health and safety at work.

COURSEWORK ACTIVITY

Carry out research to find out the current rates of income tax and VAT.

UNIT 1 — PURPOSES AND TYPES OF BUSINESS ORGANISATION

TOPIC 4 — Influence of the international environment

EXPORTS AND IMPORTS

Most businesses are likely to be affected by the international environment. A company may decide to **export** its goods to foreign countries in order to increase its sales and hopefully increase its market share. When buying raw materials, components, tools or equipment for the running of the business, the company wants to buy quality products at the lowest price which may lead them to make a decision to **import** the goods from foreign countries if they can get better or cheaper supplies from outside the UK.

Exports are goods (visible exports) and services (invisible exports) made in this country which are sold to foreign countries. **Imports** are goods and services made in foreign countries which are bought in to this country.

The **Balance of Payments** is a record of the overall results of the UK's trading activity with the rest of the world. It includes imports being bought and brought into this country and exports being sold and sent out of the country, as well as the capital flowing between the UK and other countries.

Sam and Harri need to know about the international environment

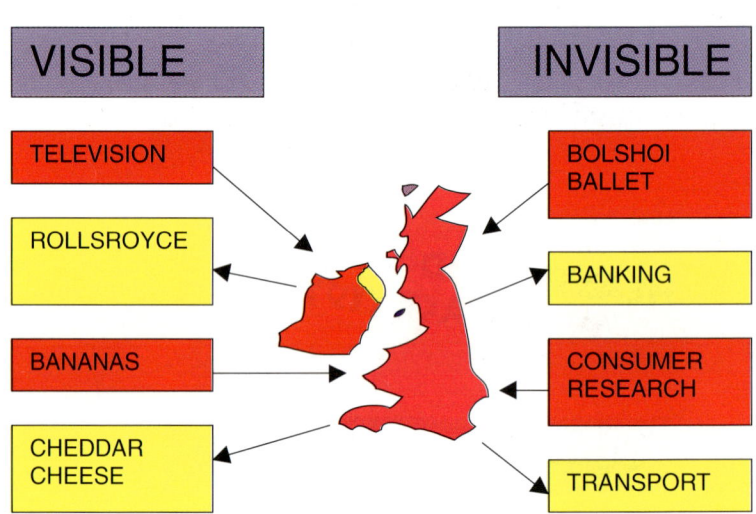

COMPETING WITH FOREIGN COMPANIES

The government can help businesses to compete with foreign companies in several ways:

- It can put tariffs on imports; that is, the government adds a tax to the price of goods made abroad but sold in this country, which could then make the imported goods more expensive to buy than UK goods.

INFLUENCES ON BUSINESS **SECTION 5**

◆ It can impose quotas on imports, i.e. the government can restrict the number of goods coming from foreign countries into the UK over the period of a year.
◆ It can try to reduce the value of the pound so that imports are more expensive and UK goods are cheaper for foreign countries to buy.

In reality the government may be unable to help. The UK is a member of the European Union (EU) and the World Trade Organisation (WTO). The former prohibits tariffs and quotas on trade between member countries; the latter limits tariffs and quotas.

The (EU) is having more and more impact on UK businesses. All businesses in the European Union have to follow EU regulations such as the health and safety regulations, employment regulations and standards set for goods and services.

Since 1993, it is easier for the countries in the EU to trade with each other, as customs controls have gone and there are no taxes on goods imported between EU member countries. European Monetary Union (EMU) will soon set up a single currency which may make trading between members of EMU easier.

KEY POINTS

■ **Exports** – businesses selling their products outside the country they are based.
■ **Imports** – businesses buying products produced outside their company.
■ Central government helps businesses to compete with foreign companies by:
  – subsidising exports
  – imposing tariffs on imports
  – imposing quotas on imports
  – influencing the exchange rates.

REVIEW QUESTIONS

1 List four ways in which the building of a new out-of-town shopping centre could affect local people.
2 State what happens to unemployment in a recession.
3 What is the difference between an import and an export.
4 Draw a diagram showing examples of products you know of that are imported and exported. Divide your diagram into visible and invisible exports and imports.

SUPER REVIEW QUESTIONS

5 Explain how the actions of local government can affect a business.
6 Explain how inflation might affect a business.
7 Explain how the government can help British businesses to export and to compete with imports.

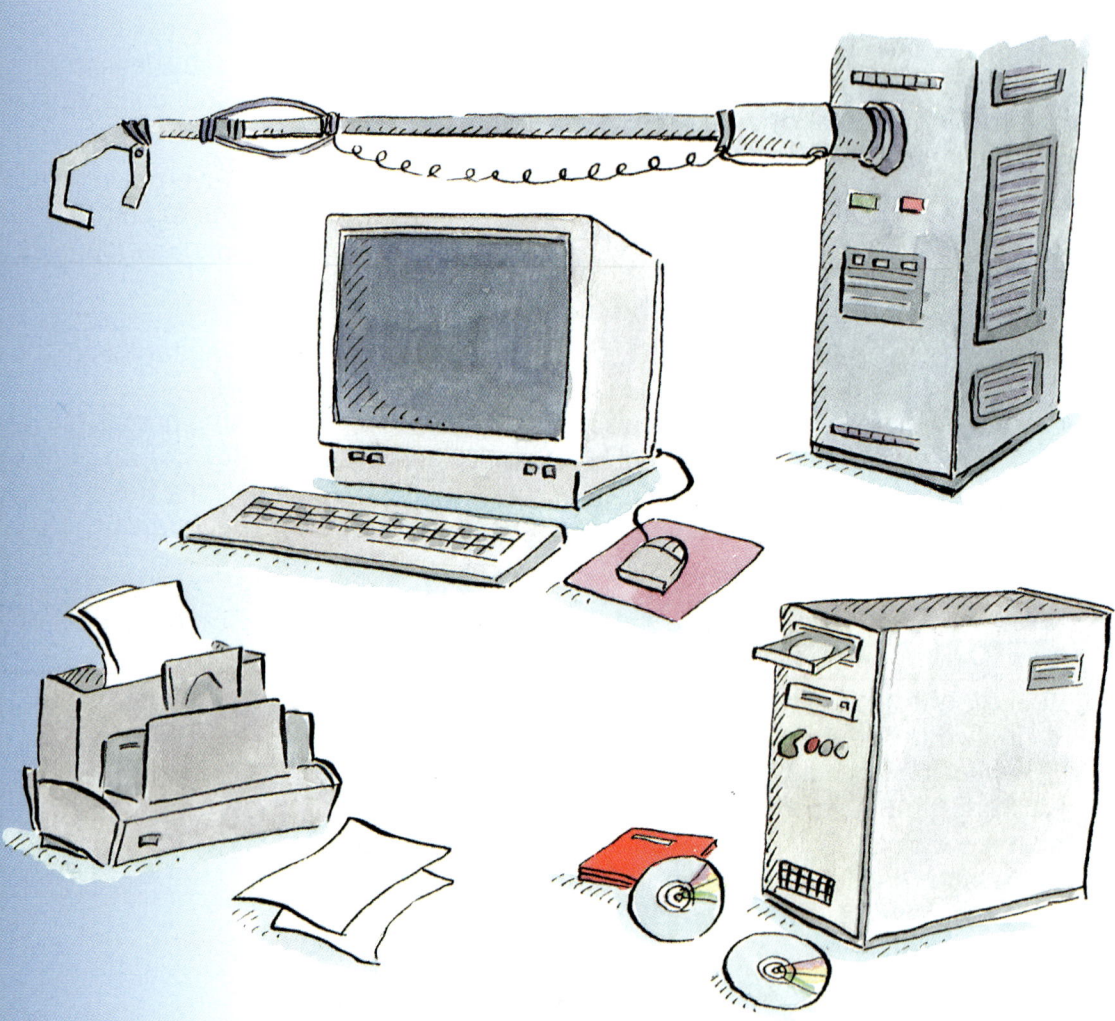

Section 6 New technology

 **LEARNING OBJECTIVES**

By the end of this section you should have learnt:
- how computers are used in a range of businesses – e.g. factories, offices, shops, warehouses or banks
- recent developments in telecommunications
- the effects new technology has had on business.

UNIT 1 — PURPOSES AND TYPES OF BUSINESS ORGANISATION

TOPIC 1: Use of computers

The introduction of the computer has brought about many changes in the running of businesses. A computer is used to store, process and communicate information for the business.

Information can be **stored** in a variety of different ways such as on a $3\frac{1}{4}$" floppy disk, a CD-ROM or magnetic tape. Information can also be **communicated** in a variety of different ways such as visual display units (VDUs), light emitting diode (LED) displays, printers, graphic plotters, sound and moving pictures.

MANUFACTURING

Computers have been introduced into factories to automate the manufacturing process. For example, in the fashion industry computers are now used in the design of clothes, with computer aided design (CAD) software packages helping the fashion designer to choose and create patterns, colours, styles in the design of their clothes. Computer aided manufacture (CAM) is then used in the cutting of the garments. The roll of fabric is automatically unrolled and placed layer on layer on the cutting table. The CAM machine is then programmed to cut out the pieces of the garments. The number of people involved in this process is minimal and far fewer than it was before CAM systems were available. Now, instead of working the machines, staff are needed to check the machine processes and reset the program for the changes in designs. This type of manufacturing process is used in many other manufacturing industries, such as car, boat, aircraft and furniture manufacturing (see Unit 5 Section 2, page 278 for further information).

OFFICE

Computers are now essential in the modern office. The **word processor** is used to produce letters, reports and notices, saving time spent correcting and repeating work by the use of such facilities as the spellchecker, editing and mail merge facilities. **Databases** are used to store information such as stock control records, personnel records or customer

Sam and Harri need to know about computers in business

CAM

NEW TECHNOLOGY SECTION 6

information. **Spreadsheets** are used to produce financial records and help predict future trends in the business. Specialised packages, such as accounts and payroll programs, are available to assist in the financial transactions and book-keeping tasks of the business.

RETAIL

Computers have replaced manual tills and other manual systems in shops. The electronic point of sale terminal (EPOS) at the checkouts in supermarkets uses a scanner to read the bar code from the product and this information is transferred by electronic data interchange (EDI) to the company's mainframe computer. This transaction is carried out at the instant the product is scanned. This is called **real time processing**. The information is used to record the sale, deduct it from the supermarket's stock levels, print out the till receipt for the customer and automatically re-order goods from the supplier. The information gathered on the computer, from the terminals, can be used by the company for a whole range of tasks: it produces regular updates of stock levels, error reports, and details on the demand for a particular product.

WAREHOUSES

Computers have been introduced in warehouses. Bar codes are put on the end of the pallets or boxes of goods. Scanners can then be used to locate the goods once they are stored in the warehouse.

FINANCE

Computers now carry out most of the work undertaken in banks. Increasingly, customers are not using cash to pay for goods. They have debit cards which have a magnetic stripe on the back. The Electronic Funds Transfer Point of Sale (EFTPOS) terminal reads the data from the magnetic stripe. Payment for goods or services is automatically transferred from the customer's bank account to the shop's bank account. Again, this is processed in real time (immediately), so payment is deducted from the customer's bank account as the transaction happens. Many financial institutions are also linked to each other worldwide, as well as their customers, for the transfer of information.

KEY POINTS

- The use of computers has meant many changes in most businesses.
- Computers can be used to:
  - store information
  - process information
  - communicate information.
- **CAD (Computer aided design)** – using computers to help design new products.
- **CAM (Computer aided manufacture)** – using computers to control machines that perform tasks automatically instead of manually.
- Computer packages used in offices include:
  - word processors – using a computer to write letters, memoranda, reports, etc.
  - databases – using a computer to store information electronically and easily searchable
  - spreadsheets – using a computer to control figures, for example financial accounts.
- Computers are used in shops and warehouses to:
  - record the sale of goods
  - record stock levels
  - locate new stock
  - produce receipts.
- Computers are used in finance to:
  - pay for goods electronically
  - pay for goods in real time.

UNIT 1 PURPOSES AND TYPES OF BUSINESS ORGANISATION

TOPIC 2 — Developments in telecommunications

COMPUTER NETWORKS

Computers in the same building or in different buildings on the same site can be linked together so that people can communicate with each other and share files such as customer databases and resources such as printers. This is called a **local area network** (LAN). Passwords are used to limit access to the information stored on the computer system to certain people or departments.

The local area network can be extended and linked to a **wide area network** (WAN). This networking of computer systems can be worldwide, using satellites to allow computers to communicate with each other via the telephone system.

There are other new communications technologies (see Unit 1 Section 3, pages 68–73) that include:

Sam and Harri need to learn about developments in telecommunication

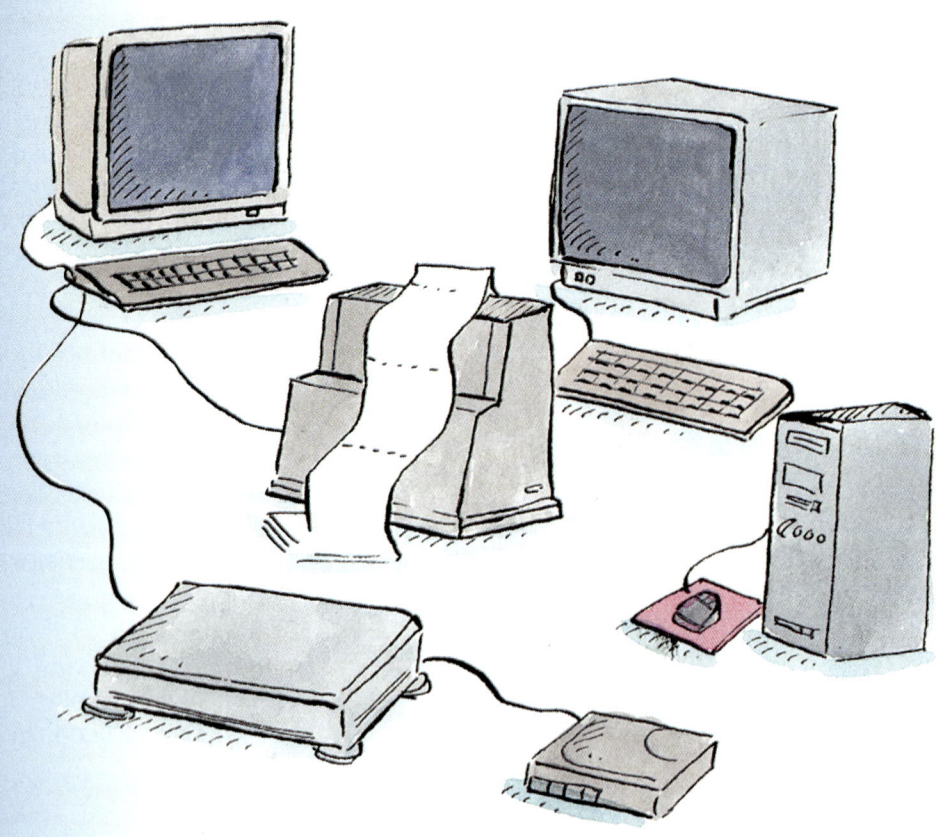

NEW TECHNOLOGY — SECTION 6

FAX

Another way that information can be communicated all around the world is by a fax machine, which sends written, numerical or graphical information from one person to another by use of a fax machine linked to a telephone line. It produces a printed copy on the receiving machine.

ELECTRONIC MAIL

Electronic mail can be transferred from one computer to another either over a LAN or the telephone system. Electronic mail can be anything from a simple text message to a fully word processed memo or report. Charts, diagrams and even video and sound clips can also be sent as part of an electronic mail message. Mail can be stored electronically or it can be printed. It is increasingly used to replace memos, and even telephone messages, and is normally cheaper and faster than the postal service.

VIDEO-CONFERENCING

Video-conferencing is another method by which people can communicate using a video camera linked to the computer which transfers moving pictures. This can allow several people to have a face-to-face meeting without having to leave their offices.

KEY POINTS

- A network consists of a number of computers linked together, allowing:
  - shared information
  - shared resources, such as printers.
- **LAN (Local Area Network)** – computers in the same building or site linked together.
- **WAN (Wide Area Network)** – computers linked together by telephone lines over long distances.
- Other developments in electronic communication include:
  - fax machines
  - electronic mail
  - video-conferencing.

UNIT 1 PURPOSES AND TYPES OF BUSINESS ORGANISATION

TOPIC 3 — Effects of new technology on business

It can cost businesses large amounts of money to invest in introducing new technology. Staff need initial training, systems have to be upgraded and staff retrained for each new system. So why do businesses take on these investments?

There are many benefits to business from the introduction of new technology.

INCREASED PRODUCTIVITY

The introduction of CAM in manufacturing industries has meant that productivity can increase because the machine can work more quickly. It does the repetitive, boring tasks that people do not want to do. It can work longer than people and more accurately. Businesses that do not invest in this new technology find themselves being left further and further behind. They become uncompetitive as their production rates and the quality of their products are not as good.

Sam and Harri need to know about the effects of new technology on business

EFFECTS ON WORKFORCE

People are now employed to supervise, control and program the machines or robots. They might work fewer hours and have more leisure time. It has, however, meant that some people now find it more difficult to find work, as many jobs that used to exist have been taken over by computers. This has led to unemployment in many areas of work but, equally, demand for specialist skilled and multiskilled workers doing jobs involving computers has increased. The introduction of new technology has meant that workers now have to be more flexible, be prepared to change direction several times in their career, and retrain in new skills as technology develops.

QUALITY CONTROL

Computers can be used in quality control checks on products. This can prevent faulty goods from reaching the consumer.

NEW TECHNOLOGY SECTION 6

EFFECTS ON COMPETITORS

Keeping up to date with new technology can help businesses to compete with their rivals by increasing efficiency. Equally, being ahead of competitor's technology can be a significant advantage.

IT in the office

IT in the computer room

IT in the science lab

IT in the CDT room

IT in the Business Studies class

KEY POINTS

New technology has had many effects on businesses:
- increased productivity
- better quality control
- increase in demand for skilled workers
- increase in unemployment for unskilled workers
- new demands for workers to be more flexible and to have more training
- new costs for acquiring or updating equipment.

COURSEWORK ACTIVITY

Carry out research to find the ways in which computers are used in the day-to-day running of your school.

This research should include finding out about how computers are used in the administration office and how computers are used by teachers in the classroom. Find out what other tasks involved in running the school or teaching are done by people instead of computers.

Use the computer to produce a report for your teacher on your findings. Make recommendations about any new jobs or tasks in school that you think would be appropriate to transfer to the computer. These recommendations could include the way administrative jobs are done or ways in which the computer could be used in more ways in the classroom.

UNIT 1 — PURPOSES AND TYPES OF BUSINESS ORGANISATION

QUESTION TIME

1. There are three types of business activity – primary, secondary and tertiary production. Draw a diagram to show one example of primary production, one example of secondary production and one example of tertiary production. Label each picture.
2. List the four factors of production. Give an example of each factor.
3. Explain the difference between goods and services. It will help to give an example of each in your explanation.
4. State and explain two advantages and two disadvantages of being a sole trader.
5. Draw out the following chart and fill in the blank spaces on control, sources of finance and distribution of profits for each type of business ownership.

Type of ownership	Control	Sources of finance	Distribution of profits
Sole trader			
Partnership			
Worker cooperative			
Franchise			
Private limited company			
Public limited company			

6. Draw an organisation chart for Trimagym plc, a company that makes fitness equipment for sports centres. The Managing Director, Richard Obugo, has a team of four financial managers who report to him. Each of these managers has either three or four production managers and they in turn control supervisors and employees.

EXTENSION TASKS

7. From the organisation chart you have just drawn, explain the span of control of the Managing Director and the chain of command within the company.
8. State and explain four main business objectives.
9. Describe how the building of a new out-of-town shopping centre in your local area could affect your local environment.
10. Explain two ways in which central government influences businesses.
11. Draw a diagram of a local area network. Describe two advantages to a company of using a computer network.

COURSEWORK ASSIGNMENT WORK

1. Select a company takeover that has taken place in recent years, for instance, Granada's takeover of the Forte group of companies. State and explain the advantages and disadvantages of your chosen takeover.
2. Select a large well-known public limited company such as Virgin, Raleigh Industries, one of the multinational oil industries, a high street fast-food chain, or a local company that interests you. Carry out research and collect details on:
   - the history of the company
   - the changes in types of ownership over the years
   - the growth of the company
   - the management structure
   - its type of business activity – primary, secondary, tertiary
   - its business objectives/mission statements
   - the influences that the company has had on the local and national environment
   - the types of new technology it uses.

   Produce an informative brochure about its development over the years which the company could use to send to Business Studies students. Use the items listed above as section headings. Use a computer to produce this brochure.

   Check the share value of the same company regularly over a period of a month and chart its progress. Evaluate the changes in its share price.

UNIT 2
Understanding Human Resources

Section 1 People in business

LEARNING OBJECTIVES

By the end of this section you should have learnt about:
- what motivates people to work
- different types of payment systems (wages and salaries)
- different types of fringe benefits
- job satisfaction
- methods that can be used to provide job improvement
- the benefits of appraisal systems (for the employer and the employee)
- laws that protect employees at work
- the implications of these laws for the employer
- the importance of human resources to business.

UNIT 2   UNDERSTANDING HUMAN RESOURCES

TOPIC 1   What motivates people to work?

We saw in Unit 1 that businesses are set up to make a profit by providing goods and services to meet consumer needs and wants. In this unit we start by asking – why do people go to work? What **motivates** them to work?

Sam and Harri need to understand motivation

MOTIVATION

If you asked ten different people you would probably get ten different answers. Starting at the most basic level, we all need food, shelter, water, warmth and clothing. To provide these we need money, and to earn money we have to go to work.

Once we have achieved these basic needs, we then begin to have other needs for working. For example:

- Many people need to feel **safe** and **secure** at work – they want to know that they have a job that will pay them a regular wage, that offers them a safe working environment and a job that is secure. Some people still look for a 'job for life', but this is increasingly unrealistic these days. Advances in technology continue to replace jobs which – at one time – relied on human resources, and at the same time create new jobs that may need different skills.

- Some people need **friendship** at work or, more importantly, to feel part of a team. They enjoy working with other people.

- Some people want **self-esteem** from work: they want status or power. They want their job to give them this prestige.

- Some people work to gain the opportunity to **reach their full potential**: they may be **creative**, like Lesley, producing her silk work, or have certain **skills**, such as being good at

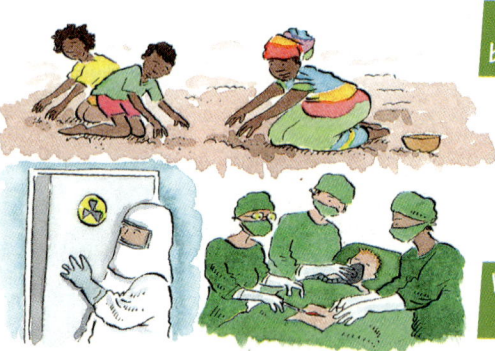

Providing basic needs

Working in a safe environment

Working in a team

Working for power and status

Working creatively

managing people, that they can use in their job of work.

So, although people want different things from work, they can be put into the general categories of:

- **basic physical needs**: earning money to provide food, shelter, clothing
- **safety needs**: a safe secure working environment, which helps workers plan their futures
- **social needs**: working and mixing with other people
- **self-esteem needs**: gaining status, power and a feeling of value
- **self-fulfilment needs**, to reach their full potential.

MASLOW'S HIERARCHY

The American psychologist Abraham Maslow developed a model of human needs to show how people are motivated to work.

This model is called a hierarchy because it starts with the basic needs at the **bottom** and climbs to the higher needs at the **top**.

Maslow believed that people start at the **bottom** of the hierarchy of needs and, as they achieve the first level, such as food and shelter, it is no longer as important and they then want to move on to the next level. It is also true, however, that if low-level needs cannot be met then the high-level needs are no longer important. For example, if you are starving, food is the only important need.

Harri's father's friend, Dave, was a supervisor at Kemet Electronics Ltd, which manufactures CD players. His job provided him with self-esteem and self-fulfilment. When Dave was made redundant, these high-level needs of self-esteem were no longer important and he went back to wanting the basic physical needs, as he worried more about how he would buy food and pay the mortgage to look after his family, without an income.

KEY POINTS

Motivations for work include:
- money
- security
- working environment
- friendship
- status
- opportunity to be creative.

Maslow's hierarchy of needs is:
- physiological
- love and belonging
- self-esteem
- self-actualisation.

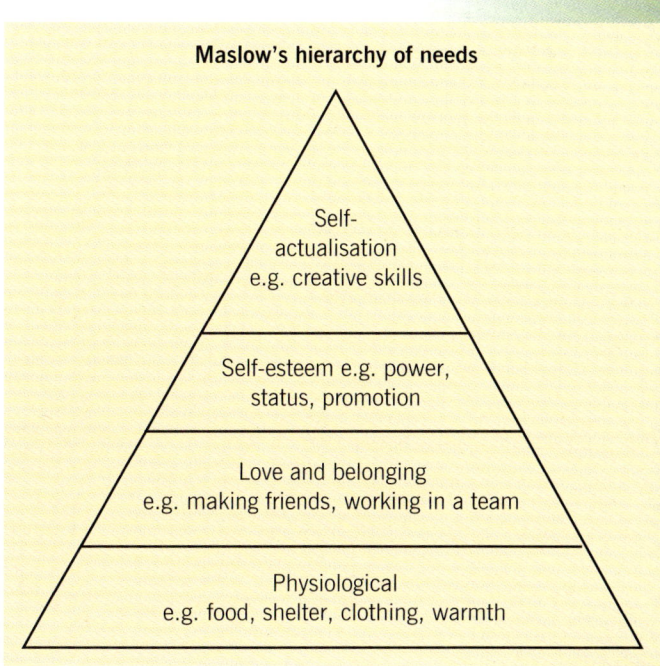

Maslow's hierarchy of needs
- Self-actualisation e.g. creative skills
- Self-esteem e.g. power, status, promotion
- Love and belonging e.g. making friends, working in a team
- Physiological e.g. food, shelter, clothing, warmth

UNIT 2 UNDERSTANDING HUMAN RESOURCES

TOPIC 2 — Types of payment system

The reward for working for a business is payment in money. There are two main types of payment – wages and salaries.

WAGES

Wages are usually paid to manual, or 'blue collar' workers. Sam's dad, Louie, is on the production line at Kemet Electronics Ltd, assembling CD players. His kind of job needs him to work either a set **number of hours** per week or to assemble a **certain number** of CD players per hour or day.

Wages are usually paid on an hourly or weekly basis. The rate of pay per hour varies according to the skills required by the job. Louie is paid £5.00 per hour and works a 37-hour week according to his contract of employment. If he works longer than this, he is paid overtime for the extra hours he works. Wages are paid weekly and the employee will receive a pay slip showing the hours worked, the statutory (compulsory) deductions made for such things as income tax and National Insurance and any voluntary deductions such as a Pension Scheme. Wages used to be paid in cash, on a set day of the week. However, nowadays, many companies pay all their employees monthly, often by credit transfer, which means the company pays money straight into the employees' bank accounts, as this is much less of a security risk for the company than having large amounts of money delivered to them every week so they can make up pay packets. This is also safer for the employees, as they do not have to carry cash home on pay day.

Sam and Harri need to know about different methods of payment

A manual worker

SALARY

A **salary** is usually paid to non-manual or 'white collar' workers such as office workers, managers and professional people, such as Harri's brother, Ken, who works as a supervisor at Kemet. The hours worked are not set, but employees are expected to work a minimum number of hours per week and are often expected to stay on at work until the job is complete.

Salaries are calculated on an annual basis and paid in monthly parts. For example, Ken is paid £24 000 a year. This is then divided into 12 equal parts and Ken is paid £2000 per month. In the past, overtime was not paid to salaried staff, but today, if they work a lot of hours above their normal working week they may be paid overtime, or receive a bonus or extra time off.

Salaries are normally paid by bank transfer at the end of each calendar month or at the end of each four-weekly period. The employee will receive a pay slip showing the monthly payment, the deductions such as income tax or National Insurance contributions that must be made, and any voluntary deductions that the employee chooses to pay, such as payment into a private pension scheme.

A white collar worker

UNIT 2 UNDERSTANDING HUMAN RESOURCES

PAY SLIPS

Pay slips are produced to show employees the total wages or salary they have been paid (gross pay), the deductions that have been withdrawn from the wages and the final amount paid to the worker (net pay).

Below is a pay slip for Ken Patel, Harri's brother. He earns £24 000 a year, which is £2000 a month. He sometimes has to work overtime.

Name Patel K				Pay Number 7756	Tax Code 500H *[B]*	NI Number HN884523K
Payments				**Deductions**		
Hours Worked	Extra Hours	Total Hours	Value £	Description		Amount £
148	0	148	2000	Income Tax *[C]* National Insurance *[D]* Pension Scheme *[E]* Charity *[E]*		353.61 177.76 90.00 40.00
		Gross Pay	2000 *[A]*	Total Deductions		661.37
				Net Pay *[F]*		1338.63

[A] **Gross Pay** is the total amount of money earned **before** any deductions have been taken off. Ken's gross pay for this month is £2000

[B] **Tax Code:** This code is calculated by the Inland Revenue and all workers are told what their tax code is by the Inland Revenue. Ken's Tax Code is 500H. The code indicates the amount of money that can be earned before income tax is deducted.

[C] **Income Tax** is the money paid to the Inland Revenue. The government uses this money to pay for such things as education, roads, defence. This is a **statutory deduction**, which means it has to be paid. Ken's income tax deductions this month are £353.61

[D] **National Insurance contributions** are paid to the government to help pay for the Health Service and Social Security. This is a statutory deduction. Ken's National Insurance contribution this month is £177.76

[E] **Voluntary deductions** are further deductions workers can **choose** to have taken from their pay. These include such items as a private pension scheme, trade union fees, AVCs (Additional Voluntary Contributions) which are extra payments into a pension scheme, private medical care contributions, savings and regular amounts paid to a charity. Ken pays £90.00 into the company pension scheme and he pays £40.00 to the Heart Foundation Charity each month.

[F] **Net Pay** is the amount of money received after all the deductions have been made, both statutory and voluntary. Ken's net pay or take home pay is £1338.63. So, although he has earned £2000, he only has £1338.63 to spend on needs and wants.

PEOPLE IN BUSINESS **SECTION 1**

REVIEW QUESTIONS
1. Explain the two main types of payment – wages and salaries.
2. What is meant by **overtime** payments?
3. What are **statutory deductions**? – give one example.
4. What are **voluntary deductions**? – give one example.

SUPER REVIEW QUESTIONS
5. Explain the five different categories of needs identified by Abraham Maslow to show how people are motivated to work.
6. Explain the difference between gross pay and net pay, on a pay slip.

KEY POINTS

- **Wage** – money paid to workers, usually manual, based on hours worked or productivity.
- **Salary** – money paid to workers, usually non-manual, based on an annual figure.
- The pay slip contains information about wages or salary for the worker, including:
  - gross pay – the amount of money due before deductions
  - tax code – the level at which the worker starts to pay tax
  - voluntary deductions – a worker can choose to pay money for other optional services such as pensions or health schemes
  - net pay – the amount of money left after all deductions.
- There are normally two types of taxes:
  - income tax – money paid to the Inland Revenue for general use by the government
  - National Insurance – money paid to the Inland Revenue specifically to fund the National Health Service and Social Security.

COURSEWORK ACTIVITY

EMPLOYEE DETAILS		DATE OF PAY WEEK 12 04 98		
Employee Name: Smith L	Employee Number: 7780	Tax Code 279 H	National Insurance Number: YH 99 76 45 B	
HOURS WORKED				
Basic Hours Worked: 37	Overtime Worked 0	Total Hours payable 37	Rate of pay: 5.00	Bonus payment 50.00
DEDUCTIONS				
Income Tax: 46.25	National Insurance: 16.60	Gross Pay: 185.00	NET PAY:	

Above is a sample of the pay slip for Louie Smith, Sam's dad.
1. State the rate of pay paid to L Smith per hour.
2. Calculate the total deductions to be taken from L Smith's gross pay.
3. Calculate the net pay for L Smith for the week ending 12 April.

UNIT 2 UNDERSTANDING HUMAN RESOURCES

TOPIC 3 — Payment systems

The amount of money paid to employees for their normal working time is called a **basic wage** or **basic salary**. However, payment for work can be calculated in other ways:

- **Time rate**: the rate of pay for every hour worked. For example, Louie Smith's time rate is £5.00 per hour for a 37-hour week. The number of hours to be worked each week is laid down in the contract. If employees work extra hours above those stated, they will be paid an **overtime rate**. This is an extra payment on top of the set rate of pay. For example, if Louie works overtime, he is paid $1\frac{1}{2}$ times his normal rate of pay. So, if the normal rate of pay is £5.00 per hour the overtime rate would be $1\frac{1}{2}$ times this normal rate, i.e. £7.50 per hour.

Sam and Harri need to know about payment systems

- **Flat rate**: a total rate of pay for a set number of hours. There are no extra payments.
- **Piece rate** or **piecework**: workers are paid for each item they produce as long as it meets the agreed quality standard. Louie could be paid a piece rate for the number of components he fits to the CD players that are assembled each day.
- **Shift payments**: if workers, such as nurses on a night shift, have to work unsociable hours, they are paid extra per hour for working this shift.

Many employees can receive additional payments on top of their basic wage or salary. There are several different systems that are used:

BONUS PAYMENTS

Bonus payments are usually linked to how hard they work. There are several different types of bonus payments:

- A **productivity bonus** is paid to a worker or group of workers who achieve a set target. Workers such as factory workers are often paid a productivity bonus to encourage them to increase output and, therefore, profits.
- A **sales bonus** is paid to workers directly involved in selling services or goods. The sales person is paid a percentage of the value of sales over a period of time, for example a car sales person could be paid 1% of the value of sales made, so if £50 000 worth of cars are sold, a £500 bonus will be paid.

CALCULATING BONUS

PROFIT SHARING

In a **profit-sharing scheme** the workers can use part of their wages to buy shares in the company which will make them part owners. The workers may then receive a dividend for investing their wages, as they are now also shareholders. Being a part owner in the company motivates them to work harder, as the more profit the company makes the higher the dividend they receive. This is also a way for owners to reduce wages and salaries, as well as receiving further investment into the company.

PERFORMANCE-RELATED PAY

Performance-related pay is similar to productivity bonuses, but normally associated with employees whose work cannot be easily measured or attributed solely to them. The member of staff will have targets and, if they meet them a bonus is paid. Achievement or non-achievement of targets often forms part of appraisal interviews.

PROFIT-RELATED PAY

Profit-related pay is another additional payment. It is calculated by looking at profit and paying a proportion of the company's profit back to the staff for their contribution to the company's overall profit.

FRINGE BENEFITS

Fringe benefits are benefits given to workers that do not appear in their pay packet. Often referred to as 'perks', these come in a variety of forms, e.g. a company car, a company pension scheme, private health care, subsidised cafeteria, or the opportunity to buy the company's products at a reduced price. Many fringe benefits are given for tax purposes as the company and the staff pay less tax on fringe benefits than on cash payments. Fringe benefits are often seen as another way of motivating workers.

KEY POINTS

Wages can be based on:
- time rate
- flat rate
- piece rate or piecework
- shift payments
- bonus payments
- profit-sharing schemes.

Salaries can be increased by:
- performance-related pay
- profit-related pay.

Fringe benefits to complement salaries can include:
- company car
- company pension scheme
- private health care
- subsidised cafeteria
- discounts on company products.

UNIT 2 UNDERSTANDING HUMAN RESOURCES

TOPIC 4 Job satisfaction

Job satisfaction is the amount of satisfaction or pleasure a worker gets from doing a particular job and doing it well.

Earlier in this unit we saw that there are a number of factors that motivate people to work. These can also lead to job satisfaction. Other factors that can also lead to job satisfaction include fringe benefits, the possibility of promotion, being given responsibility or having more flexible working hours.

Sam and Harri need to understand job satisfaction

NEEDS AND WANTS

Everyone has different needs and wants, so the factors that give a worker job satisfaction will vary.

- Some people are interested only in money. As long as the rate of pay is good this will provide them with job satisfaction, even if the job they do is a boring one.
- Other people could not do a boring job, so for them to have job satisfaction the job must be reasonably interesting, give them responsibility and perhaps the possibility of promotion.
- Some people are looking for flexibility with their job. Many people want to combine a family life with a career, so flexible working hours to fit in with their family life gives them job satisfaction as it allows them to combine going to work and being able to look after their families.
- The reality is that very few people are lucky enough to spend their working lives doing what they **enjoy** most, and this is why it is very important for people to have other interests outside of work. It is also true that many people enjoy the social aspects of work, and that good relations between colleagues are important for job satisfaction. However, we tend to go to work to make a living first and foremost. We often find that what was once the 'perfect' job becomes less attractive as we change and develop. It is essential that we keep an open mind about our future jobs, because people change as much as opportunities for work change.

JOB ROTATION

JOB IMPROVEMENT

Another way of making jobs more satisfying is by job improvement. This can be achieved in several different ways:

Job enlargement is where, instead of workers doing one repetitive job they are trained to carry out a variety of jobs. For example, workers on a car production line can be trained to carry out a variety of different tasks, to take the boredom out of the work. Many car manufacturers have adopted this way of working in recent years.

Job rotation is a similar idea. Instead of one worker doing one job all the time, the workers on one part of the production process rotate around a series of jobs on that section, again to reduce boredom.

Job enrichment is where the workers, usually working in a team, are given some say in the way a particular job is completed. This gives the workers the satisfaction of being involved in the decision-making process for a particular job. Many people like to respond to challenges at work, as it gives them the opportunity to prove that they might be able to undertake greater responsibility, or be promoted.

Teamwork can give job satisfaction; being part of a team and being involved in the decision-making within the team gives the worker a feeling of responsibility and self-esteem. Most people like to 'pull their weight' – in other words, not let the team down.

KEY POINTS

Some factors that can lead to job satisfaction are:
- fringe benefits
- possibility of promotion
- being given responsibility
- flexible working hours.

A job can be made more satisfying by:
- **enlargement** – giving workers a variety of tasks to do
- **rotation** – moving teams of workers between different tasks
- **enrichment** – giving workers more responsibility and greater involvement in making decisions
- **teamwork** – using teams of workers to increase responsibility and friendship.

REVIEW QUESTIONS

1. Name three ways that the wages can be calculated for manual workers.
2. State two ways that salaried staff can be paid extra money as well as their annual salary.
3. Name three fringe benefits that can be given to workers as well as paying them wages or a salary.

SUPER REVIEW QUESTIONS

4. Explain the difference between job satisfaction and job improvement.
5. Compare different methods that the manager might use to motivate the workers at Kemet Electronics Ltd.

UNIT 2 UNDERSTANDING HUMAN RESOURCES

TOPIC 5 Appraisal

APPRAISAL INTERVIEWS

Performance or **staff appraisal** is used by many companies, and often involves a review interview between the employee and his or her manager. The interviews are held at regular intervals, usually at least every 12 months. Appraisals are very similar to the one-on-one reviews held in school between student and teacher, where progress is discussed and targets set.

Often, a few days before the interview, the employee will be given a Review Preparation Form. This gives the employee some points to think about before the interview, in order to prepare for questions the Line Manager may ask.

Sam and Harri need to know about staff appraisal

- At the interview the employee and the appraiser (manager) will talk about, and then record, the employee's replies to a wide range of points to do with their performance at work, and future development opportunities, such as further training and promotion.

- The employee will then be assessed on his or her performance at work, over a set period of time, and given a rating, together with a brief summary of the interview.

- The appraiser will agree new objectives with the employee for the next period of time. The employee and appraiser will then sign the Review Document, as a form of agreement.

- The Review Document will then be sent on to the appraiser's manager to check and comment on. The Review Document will be placed in the employee's file for future reference.

The appraisal process gives managers an opportunity for one-to-one interviews with employees and helps them to build a better picture of the people working for them. It gives both the manager and the employee the chance to talk about any issues that may have occurred at work during the last appraisal period. It is important for the employee to be set objectives that are achievable, which will give a sense of purpose and motivation to work harder. It also gives employees a chance to discuss with management future career prospects in the company.

This is something I made in technology. I'm very proud of it.

124

PEOPLE IN BUSINESS **SECTION 1**

STRICTLY PRIVATE and CONFIDENTIAL

APPRAISAL REVIEW

Name ......*Louie Smith*.......... Job Title .. ..*Assembly worker*....... Date ...*22 April 1998*..

Overall Performance Rating: F E D C B A

Section A
The progress the job holder has made over the last 12 months against the objectives that had been set:
Louie has met two of his objectives –
He has increased the number of components assembled from 75 to 100 per day
He has trained a new employee on the assembly line work

Section B
The most important achievements of the job holder in that period of time
Highest number of components assembled in one day

Section C
The barriers the job holder has experienced that have affected his or her performance
Components not always ready at assembly point on time, slowing down assembly process
Sometimes lacks the ability to communicate problems to Line Manager

Section D
The job holder's strengths
Good timekeeper
Reliable and conscientious worker

Section E
Job development and career opportunities
Promote to chargehand when position becomes available

Section F
Performance Summary
A good worker, well motivated and a good example to other workers

Job Holder's comments:
True and accurate review

Job Holder's signature .... Date ....

Appraiser's signature .... Date ....

KEY POINTS

Appraisals give:
- managers more insight into their employees
- managers and employees the chance to:
  – discuss issues and problems
  – set objectives
  – discuss future career prospects.

UNIT 2 — UNDERSTANDING HUMAN RESOURCES

TOPIC 6 Employment laws

All organisations are legally obliged to provide equal opportunities at work for employees.

EQUAL OPPORTUNITIES

An **Equal Opportunities policy** is a statement drawn up by the employer to ensure all individuals employed by the company are treated fairly and their work is valued irrespective of disability, race, gender, health, social class, sexual preference, marital status, nationality, religion, employment status, age, or membership or non-membership of a trade union.

Sam and Harri need to learn about employment laws

EQUAL PAY

The **Equal Pay Act (1970)** requires the employer to pay males and females the same rate of pay for the same, or a similar job that has the same demands or the same skill level.

EMPLOYMENT PROTECTION

The **Employment Protection Act (1974)** led to the **Advisory, Conciliation and Arbitration Service (ACAS)** being set up to help employers and employees reach agreement and solve industrial disputes.

The **Employment Acts (1980** and **1982)** were introduced to give structure to the organisation of industrial relations. These acts reduced the powers of the trades unions.

SEX DISCRIMINATION

The **Sex Discrimination Acts (1975** and **1986)** were introduced to ensure both sexes are treated equally at work. It is illegal for employers to discriminate against men or women in:

- job selection
- terms of employment
- training and staff development
- fringe benefits
- deciding on redundancies.

CONTRACT OF EMPLOYMENT

Employers are obliged to provide every employee with a **contract of employment** within 13 weeks of appointment. This must be signed by the employer and the employee. It includes details of:

- job title
- rate and method of pay
- hours of work
- holiday entitlement
- amount of notice that must be given by the employee if they want to leave
- amount of notice the employer must give the employee if they want to dismiss them/make them redundant
- any pension scheme arrangements
- trade union rights
- details of the company's disciplinary procedures
- health and safety at work issues

Louie Smith's contract of employment is on page 130.

PEOPLE IN BUSINESS **SECTION 1**

RACE RELATIONS

The **Race Relations Act (1976)** makes it illegal for employers to discriminate against people from ethnic minorities.

DISABLED PEOPLE

The **Disabled Persons (Employment) Acts (1944, 1958** and **1981)** help disabled people to obtain employment that best suits their skills. Companies have to keep records of disabled employees and try to employ a quota of registered disabled people.

HEALTH AND SAFETY

The employer has to comply with the **Health and Safety at Work Act (1974)**. The business must draw up a Health and Safety Policy – a statement requiring **everyone**, employers and employees, to create a place of work which is both safe and healthy. The employer agrees to ensure all practicable steps are taken to ensure the health and safety of all employees, and any other people who may use the company's premises. All employees are expected to work without risking their own health or safety or that of anyone else in the company. The employers must provide suitable training in health and safety at work, in all aspects that may affect the employee whilst doing their job, e.g.

- lifting and handling goods
- dealing with waste disposal
- using knives and utensils
- using machinery and electrical equipment
- using ladders.

Employees are obliged to report to the employer any potentially hazardous situation or action. They must follow the company guidelines on fire precautions and accident preveon.

Many large companies issue their employees with a Staff Handbook that outlines the company objectives, the employees' terms and conditions of work, and health and safety policy and responsibilities.

KEY POINTS

- Legislation is used to protect employees by ensuring there is no discrimination on terms of:
  - gender
  - marital status
  - nationality
  - ethnic origin
  - disability.

- Employers must safeguard the safety and health of their employees.

- Employers must offer a contract to an employee within 13 weeks stating all details concerning employment.

COURSEWORK ACTIVITY

1. Get a copy of an Equal Opportunities policy from your school or through your family or friends.
2. Examine the contract of employment of a member of your family and note down all the details.

127

UNIT 2
UNDERSTANDING HUMAN RESOURCES

TOPIC 7 — Importance of human resources

MANAGING HUMAN RESOURCES

Managing human resources means, first of all, accepting that employees are the most important part of getting jobs done. The organisation will fail unless human resources can pull together all the people working in the company and get them to agree to work cooperatively with each other.

An alternative view is that managers have the right to manage and the people who work for them should comply with their demands, without questioning their decisions.

However, the workforce is often an organisation's biggest single investment (in other words, the greatest cost to the business). It is the job of the Human Resources department to make sure the workforce is performing efficiently, if the organisation is to succeed. The Human Resources (or Personnel) department has to strike a balance between 'laying down the law' and negotiating with employees, in order to get the best out of the workforce and, therefore, meet the company's objectives for productivity. You will learn more about human resources in the next Section.

Sam and Harri need to know about human resources

A job well done

PEOPLE IN BUSINESS   SECTION 1

CASE STUDY

The Picture House is a cinema. It is a private limited company owned by Thomas Greene and his two sons, Adam and Martin. The two sons want to expand and modernise the building and make it into a multiplex cinema with five screens.

The conversion into a multiplex cinema takes place, and is now nearing completion.

Adam and Martin now need to employ some new staff.

The structure for the new company is as follows:

Thomas, Adam and Martin Greene are all equal shareholders and members of the Board of Directors of The Picture House Ltd.

Thomas is Managing Director. Adam is the Administrative Director, in charge of the day-to-day running of the cinema. Martin is the Finance Director, in charge of the day-to-day financial aspects of the business. They will also employ a part-time accountant.

For the day-to-day running of the cinema, they will need the following staff:
- 1 full-time senior cashier
- 5 full-time cashiers
- 5 part-time cashiers
- 20 part-time cinema attendants
- 10 full-time projectionists (2 for each screen)
- 20 part-time cleaners

1. The senior cashier is paid a salary, the part-time cinema attendants are paid on time rate and the part-time cleaners are paid a flat rate. Give your reasons why you think each of these payment systems might be the most appropriate for each of these jobs.
2. Draw up a suitable contract of employment for the full-time cashier at the cinema.
3. Describe the different employment laws that could affect the employees at the cinema.
4. Adam Greene is the Administrative Director and will be responsible for employing the new staff. Explain the implications for Adam Greene, and the company, of understanding employment laws.

KEY POINTS

- Human resources management is about:
  - acknowledging the value of people
  - treating employees in an acceptable way
  - motivating employees
  - making employees feel involved in a business.
- Human resources has to balance the needs of the employee and the employer.

UNIT 2 — UNDERSTANDING HUMAN RESOURCES

CONTRACT OF EMPLOYMENT

Name .... *Louie Smith* ....

Job Title .... *Assembly worker* ....

Rate and method of pay *£5.00 per hour, paid one week in arrears every*

Thursday ....

Hours of work ... *37* ....

Annual Leave ..... *20 days* .....

Notice ... *1 week* ....

This document lays down the terms and conditions of work for employees of KEMET ELECTRONICS LTD. It is written in accordance with the Contract of Employment Act of 1972 and the Employment Protection Act of 1978.

Acceptance agreement

I hereby accept the appointment laid down in the contract and on the terms and conditions stated.

Signed ....

Date ....

Section 2 Role of human resources

 **LEARNING OBJECTIVES**

By the end of this section you should have learnt:
- the objectives of human resources
- procedures for recruitment
- the difference between a job description and a person specification
- how to draw up a job description and a person specification
- how to draw up a job advertisement
- legal requirements when producing a job advertisement
- the main parts of the job applications process
- the purpose of an interview and what format it should take
- the reasons businesses need different types of training schemes
- the main features of induction training
- the benefits of training for the employer and the employee
- the procedures for termination of employment
- how the government helps to protect employees in their workplace.

UNIT 2 UNDERSTANDING HUMAN RESOURCES

TOPIC 1 Objectives of human resources

The objectives of human resources can be described as the process of matching what the company owners want from their employees with what employees want from their work (motivation, job satisfaction, job improvement).

The employer wants to meet the demands of customers, providing them with value for money, to be efficient and to be cost-effective. These objectives can be met only through the good management of human resources. In other words, companies need:

- 'the right people in the right place at the right time'.

What do **employees** want from their work? What are their objectives?

We already know that people want rewards, both the reward of money and the reward of a satisfying job. People want to go to work feeling that they are doing something worthwhile.

How does human resource management help to meet the objectives of both employers and employees?

Sam and Harri need to know about human resources

Notice boards are often used to give employees information about promotion opportunities, social events, training courses. They are also used for employees to display advertisements, for example, items for sale, rooms to let, local events. Electronic bulletin boards may also be used for this purpose.

PROCEDURES FOR RECRUITMENT

One of roles of human resources is the **recruitment** of new staff.

The purpose of recruitment is to find the candidate who has the relevant skills, competencies and qualifications to do a particular job.

Recruitment includes the following procedures:

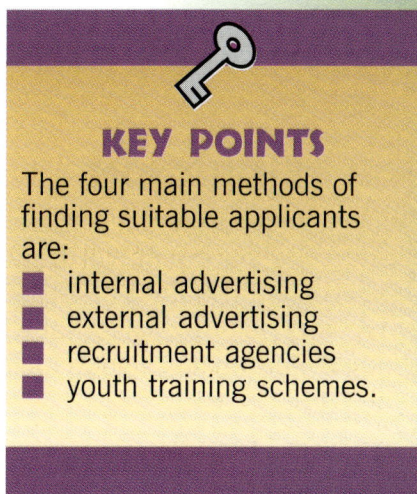

KEY POINTS

The four main methods of finding suitable applicants are:
- internal advertising
- external advertising
- recruitment agencies
- youth training schemes.

Job description
↓
Person specification
↓
Advertising the job
↓
Short-listing appropriate candidates for interview
↓
Interviews
↓
Appointments
↓
Contracts of employment

UNIT 2 UNDERSTANDING HUMAN RESOURCES

TOPIC 2: Job description and person specification

JOB DESCRIPTION

When a new job is created in a company, the Human Resources department will draw up a **job description**, usually with the relevant manager, which describes the tasks that will have to be done in that job. The job description includes such details as:

- job title
- purpose of the job
- specific duties
- other responsibilities
- job location.

Sam and Harri need to understand job descriptions and person specifications

---

JOB DESCRIPTION

1. **Job Title:**
    Trainee Manager

2. **Purpose of Job:**
    Responsible for day-to-day running of the shop

3. **Specific Duties:**
    a) *Staff rotas*
    b) *Staff payroll*
    c) *Keeping financial records*

4. **Other Responsibilities:**
    Deputise for Manager

5. **Job Location:**
    The Hobby Shop, Wallesley

6. **Responsible to:**
    Shop Manager

PERSON SPECIFICATION

After the job description has been drawn up, human resources will then produce a **person specification** which describes the sort of person needed to do the job. The person specification includes such details as:

- educational qualifications
- previous experience
- specialised skills
- personal attributes.

KEY POINTS

- It is the job of human resources to recruit employees.
- Recruitment involves:
  – creating a job description
  – advertising the job
  – choosing which applicants should get an interview
  – interviewing and choosing a person for the job.
- Human resources must make sure that recruitment follows Equal Opportunities guidelines.

PERSON SPECIFICATION

1. Job Title:
   Trainee Manager
2. Educational Qualifications:
   5 GCSEs at Grade A*–C including Maths and English
   2 'A' Levels or Advanced GNVQ
3. Previous experience:
   Part-time or Work Experience retail experience
4. Personal attributes:
   Good team member
   Leadership skills
   Good communicator
5. Specialised skills required:
   Understanding of financial accounts

COURSEWORK ACTIVITY

1. List the details from the advertisement that would have been taken from the job description, and the details that would have been taken from the person specification to make up this advertisement.
2. Now draw up a job description and a person specification for a part-time shop assistant at The Hobby Shop.

THE HOBBY SHOP

require a

TRAINEE MANAGER

To assist in the management of their new shop. The successful applicant will be responsible for the day-to-day organisation of the shop. Five GCSEs at Grades A*–C are required, plus two 'A' levels or Advanced GNVQ. He/she will be required to undertake further training in Management and Office Administration. Must work well as a team member, and have good communication skills.

Applicants should apply in writing, to:

Mrs H Scott
The Hobby Shop, High Street,
WALLESLEY WA6 9OZ   CLOSING DATE: 12 April

UNIT 2 UNDERSTANDING HUMAN RESOURCES

TOPIC 3 Recruiting

There are four main methods of finding a suitable applicant for a job:
- internal advertisements
- external advertisements
- external recruitment agencies, such as Job Centres and private employment agencies
- youth training.

The most common methods used for recruiting for a job vacancy are **job advertisements**. Details from the job description and the person specification are used to help draw up the job advertisement, such as the one drawn up for the Trainee Manager at The Hobby Shop.

Sam and Harri need to know about recruiting

INTERNAL ADVERTISING

This can then be advertised **internally**, which means looking for suitable applicants from within the organisation. These are advertised on noticeboards, in company newsletters, or on bulletin boards. Some companies also advertise internally and externally for permanent vacancies on the Internet.

EXTERNAL ADVERTISING

External advertisement means the company looks for suitable applicants from outside the company. If Alton Towers cannot recruit enough staff internally they then advertise externally using job centres or local and national newspapers. If the company is looking for a specialist or high-ranking employee it will often advertise in the national newspapers, trade magazines or on the Internet, but the majority of advertisements appear in

the local newspapers. Where there are difficulties with recruitment, some organisations may look abroad for new employees. Large companies that have subsidiary companies abroad, can bring workers from their subsidiary companies in Europe to work in this country, for a short period of time. Some schools in London have hired teachers from the Netherlands and Germany, and some nursing positions are filled by applicants from Ireland and Finland.

RECRUITMENT AGENCIES

External **recruitment agencies** are used by some companies to find suitable applicants, to save the company being involved in this part of the recruitment procedure. The recruitment agency will shortlist a number of appropriate applicants to attend for interview. The company then pays the recruitment agency or consultancy a fee for this service. Job centres also provide this service to help unemployed people back into work.

YOUTH TRAINING

Youth training is another route for recruitment, where companies accept school-leavers on training schemes. This gives the companies the opportunity to see a number of possible new employees working for them, before they actually employ any of them on a more permanent basis.

The government also provides help through such agencies as the Careers Offices, job centres and the Training and Enterprise Councils (TECs).

PRODUCING A JOB ADVERTISEMENT

When producing a job advertisement it is important that the advertisement is checked to make sure that it:
- reflects the job description and person specification for the job
- is written to be attractive to both genders and all ethnic and racial minorities
- meets the company's Equal Opportunities policy statement in its wording.

KEY POINTS
- Jobs can be advertised internally or externally.
- **Recruitment agencies** – businesses paid to find suitable applicants for a job.
- **Youth training** – employment for school-leavers, often through government schemes.

COURSEWORK ACTIVITY

A large new craft shop called The Hobby Shop is opening in Wallesley. They want skilled craftspeople to put on demonstrations and hold workshops so that the customers can come along and learn a variety of craft skills. Silk painting is one of the skills they are looking for. Limi, having started as a sole trader, is now thinking of working more hours.

Draw up an advertisement for The Hobby Shop for silk painters, lace makers and picture framers to work in the shop, giving demonstrations and running workshops for the customers, that would attract someone like Limi.

UNIT 2 UNDERSTANDING HUMAN RESOURCES

TOPIC 4 Application process

CURRICULUM VITAE

People who are interested in a particular job will then apply to the company in response to the advertisement. Depending on what the company has stated in the advertisement regarding how to apply, this is often in the form of a **letter of application** accompanied by a **curriculum vitae (CV)**.
The curriculum vitae is a document written by the applicant giving details of educational qualifications, past experience, hobbies and interests and specialist skills.

Sam and Harri need to understand job applications

CURRICULUM VITAE
PERSONAL DETAILS

Name: *Annabel Jones*

Address: *22 The Avenue*
Shipton
Wallesley

Post Code: *WA5 7BN*   Telephone Number: *01224 673645*

Marital Status: *Single*   Date of birth: *4.5.80*

EDUCATION   *Educated at Wallesley College from 1991 to 1998 including two years in the 6th Form*

QUALIFICATIONS and TRAINING
GCSEs in English (B), Mathematics (B), History (D)
Graphics (B), Business Studies (A), French (C)
and PE (D)
'A' Levels in English Language (D) and
Business Studies (D)

PREVIOUS EMPLOYMENT
No previous full-time employment but have worked weekends and holidays in a local garden centre

HOBBIES and INTERESTS
Enjoy sport and play hockey for a local club
Going out with friends to disco
Interested in embroidery and patchwork sewing

FURTHER DETAILS
Have just passed my driving test
Attending night school to do GNVQ Advanced in Retailing

Signature .... Date ....

ROLE OF HUMAN RESOURCES — SECTION 2

Many companies ask applicants to fill in a standard **application form** as this makes sure that all the information the company feels is important is included, and is in an easily accessible format.

Once the closing date has passed, all the applications are looked at and a short list will be drawn up of the applicants who appear to best meet the criteria set for the job. Remember, the whole purpose of the recruitment procedure is to find the right person for the job.

APPLICATION FORM

Below is an example of an application form which Limi Janata would fill in for the job at The Hobby Shop

---

THE HOBBY SHOP
PERSONAL DETAILS

Name   *Limi Janata*
Address   *3 Railway Terrace, Shipton, Wallesley*
Post Code   *WA3 4XZ*   Tel *01244 649321*
Marital Status   *Married*   DOB   *17/01/68*

EDUCATION and TRAINING

Educational Establishment	Start Date	Finish Date	Qualifications
Shipton High	*1979*	*1985*	*GCSEs:*
			Art (A)
			English (B)
			Math (C)
			Science (D)
			Textile (A)
			'A' Levels:
			Art (B)
			Textile (B)

PREVIOUS EMPLOYMENT
Penkraft Hobby Shop, Sales Assistant   *1985–87*
Self-employed   *1987–present*

HOBBIES and INTERESTS
Music, horse-riding, swimming

HEALTH/DISABILITIES
None

REASONS FOR APPLYING FOR THIS POST
I have been working for myself, making crafts goods from home, but I want to work more, have more access to materials and to be able to concentrate on my work instead of selling it.

Signature ....   Date ....

UNIT 2 UNDERSTANDING HUMAN RESOURCES

TOPIC 5 Interview procedures

The most common method of selecting new employees for a job is by an **interview**. Other methods that may be used to help in the selection process include:

- **aptitude tests** of verbal and numerical ability
- personality questionnaires.

Some applicants have to undertake a **practical test**, for example, bus drivers will have to take a driving test as part of their selection.

Group discussions and team building and problem-solving exercises can be built into the selection process.

At Alton Towers the selection process uses interviews, aptitude tests and group assessments. All of these processes are part of the recruitment procedure, to make sure that all applicants are given equal opportunities. A fair decision can then be reached as all applicants will have been judged on the same criteria.

Sam and Harri need to know about interviews

INTERVIEW

The interview is a face-to-face meeting between the applicants and the human resources or line manager. The applicants are asked a number of questions to try to decide if they are suitable for the job. Every applicant will be asked similar questions and their responses recorded. Often, there will be more than one person on the interview panel, and each will ask different questions.

Some general questions that might be asked at interview are ...

- Tell me a little about yourself.
- Give me an example of something you did in your previous job which made you proud.
- How well do you feel you work as part of a team?
- How well do you feel you work on your own?
- What did you most enjoy about your previous job?
- What are your greatest strengths and weaknesses?
- What do you see yourself doing in five years' time?
- What qualities could you bring to this job?
- Why do you want to work for this company?

Bus drivers need to take a driving test before they are taken on as employees

ROLE OF HUMAN RESOURCES **SECTION 2**

The interviewer will try to ask open-ended questions that do not just need a yes or no answer. Interviewees should give reasons for their answers and use examples to support them.

More specific questions related to the job will also be included.

Once all the applicants have been interviewed, their responses will be used to help the interviewers decide who is the best person for the job. The successful applicant will usually be told in writing that they are being offered the job, subject to a successful medical exam or referees' reports. Some companies also require drugs screening because of the type of job being filled.

Unsuccessful applicants will also be told, usually by letter, and within a few days of the appointment being made.

After the appointment has been made, the new employee must be issued with a **contract of employment** within 13 weeks of starting work.

KEY POINTS

The selection procedure can include

- interviews
- aptitude tests
- practical tests
- personality tests
- group discussions.
- A letter of appointment is sent to a successful applicant.
- Unsuccessful applicants also receive a letter of rejection.
- Successful applicants must receive a contract of employment within 13 weeks of starting work.

COURSEWORK ACTIVITY

You are involved in the interviews at The Hobby Shop for the selection of a person to demonstrate silk painting, and put on workshops to teach interested customers this skill.
1. State the criteria you would use to help in the selection process at the interview.
2. On the word processor, draw up an Interview Sheet to use at the interviews. Include headings for the interviewee's details and the questions to be asked.

UNIT 2 UNDERSTANDING HUMAN RESOURCES

TOPIC 6   Induction training

There are many different types of training. When new employees start work, they need to find out about the job they are going to do. This introduction to the job can be in the form of **induction training**.

In large companies, induction training can be a structured programme of between one day and one week. New employees may also be given a Staff Handbook during the induction training. In this are details about:

- the company objectives
- the employee's terms and conditions of service
- general information about the company, payment systems, training, trade union membership
- the company's Health and Safety policy.

The purpose of the induction programme is to introduce new employees to the job, to help them do the job with confidence and efficiency, and to try to encourage company allegiance from new employees.

Sam and Harri need to know about induction

Below is a sample of an induction programme that The Hobby Shop uses when their new shop assistants are starting work.

INDUCTION PROGRAMME

Introductions
Company history
Company structure
Administrative details:
- company regulations
- health and safety in the workplace
- uniform

Workplace:
- map of premises
  (showing new employee's place of work)
  - staff room
  - staff canteen
  - first aid point
  - fire exits
  - human resources office

Conditions of employment:
- rate of pay and pay point
- hours worked
- sickness and holiday pay
- pensions
- trade union rights
- breaks

Fringe benefits
- staff purchases/discount

Training:
- opportunities
- further education

Job Training on:
- customer service
- stacking shelves/presentation of goods
- pricing goods
- using bar code reader
- using cash tills
- how to deal with difficult customers
- security

KEY POINTS

- **Induction training** – training employees when they start work so they learn all they need to know about the company and their jobs

UNIT 2 UNDERSTANDING HUMAN RESOURCES

TOPIC 7 — On- and off-the-job training

Employees already working for the company may need training to:
- learn new skills
- become multiskilled
- use new technology
- improve their efficiency
- help them obtain promotion within the company.

This training can be in the form of **on-the-job training** or **off-the-job training**.

ON-THE-JOB TRAINING

On-the-job training is a method of training employees to do a job by putting them to work with an experienced worker. Apprentices learn much of their trade in this way. Trainees in professions such as accountancy or law also have a period of training with a firm after they pass their degrees before they can become fully qualified. This is often a cheap and effective method of training as long as the experienced worker is efficient. The main problem with this type of training is that the quality of work produced by the trainee may not be of a very high standard and quality.

OFF-THE-JOB TRAINING

Off-the-job training is a method of training where the employee is trained away from the workplace, often at a college or training workshop or, in a large company, in the company's own training office. Off-the-job training can be in the form of a course, leading to qualifications such as 'A' levels, GNVQs or NVQs. It can be a sandwich course where an undergraduate spends part of the time on a degree course studying at university and part of the time working with an employer. It could also be a course to train employees on new computer software, a management training course, or training on the development of a new product line.

Sam and Harri need to learn about different types of training

Apprentices can learn from people who have been doing the job for a long time

The advantages of off-the-job training are that it is undertaken by specialist trainers, and often leads to some form of qualification, which can be useful for future staff development.

Most companies provide a combination of on-the-job and off-the-job training for their employees. Training costs money, both in funding the training and in lost production whilst the training is taking place. One big concern for many employers is that, after investing time and money training an employee, the employee may decide to leave the company for a better job, having acquired their new skills and qualifications at the company's expense.

Companies in this country have been criticised in the past for their lack of investment in training. This has led to shortages of skilled workers in some areas of industry. Now large companies are realising that investing in training is important. It is an investment in the future of the company and many more resources are being used to improve training. Government-led initiatives such as Investors in People encourage employers to invest more time and money in the training and motivation of their staff. The government encourages employees to look after their own training by using tax incentives and grants to make it easier for people to pay for improving their own knowledge.

KEY POINTS

- **On-the-job training** – training existing employees as they work
- **Off-the-job training** – training existing employees outside the company.

Companies may send employees for training in new work-related skills and also personal skills such as assertiveness training

UNIT 2 UNDERSTANDING HUMAN RESOURCES

TOPIC 8 — Termination of employment

RESIGNATION

If an employee wants to **resign** (leave work) voluntarily, perhaps because he or she may have found a new job, the employer and employee must follow the rules laid down in the contract of employment regarding the length of notice that must be given. The employer should acknowledge the resignation by letter. Any items belonging to the company, such as uniforms, should be returned. Employees will be issued with a P45 form with their last pay slip. The P45 shows how much they have earned, and all deductions made from their pay.

Sam and Harri need to know about termination of employment

RETIREMENT

If an employee is about to reach **retirement** age (65), the employer should send the employee a letter confirming the retirement date. Many large companies now offer retirement seminars to help prepare employees for retirement. If the company has a pension scheme the employer will help the employee complete the pension application form.

REDUNDANCY

The company may find itself in a position where it is necessary to make some employees **redundant**. This could happen if, for example, the company has had a big fall in orders. It does not need to make as many goods and so needs fewer workers.

If this is the case, they can begin by asking employees to apply for **voluntary** redundancy. This is where the employee offers to leave the job for a cash payment. This is often the first step taken by employers if they need to reduce staff numbers. The second step may be **compulsory** redundancy. In this case the employer ends the contracts of employees whose jobs no longer exist or who are no longer needed by the company.

The government has introduced legislation to offer some protection to employees being made redundant. The company has to make a **minimum redundancy payment** to employees, based on the number of years they have worked for the company.

ROLE OF HUMAN RESOURCES SECTION 2

DISMISSAL

The company may also need to **dismiss** an employee or group of employees, for a variety of different reasons, such as:

- The employee is not capable of doing the job for which he or she was employed.
- The employee's conduct may be such that he or she has broken safety rules or endangered other employees' lives through his or her actions.
- There is a legal reason why the employee cannot be employed, e.g. he or she is an illegal immigrant.

Employees are protected against unfair dismissal by the Employment Protection Act (1978). If they feel they have been dismissed unfairly, they can appeal to an **Industrial Tribunal**. This is like a court of law, where a panel of experts listen to evidence from both the employer and the employee and come to a decision on whether the dismissal was fair or not. If they find that the dismissal was unfair the company will either be asked to reinstate the employee or, failing this, they must pay the employee compensation.

KEY POINTS

- Termination of employment can be:
  - voluntary – when an employee resigns
  - retirement – when an employee reaches a certain age
  - redundancy – when an employee is discharged because the company is abolishing the job
  - dismissal – when an employee is discharged because the company is not happy with his or her work.
- Companies must not dismiss employees unfairly.

REVIEW QUESTIONS

1. List three different types of training that a company can use.
2. Explain the purpose of each of these types of training.
3. State two reasons why an employer might want to dismiss an employee.

SUPER REVIEW QUESTIONS

4. Explain the objectives of the Human Resources Manager in offering training to the employees.
5. State and explain two reasons why employees might want to leave their job.
6. State and explain two ways in which the employer can reduce the workforce.

Section 3 Employer/employee relations

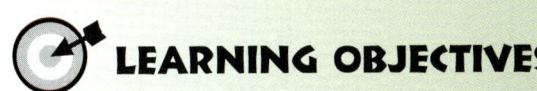

LEARNING OBJECTIVES

By the end of this section you should have learnt:
- why employers need to have good working relationships with their employees
- how employers and employees come to agreement over pay and working conditions
- the role of the trade union
- the role of employers' associations
- the meaning of collective bargaining
- types of industrial action which can be taken
- the actions available to the employer when negotiations break down.

UNIT 2 UNDERSTANDING HUMAN RESOURCES

TOPIC 1 — Industrial relations

GOOD WORKING RELATIONSHIPS

Employers need to develop good working relationships with their employees for many reasons. These include:
- If employees are content with their work and feel they are valued, they are more likely to work hard and help the company meet its objectives.
- Staffing bills are often the highest cost to a business, which means it will not want to lose good workers, in whom it has invested considerable time and money.

Sam and Harri need to know about industrial relations

INDUSTRIAL RELATIONS

Industrial relations are the interaction between the employers (this includes such people as human resources managers, supervisors, or line managers) and the employees' representatives, such as the trade union officials or the staff committee. Issues that are discussed include:
- training for employees
- equal opportunities
- shorter working hours
- pay
- production targets
- disputes and grievances
- health and safety issues in the workplace.

These two groups of people meet regularly, knowing that they may be starting on opposite sides and that each side will have to negotiate, argue, debate and put their case in the strongest possible way, before they will hopefully reach agreement.

Manual worker – member of the Transport and General Workers Union (T&GWU)

AGREEMENT OVER PAY AND WORKING CONDITIONS

The most important areas where the employer and employees need to agree are:
- pay
- working conditions.

In a large organisation it is impractical for the employer to talk to each employee individually about

White collar worker – member of the National Association of Local Government Workers (NALGO)

EMPLOYER/EMPLOYEE RELATIONS

SECTION 3

his or her rate of pay or working conditions, so in many companies this talking takes place between the employers and the employees' representatives. This representative may be a **trade union official**, or if it is a company where there is no trade union representation, the employees can elect their own spokesperson or have a staff committee.

The trade union looks after the interests of a particular group of employees. One example is NALGO (the National Association of Local Government Officers) which is a trade union for white-collar workers employed by local councils. The union puts the workers' points of view and claims for better pay and working conditions, to the employers, at regular meetings. When employers want to bring in changes in rates of pay, or working conditions, they start negotiations at these meetings, to try to reach agreement with the employees about the changes they want to introduce.

Employees may go on strike to protest against low pay. If this happens the union officials and employer's representatives will meet to negotiate an agreement. If the strike causes large disruption to the public, then the employers will feel under more pressure to come to an agreement that will stop the strike. See pages 154–5 for more information on industrial action.

THE ROLE OF THE TRADE UNION

The trade union's main role is to secure the best possible working conditions for its members, and to promote and protect their interests. That is why many people join trade unions. It is also much easier for the employees if they combine together as a group rather than trying to negotiate pay and conditions individually. This is known as **collective bargaining**.

In addition to negotiating pay and working conditions, the trade union can:
- support training and opportunities for further educational qualifications
- organise legal representation for members of the union who feel they have been unfairly dismissed
- provide some pay to workers during strike action.

Most trade unions are members of the **Trades Union Congress (TUC)**. The Trades Union Congress cannot tell unions how to run their business, but they do represent the unions, through the General Council, in discussions with the government to try to influence government policy on a wide range of issues. The Trades Union Congress meets once a year at a conference to discuss these issues.

Employer/employee negotiations over pay

EMPLOYERS' ASSOCIATIONS

As we have seen, the trade union is a body of people that represents the **employees'** interests. An employers' association is a similar body that represents **employers'** interests. For example, the Engineering Employers' Federation is a body that supports and represents employers in the engineering industry. The main roles of the employers' associations are:
- to represent the employers in negotiations with trade unions
- to give employers help and advice on such things as training, health and safety matters.

The **Confederation of British Industries (CBI)** is a national organisation set up to represent the interests of the employers from **all areas** of industry and commerce, in discussions with the government, trade unions and other interested groups.

COLLECTIVE BARGAINING

The process where employers' and employees' representatives negotiate pay and working conditions is called collective bargaining.

This can be at **local** level, where bargaining for pay and conditions takes place within the organisation, and the managers and trade union representatives or shop stewards working in the organisation are involved in the negotiations. It can also be at **national** level, where there are issues that might affect a whole industry, and here the national union representatives and the employers' association will discuss the issues through collective bargaining. For example, nurses now have to negotiate their pay rises on two levels. The government agrees a minimum pay rise for all nurses across the country, and this can then be renegotiated at a local level, with their local health authority for a further increase in their pay. These negotiations also involve discussions on broader issues, such as:

- conditions of employment
- basic pay
- overtime pay
- bonus schemes
- health and safety issues in the workplace
- training
- equal opportunities
- redundancy and dismissal.

COURSEWORK ACTIVITY

Find out if any members of your family or a friend's family, or perhaps one of your teachers at school, are members of a trade union.

1. Interview them and find out:
   - why they joined the union
   - if they attend union meetings
   - the advantages and disadvantages of being in a trade union.
2. Give your own opinions on the importance of the trade union in the workplace.

KEY POINTS

- Employers and employees need good working relations.

- Industrial relations concerns issues such as:
  - training
  - employees' rights
  - working hours
  - pay
  - production
  - health and safety.

- Employees group together to negotiate collectively through a trade union.

- Trade unions exist to help employees with:
  - disputes over pay and working conditions
  - training
  - health and safety
  - equal opportunities
  - legal representation.

- There are also associations which help employers in similar ways.

- **Collective bargaining** – where employees band into a group to negotiate conditions of work with the employer.

UNIT 2 UNDERSTANDING HUMAN RESOURCES

TOPIC 2 Industrial action

TYPES OF INDUSTRIAL ACTION

When the employer and employee representatives meet to discuss pay and working conditions, it is hoped that agreement can be reached. In many companies today employees see themselves as stakeholders in the company and so are more likely to compromise. However, sometimes agreement cannot be reached – this is called an **industrial dispute**. For example, the employer might argue that the business cannot afford to give the employees a pay rise because recent increases in interest rates have made their prices uncompetitive abroad.

Sam and Harri need to understand industrial action

The trade union may then try to put pressure on the employer to reach agreement through some form of **industrial action**. There are a number of laws governing industrial action and the unions are also obliged to consider them. Some types of industrial action include:

- **Work-to-rule** – the employees will go about their work by strictly following the rules that apply to their job. This is sometimes described as a **go slow** because this type of action invariably slows down the production rate.
- **Overtime ban** – the employees work exactly to the hours in their contract of employment and refuse to do any overtime.
- **Boycott** – the employees refuse to undertake a particular duty or use a particular machine or piece of equipment that the employers might be trying to introduce.
- **Strike** – the employees stop working altogether. A strike can be an **official strike** in which case it has been agreed with the union. An **unofficial strike** is when the employees stop work but they do not have the backing of the union.
- **Sit-in** – the employees try to protect their jobs by occupying the workplace. This is often used when a business is threatened with closure and the workers feel that this type of action might influence the owners.

Agreement reached on new rates of pay

Employers can also take action against the employees in an industrial dispute:
- They can threaten to close loss-making parts of the business and make the employees redundant.
- They can sack workers who refuse to work.
- They can suspend workers, which means that they can be sent home without pay for a period of time.
- They can use a lock-out, which means that the employers shut the premises and stop the workers coming to work.
- They can stop a previously agreed pay rise.

CONCILIATION AND ARBITRATION

In the Employment Protection Act (1974) a body of people was set up to help employers and employees reach agreement and help them solve their industrial disputes. This body is called the **Advisory, Conciliation and Arbitration Service (ACAS)**.

ACAS is made up of representatives from the trade unions, representatives from the CBI and some independent experts on industrial relations.

If approached to help solve a dispute, ACAS can help in the following ways:
- It can meet each side separately and listen to their arguments, and then try to get the employer and the union to meet together – this is called **conciliation**.
- It can suggest a solution, but neither side has to accept the proposal – this is called **mediation**.
- It can get both sides to agree in advance to accept the solution that ACAS puts forward – this is called **arbitration**.

REVIEW QUESTIONS

1. List two types of industrial action that are available to the employee during an industrial dispute.
2. List two types of action available to the employer during an industrial dispute.

SUPER REVIEW QUESTIONS

3. Explain the difference between arbitration, conciliation and mediation.
4. Explain the advantages to a business of working closely with the trade unions.

KEY POINTS

- **Industrial dispute** – when discussions between employers and employees fail.
- Employees can:
  - work to rule
  - refuse to do overtime
  - boycott
  - strike
  - stage a sit-in.
- Employers can:
  - make workers redundant
  - sack workers
  - suspend workers
  - lock workers out
  - stop a pay rise.
- The Advisory, Conciliation and Arbitration Service (ACAS) can offer:
  - conciliation – helping the different sides to discuss a settlement
  - mediation – suggesting a settlement and letting the different sides discuss it
  - arbitration – deciding on a settlement that both sides have agreed to accept.

UNIT 2: UNDERSTANDING HUMAN RESOURCES

QUESTION TIME

PART-TIME CLEANER

wanted for

Supacosts plc

Hourly rate – £4.00
25-hour week + overtime
(includes bonus scheme and weekend work)

For further information write to:
PO Box 32
Northbury
NO34 9JN

TRAINING OFFICER

wanted for

Supacosts plc

Salary £15,000
+ package of company benefits

*We are looking for a person who is:
well qualified, experienced,
a good communicator,
smart in appearance,*

Apply in writing, with full CV
For further information write to:
PO Box 32
Northbury
NO34 9JN

Study the advertisements above, which have been drawn up by the Human Resources Manager at Supacosts plc, for a cleaner and a training officer.

The cleaner is paid wages and the training officer is paid a salary.

1. Explain how the cleaner's wages will be calculated and paid, and how the training officer's salary will be calculated and paid.
   The manager is given a package of company benefits.
   The cleaner can be paid a bonus for the work they do.

2. List the company benefits that could be given to the training officer. Explain how the cleaner's work could be calculated so that he or she earns a bonus.

3. Employees need job satisfaction to be happy at work.
   State and explain three different things that Supacosts plc could do to motivate its employees, which could then lead to more job satisfaction.

4. Draw a flow chart to show the recruitment procedures that Supacosts plc would use to appoint the cleaner.

5. Draw up an appraisal form that could be used by Supacosts plc to monitor the performance of its staff.

EXTENSION TASKS

Most large companies have a Human Resources department.

6 Evaluate the importance of human resources to Supacosts plc.

7 State and explain the objectives of human resources in Supacosts plc, and how they fit in with the company objectives.

8 Draw up a set of guidelines for the employees on their legal rights at work. Use the word processor to produce these guidelines. It should include sections on:
- the contract of employment
- the length of notice needed
- the Race Relations Act
- the Sex Discrimination Acts
- the Disabled Persons Act
- the Equal Pay Act
- the Health and Safety at Work Act
- the Employment Protection Act.

UNIT 2 UNDERSTANDING HUMAN RESOURCES

COURSEWORK ASSIGNMENTS

The owners of The Hobby Shop have interviewed six people for the post of Trainee Manager. They have appointed Amy Wing. They now need to confirm the appointment with Amy, organise an induction programme for her and draw up her contract of employment.

She is to be responsible for the day-to-day running of the shop, which will include keeping all the financial records up-to-date and organising the staff payroll and staff rotas. Your task is to:

1. Write a letter offering the post to Amy Wing.

2. Draw up an induction programme for the owners to use with their new manager.

3. Draw up a contract of employment for Amy.

4. Evaluate the benefits of induction training, on-the-job training and off-the-job training to the owners, and also to Amy as an employee of the company.

The Hobby Shop will employ a lot of workers, because it is open seven days a week and does not close until 8.00 pm. The owners decide it would be useful to have a Recruitment Guide to send to prospective employees. It will give details of the company's procedures for recruitment.

5. Produce this guide on the word processor, in the form of a leaflet. The leaflet should include the following information:

Section 1	Applying for a job	Use of application forms only
		Procedures for unsuccessful applicants at application form stage
		Timescale for whole of selection procedure
		Shortlisting
Section 2	Tests	Aptitude tests
		Role play
Section 3	The interview	Interview personnel
		Informing successful applicant
		Informing unsuccessful applicants
Section 4	The appointment	Details of start date
		Details of induction programme
		Contract of employment

6. Role play:

   Kemet Electronics Ltd have been negotiating restructuring the working day with the trade unions. They want to change the employees' shift patterns.

   They want to introduce weekend working on the assembly line, which will mean that some weeks the workers will have days off in the week instead of at the weekend.

   The days off will be different each week and will be worked out on a rota. The workers will not be working any extra hours each week, but they will have to work some weekends.

   Work with a partner, with one taking on the role of the employer and the other the role of the trade union representative. Write out the arguments you will put forward.

7. Kemet Electronics Ltd and the trade union cannot agree on the restructuring. They decide to go to ACAS. Describe the different ways in which ACAS can try to help the employer and the union to reach agreement.

UNIT 3
Sales and Marketing

Section 1 Marketing

 **LEARNING OBJECTIVES**

By the end of this section you should have learnt:
- the purpose of marketing
- the objectives of marketing
- how a business identifies its market segment
- the difference between a market segment and a niche market
- the 4Ps
- the constraints there are on marketing
- the legislation there is to protect the consumer
- the importance of marketing to the business.

UNIT 3 SALES AND MARKETING

TOPIC 1 — What is marketing?

Marketing is: ' ... the management process responsible for identifying, anticipating and satisfying consumer's requirements profitably'.
(from the Chartered Institute of Marketing)

Other definitions of marketing include:
- 'Marketing is about creating customers by looking at all your activities through their eyes and giving the customers what they want and at a profit.'
- 'Marketing is not just selling, it is about what a company believes about its products, it is about objectives and goals, it is the driving force for all the people who work there.'

Sam and Harri need to understand marketing

So, from these definitions we can see that marketing activities include:
- carrying out **market research** to find out customer needs and wants
- producing a **product** that meets customer needs and wants
- calculating the **price** that meets customer demand
- producing the right **quantities** to supply customer demand
- **promoting** the new product to the customer
- distributing the product to the right **place** that is convenient for the customer to buy it.

Without marketing, the company could find itself trying to sell a new product that few people want. This sort of mistake can lead to big financial losses, because the company will have spent a lot of money developing and setting up the new product and promoting its launch. This shows just how important marketing is to the success of the whole company.

MARKETING **SECTION 1**

When companies are struggling and sales may be falling, financial managers are often tempted to cut back on marketing first. This has often been the case in recent years, whilst the country has been in a recession. It is probably the worst time of all to cut back, as in a recession competition is at its highest, with lots of companies chasing a few customers, and so successful marketing is even more important.

KEY POINTS

Marketing is used to:

- get current information about customers
- predict future trends
- produce the right products
- increase sales.

MOST BASIC FORM OF MARKETING: OWNER DISPLAYING GOODS ON STALL TO ATTRACT CUSTOMERS.

UNIT 3 SALES AND MARKETING

TOPIC 2 Marketing objectives

The main objectives of any Marketing department in a business are:
- to look at the company's current market all the time, and be aware of things happening outside the business. For example, if your company makes washing-up liquid and there is a large rise in the sale of automatic dishwashers this would be important for your market
- to find out consumer needs and wants by carrying out market research activities
- to try to increase the company's market share.

These objectives can be achieved by the company if only they are always trying to make sure that they are making the right **product**, selling it at the right **price**, selling it in the right **place** and **promoting** it at the right time. These are called the 4Ps (see page 168 for more information).

Two examples of companies you have studied in previous units, who have changed their marketing mix to meet consumer demands are Rapid Travel and Alton Towers.

Sam and Harri need to understand the main objectives of marketing

ALTON TOWERS

Alton Towers has made changes to the theme park in recent years. Market research shows that many more families now visit the theme park. Before, the market had been targeted mainly at the late teens and early twenties with rides such as Nemesis and the Corkscrew being the main attractions. The management decided to invest money in the introduction of a range of new rides and attractions that particularly appealed to families, e.g. Old Macdonald's tractor ride, Toyland Tours and the Doodle-doo Derby, all of which are targeted specifically at young children.

As a result of this investment in new product development, new promotion and marketing strategies, Alton Towers has seen an increase in visitors, which has meant an increase in revenue for the company.

MARKETING SECTION 1

RAPID TRAVEL LTD

Rapid Travel Ltd has recently introduced a cruise section to its business. People are retiring earlier, the cost of living is quite low and people have more money to spend from such things as the windfall shares, so they are looking to spend some of this extra money on luxury items like holidays. At the moment there is a trend towards all-inclusive holidays, and so the introduction of the cruise section is meeting this new consumer demand. Rapid Travel is marketing this new section as an exciting and affordable alternative to the beaches of Spain and Greece which have been popular for so long.

To promote this new business, Rapid Travel sends mail to all its regular customers with details of cruises in locations around the world with different cruise lines and varying prices. It also has big promotions of cruising holidays displayed in its windows.

KEY POINTS
A marketing department:
- looks at the current market
- finds out customer needs
- increases market share

BROCHURE

SUMMER 20X1
- 14 nights
- £1340 all inclusive
- five meals a day

Sport
- swimming
- quoits
- volleyball
- fully-equipped gym

Entertainment
- cinema
- cabaret
- comedy
- dancing

★ 5 bars ★
★ 5 restaurants – including French and Italian ★

NEED A BREAK?

WHY NOT GO ON A CRUISE?

COME IN TO RAPID TRAVEL AND PICK UP A BROCHURE

Economy inside cabin
- 2 single beds
- desk
- easy chair

Standard inside and outside cabins
- 1 double bed
- 2 single beds
- sofa
- table
- 4 chairs

Luxury stateroom – outside only
- 1 king-size bed
- 1 double bed
- 2 sofas
- 2 easy chairs
- ensuite round bath
- balcony
- mini-bar

All cabins come with ensuite shower, WC and basin

UNIT 3 SALES AND MARKETING

TOPIC 3: Identifying market segments

WHAT IS MARKET SEGMENT?

If a company sells its products to a wide range of people, known as its **market**, it can divide them up into **segments** or smaller groups. This then allows the company to make different products to meet each different group's specific needs.

For example, Raleigh Industries makes bicycles. Forty years ago, you could buy a man's bicycle, a woman's bicycle or a junior bicycle. Then the firms that make bicycles, such as Raleigh, found out that people wanted to do different things with their bicycles, for example:

- some wanted to ride a bike to work
- some wanted them purely for leisure
- some wanted bicycles designed for road use or racing
- some wanted bicycles that could be used anywhere.

The idea of making different bicycles to meet different purposes was developed. This means that the market was broken down into segments.

Raleigh's **market segment** includes:

- tricycles for toddlers
- play bikes for 3–7-year-olds
- action bikes for the teenage market
- Raleigh made-to-measure bicycles made to individual customer's orders
- racing bicycles for professional cyclists.

Sam and Harri need to know about market segments

HOW ARE MARKETS SEGMENTED?

There is a variety of ways in which the market can be segmented:

◆ **Age** – Raleigh can segment by age by producing a range of bicycles for toddlers, teenagers, adults.
◆ **Gender** – women's and men's bicycles have different designs.
◆ **Socio-economic grouping** – segments the population according to social status and occupation. People in the higher grades are more likely to be able to afford the made-to-measure bicycle, where each one is built individually to match the customer's size, weight, and preferences for particular components on the bicycle.
◆ **Geography** – people living in built-up areas are more likely to want a road bike, whereas those living in rural areas are more likely to want an off-road bicycle like a mountain bike.

KEY POINTS

■ **Market segment** – a group of people in a market, which can be based on:
  – age
  – gender
  – socio-economic grouping
  – geography

Below is a table showing the different socio-economic groupings:

Social grade	Social status	Head of household's occupation	Approximate % of total UK population
A	Upper middle class	Managerial, professional and administrative jobs such as solicitors, doctors, company directors	3.5
B	Middle class	Middle managers such as department managers, teachers	12–13
C1	Lower middle class	Supervisory or clerical workers such as junior managers and foremen	22
C2	Skilled working class	Skilled manual workers such as electricians, plumbers	32–33
D	Working class	Semi-skilled and unskilled workers such as production line workers, cleaners	19–20
E	Poorest in society	Long-term unemployed, casual workers, state pensioners	10

The table shows that households can be divided broadly into six different categories. Each category is organised according to the occupation of the head of the household. It can also be used to gain a rough indication of income ranges in each category. These socio-economic groupings are one of the most important ways used to divide up the market, as they reflect consumers' lifestyles and likely levels of disposable income.

UNIT 3 — SALES AND MARKETING

TOPIC 4: Market segment and niche markets

MARKET SEGMENT

A **market segment** is a part of the whole market that has similar characteristics. The market for a particular product might be segmented by such characteristics as – age, income, socio-economic group, sex, geographical location or lifestyle of the consumer. By dividing the market into segments like this the business can target its products and marketing campaigns more accurately at that particular group of people.

For example, compare an advertisement for a can of Coke with an advertisement for Nescafé Gold Blend coffee. The Coke advertisement is targeted specifically at the teenage/under-25s market whereas the coffee advertisement is targeted at the over-25s.

Sam and Harri need to understand market segments and niche markets

Teenage market

Over-25s market

MARKETING SECTION 1

NICHE MARKET

A **niche market** is an even smaller part of the market, it is a section within a market segment. It is an even smaller group of consumers whose needs and wants can be clearly identified. Niche marketing has been introduced by companies because there are many groups of consumers who can be identified as having very specific needs, but the numbers in these groups are small.

For example, vegetarians could be identified as a market segment within the food industry, but producing foods made specifically from soya is providing for a niche market within the vegetarian market segment.

KEY POINTS

- **Niche market** – a smaller, even more specific part of a market segment

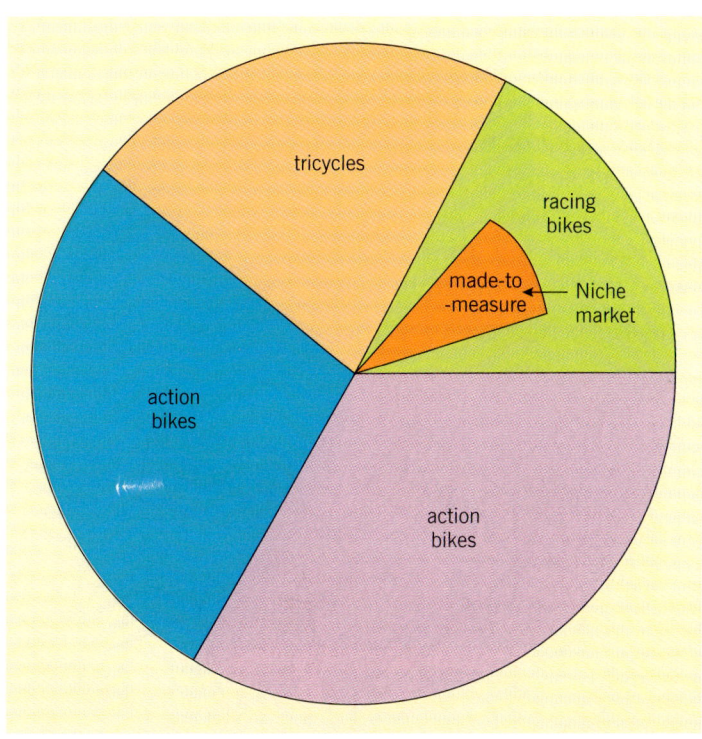

A bicycle manufacturer would produce a number of different types of bicycles for different markets, for example, tricycles for toddlers and action bikes for teenagers. They might also produce bicycles for a niche market, for example, made-to-measure bikes for professional racers.

UNIT 3 SALES AND MARKETING

TOPIC 5 — Marketing mix

When marketing a new product it is important that a company put together the right mix of:
- the right **product**
- at the right **price**
- in the right **place**
- using the best method to **promote** the product.

These are often called the 4Ps: product, price, place, promotion.

Different goods and services need a different emphasis from each of the 4Ps. For example, Marks & Spencer uses mail shots to promote its goods, but it does not advertise on television, putting much more emphasis on producing high-quality goods and selling them at reasonable prices – right product, right price. Soft-drink manufacturers spend a lot of money on promotion – advertising on television and designing attractive packaging for their goods. They also make sure you can find their brand of soft drink on the shelves on the local supermarket – the right place.

This different use of the 4Ps is referred to as the **marketing mix**.

Sam and Harri need to understand what is meant by marketing mix

MARKETING SECTION 1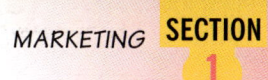

To put together the right mix a company needs the following:

- **Product**: the company must have a product that customers want, and are prepared to pay for. The company may want to emphasise that the product is of a high quality, suitable for a particular purpose, has particular design features such as its size, weight, shape and materials used, that it is value for money, or perhaps it will improve the consumer's own image.
- **Price**: the company needs to know the price the customer is prepared to pay for the product. It must also be a price that enables the company to make a profit (you can read more about pricing methods in Section 4).
- **Place**: the company needs to make sure that the product is being sold in the right type of retail outlet. For Raleigh, this could be a specialist shop, such as a bicycle shop, or a large hypermarket which sells a wide range of goods, including bicycles. The decision is made by working out the type of customer who uses that particular outlet, and then choosing the right product to match that type of customer. Some manufacturers are increasingly choosing mail order and even the Internet to sell their products. Busy people often do not have the time to go to the shops; they prefer to browse through catalogues in the comfort of their own homes when buying goods.
- **Promotion**: the company needs to make sure the customer knows about the new product. The method can range from word-of-mouth to expensive advertising campaigns to inform the customer about the company's products.

The marketing mix must be right to attract the target market. Companies hope that by getting the marketing mix right they will have a competitive edge over their rivals. Large companies will often employ specialist firms such as market research agencies and advertising agencies to help them put together the right marketing mix.

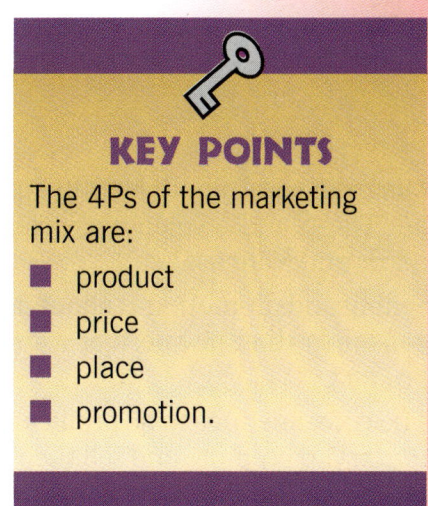

KEY POINTS

The 4Ps of the marketing mix are:
- product
- price
- place
- promotion.

REVIEW QUESTIONS

1. Explain the difference between a market segment and a niche market.
2. Describe each of the 4Ps.

SUPER REVIEW QUESTION

3. Explain the importance of the marketing mix to a company like Raleigh Industries.

UNIT 3 — SALES AND MARKETING

TOPIC 6 — Protecting the consumer

Marketing is all about identifying consumer needs and wants and developing a product to meet those needs and wants.

Selling and promotion is about persuading the consumer that they need or want to buy your product.

The consumer has to be protected against companies that try to promote and sell their products through misleading or dishonest claims and descriptions of their products. As a result measures have been introduced to protect the consumer, ranging from voluntary codes of practice to legislation.

Sam and Harri need to know about consumer protection

LEGAL PROTECTION

There are many laws that apply specifically to the ways companies promote and sell their goods. Below are some of the most important ones.

The **Trade Descriptions Act** – makes it an offence to describe goods falsely, for example, to say a garment is pure wool when it contains 20 per cent of a man-made fibre is illegal.

The **Sale of Goods Act** – makes it an offence to sell goods with defects. Goods must be of 'merchantable quality' which means they must be free from faults, fit for the purpose for which they were made and as described.

CERTIFICATION TRADE MARK
PURE NEW WOOL

The **Consumer Protection Act** – makes it an offence to sell any unsafe goods that might endanger life or cause injury, or could cause damage to property. For example, some toys have been found to have buttons that could come off easily and on which a child could choke.

The **Weights and Measures Act** – makes it an offence to sell goods that are not of the actual quantity declared on the product. For example to sell a packet of crisps that should weigh 25 g when it actually only weighs 15 g is breaking the law.

The **Food and Drugs Act** – it is an offence to sell any food that is not fit for human consumption. This applies to the contents of food and medicines.

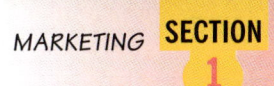

MARKETING SECTION 1

Packaged foods must carry ingredients labels and some goods have to carry warnings about the way they should be handled or cooked.

The **Food Safety Act** – this gives Environmental Health Officers the power to close down businesses where food is not being prepared hygienically.

The **Consumer Credit Act** – states that businesses must state the true annual rate of interest being charged to customers buying goods on credit. Customers must also have a period of time to change their minds after signing hire purchase contracts at home.

VOLUNTARY CODES OF PRACTICE

As well as laws protecting the consumer, there are other constraints on the way organisations behave that have implications for marketing. Several industries and associations have **voluntary codes of practice** which they are expected to follow. The Press Association has a code of practice governing newspapers. Travel agents also have their own code of practice which is monitored by ABTA (the Association of British Travel Agents).

One of the most successful voluntary codes of practice applies to advertising. The **British Code of Advertising Practices** was drawn up in 1962 to monitor all printed and cinema advertising. The code states that all advertisements must be 'legal, decent, honest and truthful'. The Advertising Standards Authority is responsible for supervising the British Code of Advertising Practices, and if it considers that an advertising company has not kept up the standards agreed it can ask all the newspapers, magazines and cinemas to refuse to use the advert. This code of practice does not apply to radio or television advertising.

The Independent Television Commission (ITC) was set up in 1990 to control television advertising.

KEY POINTS

Governments pass laws to protect the consumer from:

- false descriptions of goods
- faulty or dangerous goods
- goods that can affect consumers' health.

171

UNIT 3

SALES AND MARKETING

TOPIC 7 — Ethical constraints

PRESSURE GROUPS

Pressure groups can also put constraints on businesses. In recent years, several companies have been forced to change their advertising methods due to public demand.

A series of Benetton advertisements met with strong public disapproval and were eventually withdrawn. The government has put pressure on cigarette companies by banning cigarette advertising on television. It has now taken this ban one stage further with the banning of cigarette companies advertising their sponsorship of major sporting events such as the World Snooker Championships.

Sam and Harri need to know how ethical constraints work

Other areas of marketing that have been affected by public pressure are:

- The use of animals in testing for medicines and cosmetics; many companies now feel it is important to declare that they do not use animal testing on their products as they want consumer approval; the Body Shop led the campaign to have the testing of cosmetics on animals banned.

- The reduction of packaging on goods and the recycling of packaging materials to protect the environment; companies want consumer approval so will advertise the fact that they recycle their packaging on the packaging itself. Again the Body Shop was a leader in recycling its packaging, as well as reducing the amount of packaging and labels used on its products.

HELP AND ADVICE FOR CONSUMERS

If consumers feel they need advice on consumer legislation there are a number of official and unofficial bodies which have been set up to protect consumers.

The **Office of Fair Trading** has wide-ranging powers to investigate complaints about misleading descriptions and prices, inaccurate weights and measures, consumer credit problems and safety of goods. With any business that it feels is working against the consumer's interests, it has the power to ban their goods or services.

The **Consumers' Association** tests a wide range of goods and services. It publishes the magazine *Which?* where it reports on investigations and tests it has carried out on the consumer's behalf. Other unofficial bodies that exist to protect consumer rights are – the BBC's *Watchdog* series of programmes, the Citizens' Advice Bureaux, and Consumer Advice Centres (see Unit 1 Section 5, pages 93–94 for further information).

KEY POINTS

- Companies can also be constrained by:
  - voluntary codes of practice
  - pressure groups
  - public opinion.
- Consumers are represented by official government organisations and other unofficial bodies.

REVIEW QUESTIONS

1. List the laws that protect the consumer against:
   - goods being sold underweight,
   - goods not being accurately described,
   - goods that are unfit for human consumption.
2. State one example of where the Food Safety Act might be used. State who would enforce this law and what action they might take.

SUPER REVIEW QUESTION

3. Explain the difference between legislation that is a constraint on marketing, and a voluntary code of practice that might be a constraint on marketing.

Section 2 Market research

 **LEARNING OBJECTIVES**

By the end of this section you should have learnt:
- the purpose of market research
- the different methods used for market research
- different ways that can be used to collect data
- the different methods of sampling
- designing a market research questionnaire
- how to collect, record, analyse and interpret the data from the questionnaire.

UNIT 3 SALES AND MARKETING

TOPIC 1 Purposes and methods of market research

PURPOSES OF MARKET RESEARCH

Companies need to know what the consumer needs and wants to buy. Some companies develop and launch a product and then embark on a heavy promotion and advertising campaign to convince the consumer they want the product. This type of company is called a **product-orientated** company.

Some companies first go out and find out what consumers want and then develop the product to meet their needs. This type of company is called a **market-orientated** company. Many businesses today think that they are likely to do well if they are market-orientated so they generally listen to what consumers tell them they want.

To find out what the consumer wants, companies have to carry out **market research**.

Market research is the gathering, presenting, analysing and interpreting of data about the market's (people's) demands for goods and services.

Sam and Harri need to understand market research

3	MEDIA			
1	How many hours television, on average, do you watch per week? 0-2 hrs 1 ☐ 2-10 hrs 2 ☐ 10-15 hrs 3 ☐ 15+ hrs 4 ☐			
2	Which of the following daily newspapers do you read regularly?			
	Daily Express	01 ☐	Independent	07 ☐
	Daily Mail	02 ☐	Star	08 ☐
	Daily Mirror	03 ☐	Sun	09 ☐
	Daily Telegraph	04 ☐	Times	10 ☐
	Financial Times	05 ☐	Today	11 ☐
	Guardian	06 ☐	Other	12 ☐
3	Which of the following Sunday newspapers do you read regularly?			
	Independent on Sunday	01 ☐	Sunday Mirror	07 ☐
	Mail on Sunday	02 ☐	Sunday Post	08 ☐
	News of the World	03 ☐	Sunday Telegraph	09 ☐
	Observer	04 ☐	Sunday Times	10 ☐
	Sunday Express	05 ☐	The People	11 ☐
	Sunday Mail	06 ☐	Other	12 ☐
4	What kinds of books do you like to read?			
	Fiction		**Non-fiction**	
	Classical	01 ☐	Biography	09 ☐
	Contemporary	02 ☐	Cookery	10 ☐
	Crime	03 ☐	Gardening	11 ☐
	Fantasy	04 ☐	History	12 ☐
	Romance	05 ☐	Popular Science	13 ☐
	Science Fiction	06 ☐	Travel	14 ☐
	Western	07 ☐	War	15 ☐
	Other	08 ☐	Other	16 ☐

METHODS OF MARKET RESEARCH

There are several ways of collecting the data. Some large companies have their own marketing department whilst others employ outside agencies to do the research for them.

The two main methods of market research are:
- desk research
- field research.

KEY POINTS
- To find out what consumers want or need a company has to do market research.

UNIT 3 SALES AND MARKETING

TOPIC 2 Desk and field research

DESK RESEARCH

Desk research is gathering together existing data that has already been collected and published for another purpose. This is also called **secondary research**.

Using desk research is a relatively cheap and quick way to gather data that already exists. For example, data can be collected by using the company's own sales figures. Supermarkets use the data collected from their sales tills to determine such things as trends and loss leaders. Companies can also use published sources of information:

◆ **Market research agencies** who collect data, analyse it and publish the results in journals. This can then be bought by companies who need information on current consumer markets.

◆ The **Office of Population Censuses and Surveys** carries out a census every ten years for the government, and this data is available to companies. It includes such details as age groups in different areas, where people live and employment statistics.

◆ **Public libraries** have many different types of reference books, and many also have CD-ROM facilities.

◆ Some **newspapers and magazines** provide information on market trends.

Sam and Harri need to know about desk and field research

PUBLIC LIBRARIES CAN BE USEFUL FOR MARKET RESEARCH.

MARKET RESEARCH

FIELD RESEARCH

Field research is gathering new data **direct** from the consumer by carrying out surveys based on structured questionnaires or interviewing a sample of people. This is also called **primary research**. Field research can be carried out in a variety of ways.

- **Questionnaires** are often used by companies. Market researchers are employed to ask questions of the public, either by face-to-face interviews in such places as shopping centres, or by door-to-door interviews. Alternatively, the questions can be asked over the telephone or the questionnaires can be posted to people's homes.

- **Focus groups** can be used. These are small, carefully chosen groups that discuss a variety of topics of common interest. It is hoped this will encourage those taking part to be more open about their needs and wants. Focus groups are often used by political parties to find out what policies are popular.

- **Test marketing** can be carried out by producing a small run of a new product and testing it in one small area of the country before opening it up to the full market. For example, consumers have recently been testing new scanners in Tesco supermarkets. Customers scan each individual item themselves as they put it in their basket. When they have finished their shopping the scanner gives them the total amount they have spent on their shopping and this is then deducted from their bank account electronically, saving the customer queuing at the cash till.

- **Consumer panels** can be used. Groups of consumers are asked to test a new product and comment on their findings before the product is put on the open market. This method of research is often used to gauge reaction on new products such as toiletries and food products.

KEY POINTS

Market research can be

- **desk** – using existing data from the company or other sources
- **field** – collecting data from consumers by questionnaires, test marketing and consumer panels.

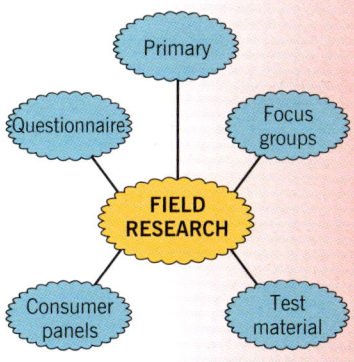

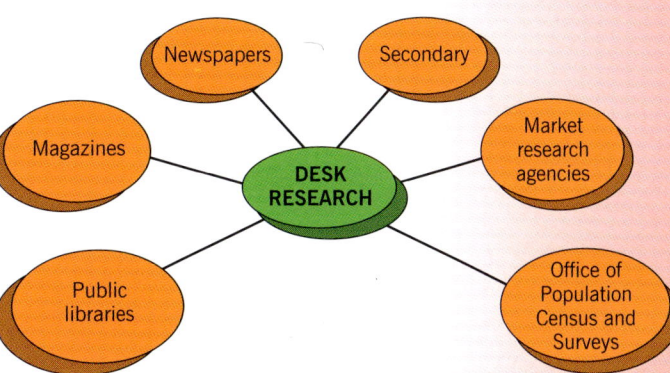

UNIT 3 SALES AND MARKETING

TOPIC 3: Sampling and questionnaires

METHODS OF SAMPLING

When carrying out market research it is not practical to question everyone who might use the product, so companies try to select a representative **sample** of the public. Usually a few thousand people will be questioned and there are two main methods of choosing a sample:

- random sampling
- quota sampling.

Random sampling does not mean just picking anyone to answer questions. It is a system of selecting people so that everyone has an equal chance of being selected. The areas in the country that are to be researched are chosen at random, usually by computer. The people to be interviewed are also chosen at random. This can be very time-consuming and it may often give an unbalanced result as there is no control over the selection of the people being interviewed.

Quota sampling is the method more often used. Market researchers have to interview an agreed number of people in a day. The number of people questioned depends on the time needed to ask each questionnaire. From the people questioned there must be a set number in each of the categories of – gender, age range, e.g. 18–25, 26–35, 36–50, 51–64, 65+ and social grade, that is A, B, C1, C2, D and E.

Sam and Harri need to understand sampling

1 Which daily newspaper do you usually read?

Daily		You		Ptnr
Daily Express	01	☐	28	☐
Daily Mail	02	☐	29	☐
Daily Mirror/Record	03	☐	30	☐
Daily Telegraph	04	☐	31	☐
Financial Times	05	☐	32	☐
Glasgow Herald	06	☐	33	☐
Guardian	07	☐	34	☐
Independent	08	☐	35	☐
Scotsman	09	☐	36	☐
Star	10	☐	37	☐
Sun	11	☐	38	☐
Times	12	☐	39	☐
Today	13	☐	40	☐
Welsh Times	14	☐	41	☐

2 What kind of home do you live in?

Detached house	1	☐
Semi-detached house	2	☐
Terraced House	3	☐
Flat/Maisonette	4	☐
Bungalow	5	☐

3 How many bedrooms does your home have ☐

4 Is your home

Owned	1	☐
Privately rented	2	☐
Council/Housing Ass.	3	☐

Extract from a multi-response questionnaire

DESIGNING A QUESTIONNAIRE

For questionnaires to be useful they must be written with a set objective in mind: for example, to find out if there is enough demand for a new design of trainers. The questionnaires must have clear, simple **unambiguous** questions.

The questions should be **closed** questions, which means the interviewee is given a limited number of possible answers. The simplest is a question that requires a straight Yes/No answer.

The question can be a **multi-response** question which provides the interviewee with a range of possible answers to choose from. For example:

How often do you rent a video?
- [ ] More than twice a week
- [ ] Weekly
- [ ] Less than four times a month

The question can ask the interviewee to give their opinion on something on a **scale of preference**, for example to assess a product on a scale of 1 to 5, where

1 = Very poor
3 = Average
5 = Very good

The advantage of using closed questions on a questionnaire is that they provide simple, short positive responses that make the data easy to handle when it is being analysed.

Having written a questionnaire, it should be tested on a small sample of people, to check that the questions have been understood and they are providing the right types of responses. If not, the questionnaire should then be modified, where necessary, before being used on a full quota of consumers.

KEY POINTS
- The two main types of sampling used for market research are:
  - **random** – selecting people and area by random
  - **quota** – selecting a set number of people based on age, gender etc.
- Good questionnaires should:
  - have a set objective
  - be unambiguous
  - have closed questions
  - be tested before use.

COURSEWORK ACTIVITY

- Choose a well-known maker of trainers.
- You work in the Marketing department of this company. You want to develop a new trainer to sell to the teenage market.
- Your first task is to carry out market research to be sure that there is a demand for another new product on the market.

Use the word processor for this work.

1 State your objectives in using this questionnaire, e.g. what is the market for these new trainers, consumer reaction to your current products, details about competitors' products.

2 Design your questionnaire. Test it on two or three people to check that it works, then carry out any modifications.

3 Conduct your questionnaire. Question at least 20 people. You are to use quota sampling, so make sure that your quota includes a range of categories such as male and female. Make sure you question people in the age range you are targeting for your new trainer.

4 Record the results. Collate the results gathered and select the most appropriate method to present the findings, e.g. table, graph, database or spreadsheet.

5 Write a report on your findings. Your report should include details of the questionnaire, the sample of people chosen, the main findings from the questionnaire. Include the details of your results in your report. Make recommendations on the viability of the development of the new product.

Section 3 The product

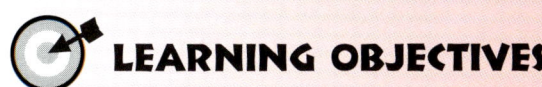
LEARNING OBJECTIVES

By the end of this section you should have learnt:
- the features that make up a product
- how to draw and explain the product life cycle
- the benefits of brand names to the manufacturer
- the possible reasons for an increase in sales of own label products
- the importance of packaging
- the effect of pre-sales and after-sales service on a product.

UNIT 3 — SALES AND MARKETING

TOPIC 1 — What makes a product?

The whole purpose of marketing is to find out what the consumer needs and wants and to satisfy that demand. The product is the most important part of the marketing mix and it must have features that make it attractive to the consumer to buy.

MAIN FEATURES

The features that make up an attractive product include such things as:

- **Reliability** – the product must be fit for the purpose it was designed for and do the job well, e.g. the VW Golf motor car is well known for its sturdiness.
- **Quality** – the product must be of a certain standard, e.g. Marks & Spencer always prides itself on the quality of its goods.
- **Value for money** – the product must provide good value compared with goods produced by competitors, e.g. Tesco is currently the leader in the supermarket race to provide the customer with the complete shopping experience, with all the extra facilities it provides for its customers.
- **Design** – the size, colour, weight, shape should be attractive and appropriate to the product, e.g. IKEA furniture stores are modern, colourful and innovative in their designs.
- **Image** – the product should create an image, such as fun, modern, e.g. the Sony Playstation.
- **Status** – the product may be bought because the consumers feel it gives them added status, e.g. Umbro sportswear has become fashionable due to France 98.

Sam and Harri need to know what makes a product

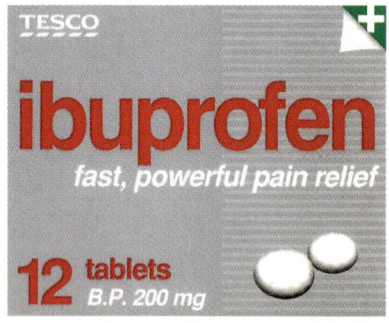

OTHER FEATURES

Other features that can be added on to a product to make it more attractive to the consumer include such things as:

- **Pre-sales service** such as credit facilities – to help the consumer buy the product the retailer can offer credit to allow payment to be spread over a period of time. This can vary from 0 per cent finance to no deposit or 3–5 years to pay. This is used for expensive items such as cars and furniture.
- **After-sales service** – machinery and equipment can be sold with the facility to have the products serviced after they have been purchased. For example, when buying a new car the manufacturer will recommend the car is serviced after a set period of time or after so many miles of use. The first service is often free as an added incentive.
- **Manuals** – for equipment such as computers, video recorders or dishwashers that needs to be properly operated, instruction books on assembly and use are provided.
- **Guarantees** – some products have guarantees against wearing out for a certain period after the purchase. The company will either replace the entire product or simply repair it. Guarantees are also used as a sign of quality, on some foods, for example.

KEY POINTS

- The most important part of the marketing mix is the product.
- Features which make an attractive product include:
  - reliability
  - quality
  - value for money
  - design
  - image
  - status.
- Products can have extra features to make them more appealing such as:
  - pre-sales service
  - after-sales service
  - manuals
  - guarantees.

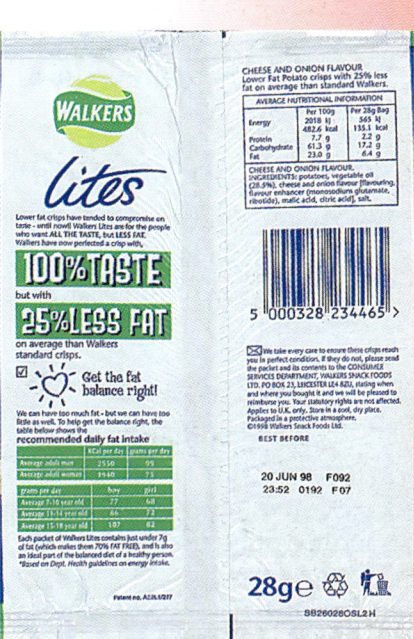

UNIT 3 SALES AND MARKETING Used in Exam

TOPIC 2 — Product life cycle

Any new product will have an expected **life cycle**. This is the amount of time the manufacturer expects the product to sell. This life cycle is made up of a series of stages.

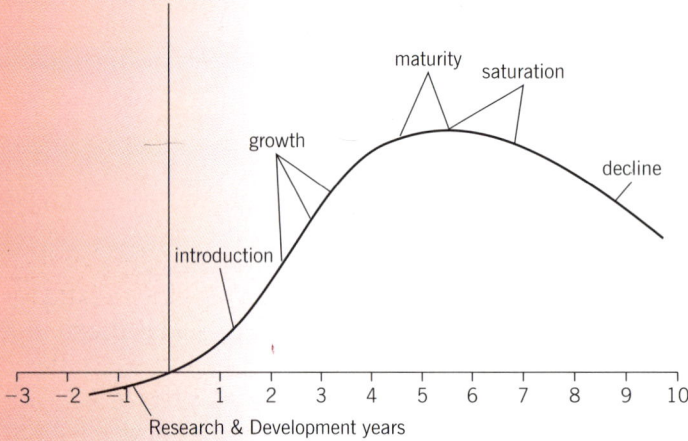

Sam and Harri need to know about product life cycle

STAGES OF A PRODUCT LIFE CYCLE

Stage 1 – Research and development
The company invests a lot of money into researching the market for the new product, developing it and market testing the product. At this stage of the life cycle the product is making no money for the company, it is actually costing money for the development.

Stage 2 – Introduction
The product is launched on the market. A promotion campaign and a large amount of advertising will take place at this stage. The product is still making a loss for the company.

Stage 3 – Growth
The product becomes known in the market. Sales should start to increase. Advertising is still continued, but less frequently than at the launch. The product should begin to make a profit.

Sometimes a company may restyle a product to extend its life cycle a little bit longer

THE PRODUCT **SECTION 3**

Stage 4 – Maturity/saturation

The product is now well established in the market. Advertising will be used to remind the consumer about the product. This is when the product reaches its peak and is at its highest profit level. Companies will try to maintain this stage as long as possible. They may introduce new models, or revitalise the advertising campaign to try to promote further sales.

Stage 5 – Decline

The product begins to lose its edge. More rival products are introduced to the market. The product has become out of date. Sales begin to fall. Profits also begin to fall.

Stage 6 – End of product line

The product is taken out of production. The last products are often sold at a reduced price to move them from the shelves, meaning a further reduction in profits.

Businesses try to have a range of products at different stages of their life cycles so that all the products do not reach the end of the line at the same time. They try to make sure that there are always some products at the mature stage and some in the introductory and growth stages.

KEY POINTS
The stages of the product life cycle are:
- research and development
- introduction
- growth
- maturity/saturation
- decline
- end of line.

REVIEW QUESTION

Look at the life cycle drawn for the Ford Escort car.
1. Describe the stages of the life cycle for the car.

SUPER REVIEW QUESTION

2. Explain the actions that could be taken by the company at each stage of the product's life cycle to try to boost sales.

UNIT 3 SALES AND MARKETING

TOPIC 3 — Brand names

A **brand name** is associated with large, long-established companies such as Kellogg's or BMW. These companies have well-known products that are instantly distinguishable from their competitors. They also have attributes associated with their brand names. BMW, for example, is associated with quality and status.

Sam and Harri need to know about brand names

CREATING A BRAND NAME

To create a brand name requires starting with a very good product and distinguishing it from its rivals. This might be achieved by making the design of the packaging bold, attractive and instantly recognisable; or through advertising, so that the consumer relates the name to good and consistent high quality. Symbols are also used – all car companies have a different symbol that they put on the bonnet of their cars.

BRAND LOYALTY

By creating this brand image the manufacturer hopes that it will create **brand loyalty**, encouraging the consumer to continue to buy its product in preference to that of its rivals.

If the manufacturer is able to develop a strong brand name it may be able to sell its products at a premium price. This is a price higher than that of its competitors. The consumer is prepared to pay the higher price, because he or she feels the branded product is of a higher quality, and also branded products are advertised more, and so the consumer is more aware of their existence. If the manufacturer has a strong brand image, it might be able to transfer the customer's loyalty to other goods it makes. For example, Mars and Bounty chocolate bars have been very successfully developed into ice cream bars.

THE PRODUCT SECTION 3

OWN-BRAND GOODS

Own-brand labels are goods that carry the name of the retailer that sells them. For example, Asda, Sainsbury and Tesco all sell their own-brand label goods. They are in direct competition with the named brand goods such as Kellogg's, that they also sell on their shelves.

Many supermarkets already sold their own-brand goods for some items, e.g. corn flakes and baked beans. The most important attraction of these goods was their lower price. Places such as Kwik Save have taken this idea one stage further and advertises its 'no frills' goods at even lower prices. Often these own-brand goods were not as good as the brand-name goods. Then supermarkets became more competitive with each other and this meant they had to improve the quality of their own-brand goods. Sometimes they even had the manufacturers of branded goods making especially for them. Many people were surprised when Sainsbury's decided to launch its own-brand cola. Everyone felt that Pepsi and Coke had cornered the market and no other brand could touch them.

But they were wrong, because Sainsbury's spent time and money developing a good (and cheaper) own-brand cola and their sales rocketed. Since then business people have realised that own-brand goods can compete with and beat branded goods. Also, the fact that Sainsbury's has a reputation for quality goods helped it win over consumers.

KEY POINTS

- Brand names identify a product.
- Retailers sell own-brand goods, often cheaper.

UNIT 3 SALES AND MARKETING

TOPIC 4: Packaging

IMPORTANCE OF PACKAGING

Packaging is important as it is needed to deliver the goods to the consumer in a safe, hygienic condition. Cakes often have several layers of packaging to protect them from being crushed and to make sure that they reach the consumer in a good condition. Further packaging may be needed to help the retailers store the products easily and safely on the shelves.

The packaging may be used by the manufacturer to promote the goods, as the colour, design or lettering may make the product more attractive and noticeable to the consumer on the shelf.

The packaging can also be used to pass on details of contents, ingredients, weight, care instructions, etc. some of which are now a statutory requirement.

Sam and Harri need to know about packaging

THE PRODUCT SECTION 3

PROBLEMS OF PACKAGING

However, packaging can also create problems for the manufacturer, as it adds to the cost of producing the goods. Excessive packaging has been a target for consumers in recent years, as they become more sensitive to environmental issues. The packaging creates problems with its use of natural resources and with its disposal afterwards. Many companies have now undertaken to recycle as much of their packaging as possible.

KEY POINTS
- Good packaging is an important part of the product.

COURSEWORK ACTIVITY

Research budget-price aftershaves or perfumes and expensive, luxury aftershaves or perfumes.

1. Look around the toiletries section in Boots or a large department store. Make a list of all the brand names of toiletries that you can find.
2. Make a note of the prices of each of the brand-name goods you have listed. Also make a note of the price of own-brand toiletries. Produce a spreadsheet and graph of the different brands and their prices.
3. Make notes on the effectiveness of the packaging on each of the toiletries, including the own-brand goods. Your notes should include details on:
   - the packaging that had most impact and why
   - whether or not the packaging would influence you if you were buying
   - the differences there were in information on the packaging of the different toiletries
   - the image created by the packaging and overall presentation of the two different products.

Section 4 The price

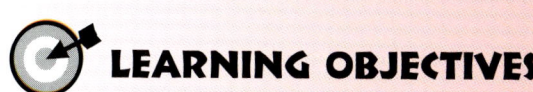
LEARNING OBJECTIVES

By the end of this section you should have learnt:
- the factors that affect prices
- the meaning of cost plus concepts
- the difference between mark-up and margin
- some different pricing strategies that companies can use.

UNIT 3 SALES AND MARKETING

TOPIC 1 — Pricing methods

IS THE PRICE RIGHT?

Businesses use marketing to find out consumer needs and wants so that they can react and provide for those needs and wants. The business is in control of the products it makes and sells. It does not have as much control over the price it charges for its products. There are two important factors that affect the price a business can charge. These are:

- the actual cost of making the goods
- the price charged for similar goods in the marketplace.

An organisation will not stay in business very long if it makes a loss on every item it sells. Nor will it stay in business very long if it charges four times as much as its competitors for similar products.

Sam and Harri need to understand methods of pricing

PRICING METHODS

When deciding on the price to set for goods the business will take into account three main factors:

- the cost of producing the goods **(cost plus pricing)**.
- the price of similar goods being sold by competitors **(competition-based pricing)**
- how the price set can be used to help increase market share **(destroyer pricing)**.

These three factors can lead to the business using different pricing methods to calculate the selling price for their goods.

There are various factors that go towards deciding the price of a product. For example, labour, the cost of importing the materials – including exchange rates and duty – and the cost of exporting goods. Other factors include overheads, the price of the competition and the price the consumer is willing to pay

COST PLUS PRICING

Cost plus pricing means taking the **direct** costs of producing the goods and adding a percentage of the **indirect** costs such as overheads (e.g. rent, heating, etc.). A **percentage mark-up** is then added on to calculate the selling price. The amount to be added may be worked out by taking into account the market demand for the goods and the price being charged by the company's competitors.

It is often difficult, however, to work out exactly what one item costs to make. Most large organisations employ management accountants to help with pricing, but here is a simplified version of how it might work:

A manufacturer makes a pair of jeans:

	£
Material	15
Labour	10
Overheads	15
Total cost	40

The manufacturer marks up all its retail prices by 50%, which gives it a retail selling price of £60. The **profit margin** is the difference between the selling price and the manufacturing cost for one unit. The jeans manufacturer could reduce the price to £50, which would cut the profit margin in half. However, if that increased sales then **profits** could be higher, even with a smaller profit margin. See Unit 4 Section 1, pages 230–231 for further information.

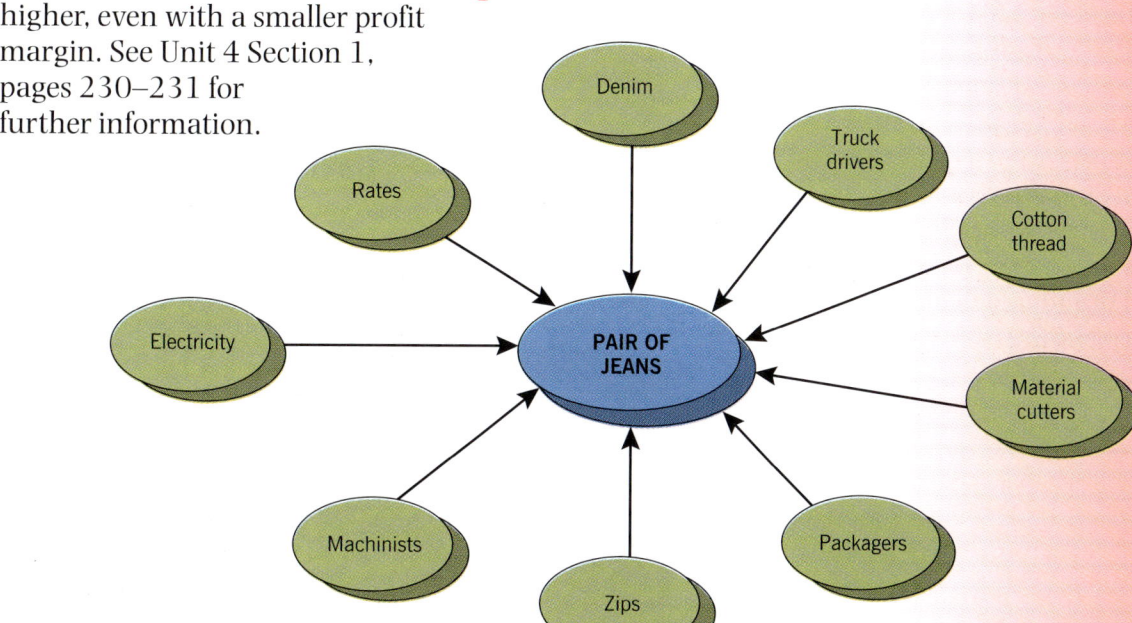

COMPETITION-BASED PRICING

This is when the business decides to set its selling price at a similar level to that of its competitors even if this means a smaller profit margin. When a new product is brought on to the market, the business may decide to sell its product at a lower price than that of its competitors to begin with, to gain a share of the market. This is called **penetration pricing**.

The opposite of penetration pricing is **creaming** or **skimming**. This is when the business sets its prices high to begin with, and then lowers the price later on. This is often used with new, high technology products. Computers, calculators, video cameras and digital cameras were all very expensive to buy when they first came on the market. They were made for a niche market – people who were very often enthusiasts willing to pay a high price. Then, in order to attract a wider audience, and get into the mass market, the manufacturers had to reduce their prices.

Businesses can also use pricing to try to attract customers away from their competitors.

For example, if a customer is tempted to buy Gold Blend coffee because there is a special offer, for example, 'buy one, get one free', the customer is attracted away from the competition. Also, as they have two jars of coffee to use, by the time they want another one they may have forgotten their old brand and will therefore keep buying Gold Blend in the future.

Buy 1 bottle of shampoo
Get 1 bottle of conditioner
half price!

100 EXTRA POINTS
If you buy 2 JARS

Buy 6 videos and get **15%** discount

3 for the price of 2!

Today only! save up to 50% on selected TVs and videos

THE PRICE SECTION 4

DESTROYER PRICING

This involves selling goods at a very low price to try to destroy competition. In recent years many of the national newspapers have used this type of pricing to reduce competition. *The Times* sold their newspaper at 10p a copy for a period of time, when their competitors were charging 40–50p per copy, to try to attract customers to buy their product.

KEY POINTS

- The factors which influence the price of a product are:
  - the manufacturing cost
  - the price of similar products
  - the effect of price on the market.
- The manufacturing cost is calculated by:
  - **direct costs** – costs related to the product, such as raw materials
  - **indirect costs** – costs related to overheads.
- **Competition-based pricing** – setting prices similar to competitors.
- **Penetration pricing** – setting prices lower to increase market share.
- **Creaming** or **skimming** – setting prices higher to appeal to a niche market.
- **Destroyer pricing** – setting prices very low to drive competitors out of business.
- **Cost-plus pricing** – setting prices based entirely on the manufacturing cost.
- **Profit margin** – the difference between the cost of producing one unit and the selling price
- **Mark-up** – the amount by which the cost of producing one unit is increased, usually expressed as a percentage, i.e.
  - A 10% mark-up on a product that costs £100 to make makes the selling price £110.

TOPIC 2: Other factors that affect prices

VALUE ADDED TAX

Value Added Tax (VAT) must be added to most goods and services. There are exceptions such as basic foods, children's clothes and footwear, books and newspapers. VAT is a tax levied by the government, at a rate of 17.5 per cent in the UK for most products.

CUSTOMS AND EXCISE DUTIES

The government puts **customs and excise duties** on a range of goods such as alcohol, tobacco and petrol, and Stamp Duty on the sale of houses. These all have to be added to the price of the goods and the business has no choice in this.

Sam and Harri need to know about other factors that affect prices

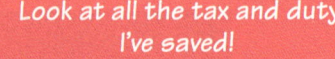

Look at all the tax and duty I've saved!

THE PRICE **SECTION 4**

ECONOMIC POLICY

The general economy of the country can also affect prices, depending on the government's economic policies and other factors such as inflation (see Unit 1 Section 5, pages 91–102 for more details).

EXCHANGE RATE

The exchange rate for the pound can also affect the price of goods and services. The exchange rate is the value of the pound when buying foreign currencies. If the pound is strong (worth more against foreign currencies), it means businesses have more money to spend when **buying** goods from abroad. But it makes it more difficult to **sell** abroad because the strong pound makes UK goods more expensive to buy in foreign countries. The changes in the value of the pound against foreign currencies can have a great influence on prices, but businesses have no control over exchange rates. They just have to learn to accept them and adapt their prices to match the changes in exchange rates.

KEY POINTS

- Other outside factors can affect costs, such as:
  - taxes
  - inflation
  - exchange rates.

REVIEW QUESTION

1. Explain the difference between mark-up and profit margin.

SUPER REVIEW QUESTION

2. State and explain the external factors that influence and affect businesses when calculating the price to set for their goods.

Australian Dollar	1.26430	Austrian Schilling	10.46900	Bahamian Dollar	1.00010
Barbados Dollar	2.01100	Belgian Franc	30.65000	Bermudian Dollar	1.00010
British Pound	0.64675	Canadian Dollar	1.36730	Chilean Pesos	410.70000
Chinese Renmimbi	8.31700	Danish Krone	5.73800	Dutch Guilder	1.67000
Egyptian Pounds	3.39500	Finnish Markka	4.52000	French Franc	5.04700
German Mark	1.48800	Greek Drachma	236.00000	Hong Kong Dollar	7.73800
Hungarian Forint	149.00000	Icelandic Krona	66.31000	Indian Rupee	35.45000
Indonesian Rupiah	2330.00000	Irish Pound	0.62212	Israeli New Shekel	3.17800
Italian Lira	1510.00000	Jamaican Dollar	34.00000	Japanese Yen	108.26000
Malaysian Ringgit	2.48800	Mexican New Pesos	7.61300	New Zealand Dollar	1.44200
Norwegian Kroner	6.40400	Pakistani Rupee	35.21000	Philippines Pesos	26.17000
Polish Zloty	2.70500	Portuguese Escudo	153.00000	Russian Ruble	5160.00000
Saudi Arabian Riyal	3.75000	Singapore Dollar	1.41700	South African Rand	4.38700
South Korean Won	813.90000	Spanish Peseta	125.40000	Swedish Krona	6.61500
Swiss Franc	1.21700	Taiwan Dollar	27.60000	Thai Baht	25.30000
Trinidad/Tobago Dollar	5.73500	Turkish Lira	83900.00000	US Dollar	1.00000
Venezuelan Bolivar	470.00000				

Section 5 The place

 **LEARNING OBJECTIVES**

By the end of this section you should have learnt:
- the importance of distribution
- the channels of distribution
- the functions of the wholesaler in the channels of distribution
- some of the new channels of distribution
- the functions of a retailer
- the different types of retailers.

UNIT 3 SALES AND MARKETING

TOPIC 1 Distribution

IMPORTANCE OF DISTRIBUTION

The next part of the marketing mix is **place**. This can be seen in two ways: choosing the right place to **sell** the goods; and deciding the best way to **distribute** or transport the goods to get them to the right place. If an organisation does not get its distribution right then all its other work is useless, because its customers cannot buy its goods or enjoy its services. If you have the best new CD player on the market, praised in every hi-fi magazine, but your warehouse cannot package it properly and it reaches the public damaged, your company will lose lots of potential customers.

Effective **distribution** needs business decisions on:

- which channels of distribution to use – wholesaler, retailer, customer
- which method of distribution to use – road, rail, air, sea
- how to get the products to the right place at the lowest cost.

Sam and Harri need to understand distribution

CHANNELS OF DISTRIBUTION

The ways the manufacturer gets its products to the customer are called the **channels of distribution**. The most common channel of distribution is:

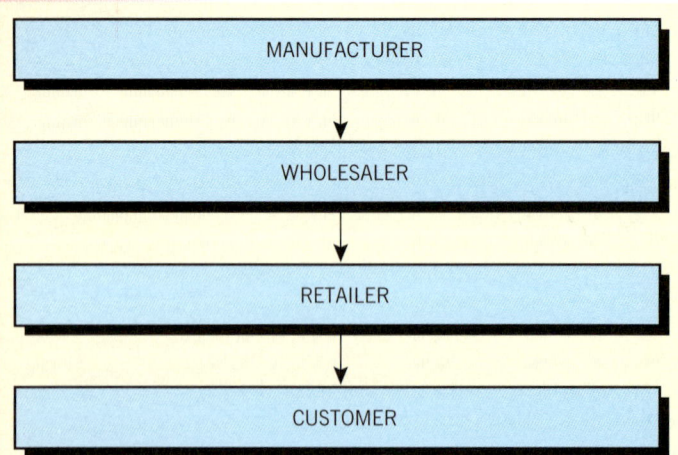

MANUFACTURER
↓
WHOLESALER
↓
RETAILER
↓
CUSTOMER

It is important that the manufacturer finds the most effective channel to distribute its goods to the consumer.

Generally, the shorter the link between manufacturer and customer, the cheaper it is to distribute the product and therefore the price of the product can be lower. The more links there are in the channel of distribution the more expensive the goods will be to buy, as the more people involved in getting the goods from the manufacturer to the consumer, the more people who want a part of the profit for handling the goods.

All of these costs have to be included in the price. Also, the longer the distance from the manufacturer to the next link in the channel of distribution, the more expensive it will be to transport the goods. There is also more chance of damage to the goods, or theft. Perishable goods have to be moved very quickly if they are to reach the consumer in good condition. However, for many manufacturers it is not cheaper to distribute direct – it would be impractical for a company such as Kellogg's to deliver its goods to every supermarket in the country, so it uses wholesalers or regional distribution centres (explained later in this section).

FUNCTIONS OF THE WHOLESALER

Manufacturers find it expensive to sell their goods in small quantities direct to retailers, so traditionally have use a **wholesaler**.

Wholesalers buy goods in large quantities from the manufacturer, getting discounts for the size of their orders. They then sell the goods to to retailers in smaller quantities.

Some will offer transport and credit facilities to retailers.

The customer can then buy goods from the retailer in individual or small quantities, appropriate to their needs.

KEY POINTS

- Decisions about place include:
  – where the goods are sold
  – how the goods are distributed.

- **Channels of distribution**
  – the routes that products follow to get from the company to the consumer, typically:
  – manufacturer
  – wholesaler
  – retailer
  – customer.

- The main functions of wholesalers are:
  – buying goods in bulk
  – selling goods in smaller quantities
  – offering credit and delivery services.

UNIT 3 SALES AND MARKETING

TOPIC 2 — Changes in channels of distribution

There are many more methods used today to distribute goods from the manufacturer to the consumer. The wholesaler has been missed out in many cases and the manufacturer employs a range of different methods for distributing its goods to the consumers.

Sam and Harri need to know about changes to the traditional channels of distribution

DIRECT SELLING

Many small manufacturers sell direct to the consumer. Lesley Jerome, sells her silk scarves direct to the consumer when she takes her products to the craft fairs and sells them herself.

MAIL ORDER

Mail order is another method of direct selling. The manufacturer produces a catalogue of goods and the consumer buys direct from them and the goods are delivered by courier or delivery service. Grattans, Kays and the Next Directory are all examples of companies that sell direct to their customers via a mail order catalogue. The Internet is also a rapidly developing high-tech electronic mail order facility.

NETWORK MARKETING

Some manufacturers use a network of people to distribute their goods to family and friends by holding parties or meetings in their houses. It is hoped that some of the people attending the party will then volunteer to hold another party. This is how the network continues to develop. Tupperware and Avon cosmetics have been sold for many years using this method.

THE PLACE **SECTION 5**

WAREHOUSE CLUBS

The idea of warehouse clubs has been brought over from the USA. Members of the public pay a fee to shop in big warehouse outlets. The warehouses sell goods in bulk. You cannot buy goods in the warehouses if you are not a member. An example of a warehouse club is Cosco at Thurrock in Essex.

CASH-AND-CARRY WAREHOUSES

Cash-and-carry warehouses were originally wholesalers selling goods on to small retailers. They broke bulk from large manufacturers and the small retailers bought from them, paid cash and took the goods away to sell to consumers. No delivery service was offered by the wholesalers. This idea has now been expanded to include the general public as direct customers. Large warehouse stores have been built in out-of-town shopping centres that sell to small tradespeople as well as the general public.

KEY POINTS

Other types of distribution channels include:
- direct selling
- mail order
- network marketing
- warehouse clubs
- cash-and-carries.

REVIEW QUESTION

1. Identify the different channels of distribution in the above pictures.

UNIT 3 SALES AND MARKETING

TOPIC 3 Retailers

TYPES OF RETAILERS

Goods can be sold to the consumer through a wide variety of different outlets.

- A **vending machine** sells goods direct to the consumer. The goods are purchased by putting the correct money into the machine, choosing an item from the goods on display and the goods are then ejected from the machine. They are found in bus stations and in shopping centres, and are useful when the shops are closed.

- A **mobile shop** is often used in country areas where there are not many shops. Mobile shops can sell fruit and vegetables, fresh fish, fresh meat, etc. They travel round the streets to sell their goods.

- A **market** is a series of stalls, usually on open ground and held once or twice a week. Markets can sell a range of goods from food to clothes to furniture.

- An **independent store** is a small shop, usually owned and run by one person.

- A **chain store** is a group of stores selling the same range of goods in a number of different towns and cities, for example, Marks & Spencer, Woolworth's.

- A **department store** is a large store, usually in the town centre. It sells a wide range of goods, and often leases out floor space to other companies to sell inside their stores. Some Debenhams department stores, for example, have a Planet outlet in them. This is not part of the Debenhams company, it it just using the store.

Sam and Harri need to know about the different types of retailer

THE PLACE SECTION 5

- A **supermarket** is a large store usually selling mainly food items and some household goods.
- A **hypermarket** also sells food, but it is all on one floor and increasingly it is located in out-of-town centres. It offers car parking facilities alongside the stores, for example, Sainsbury's, Tesco, Asda. Other customer facilities can include a photograph booth, baby room, cafeteria and even a toddlers' play area.
- A **discount warehouse** is a large store where the prices are usually lower than other stores selling similar goods. They are often located on the outskirts of the town selling such things as DIY goods, electrical goods or car accessories, for example, B&Q, Currys, PC World.
- A **shopping mall** is a collection of different shops and owners gathered under one roof. They have their own free car parking facilities and offer a wide range of goods and services to the public, such as restaurants and bars, crèche facilities, direct transport links with all the local areas, Examples of large shopping malls are the Metro Centre in Newcastle, Meadowhall in Sheffield and Lakeside in Essex.

KEY POINTS

Consumers can be sold goods through:
- vending machines
- mobile shops
- markets
- independent shops
- chain stores
- department stores
- supermarkets
- hypermarkets
- discount warehouses
- shopping malls.

REVIEW QUESTIONS

1. Make a list of all the different types of outlets you can think of in your local area, e.g. vending machines.
2. Explain the difference between mail-order and network marketing, when distributing goods.

SUPER REVIEW QUESTIONS

3. Explain the advantages to the manufacturer of using a wholesaler, when distributing their goods.
4. Explain the advantages to the customer of having a shopping mall in their local area.

UNIT 3 SALES AND MARKETING

TOPIC 4 — Methods of distribution

There is a range of methods used to distribute goods. Each has its advantages and disadvantages.

ROAD

Using road transport means the company can give door-to-door delivery. It can be contracted out to transport companies and can be the cheapest and quickest form of delivery over short distances but it is subject to traffic jams; lorries can be held up abroad; drivers can drive for only a set number of hours each day.

Sam and Harri need to know about different methods of distribution

RAIL

Rail can be quick and efficient for long distances but it cannot deliver to the door. This means that goods have to be loaded and unloaded several times, as road transport will also have to be used to take the goods the last few miles to the customer.

AIR

Distribution by air is fast but probably the most expensive form of transport. It is limited as to the size of cargo it can carry. This is ideally suited to perishable goods such as fresh fruit and vegetables or small expensive goods.

SEA

Sea distribution is cheap for carrying goods very long distances. It is used for transporting heavy, bulky loads that cannot be accommodated by air.

THE PLACE SECTION 5

REGIONAL DISTRIBUTION CENTRES

Regional distribution centres are another form of warehouse. They were originally used by supermarket chains as a central point in a region of the country where all their goods could be stored and delivered to the supermarkets in that particular region. The manufacturers all delivered their goods to the distribution centre by road, and then the supermarket chains used their own fleet of lorries to deliver the goods to all their outlets in that particular region. This idea has grown in recent years with independent companies setting up distribution centres to deliver a company's goods for it in the different regions of the country. It is an idea that is now used by manufacturers as well as the large retailers for distributing their goods.

KEY POINTS

- The main methods of distribution are:
  - road
  - rail
  - air
  - sea.
- Regional distribution companies are used to:
  - store goods for more than one outlet in one place
  - deliver goods to different outlets.

REVIEW QUESTIONS

1. List the four most common channels of distribution.
2. State the three main functions of a wholesaler.
3. List the four main methods of distribution.
4. Why do you think a company might use regional distribution centres.

SUPER REVIEW QUESTIONS

5. Give one advantage and one disadvantage of each of the four main methods of distribution.
6. State which distribution channels you would choose for each of these goods:
   a) potatoes from Shropshire to London
   b) oil from the Middle East
   c) diamonds from South Africa to England
   d) daffodils from Jersey to Amsterdam.

Section 6 Promotion

LEARNING OBJECTIVES

By the end of this section you should have learnt:
- the meaning of promotion
- the different methods of promotion available to businesses
- trade promotions
- the effect of sales promotions on purchases
- the main purposes of advertising
- the role of advertising agencies
- the contents of an advertisement.

UNIT 3 — SALES AND MARKETING

TOPIC 1 — What is promotion?

Promotion is the last part of the marketing mix. It is all about informing the consumer about the product – what it is, what it is for – and then persuading the consumer to buy it.

There are a number of techniques that can be used to promote products:

- packaging
- advertising
- sales promotion
- sponsorship
- public relations.

Sam and Harri need to understand promotion

SALE SALE SALE SALE SALE
SATURDAY ONLY

WIDE-SCREEN TVS
25% OFF
£250-£800

PORTABLE TVS
30% OFF
£100-£300

COFFEE MACHINES
30% OFF
£70-£200

FRIDGE-FREEZERS
50% OFF
£200-£500

FRIDGES
25% OFF
£80-£300

IRONS
10% OFF
£7-£45

MICROWAVES
20% OFF
£70-£18

COOK
50% O
£200

PROMOTION SECTION 6

PACKAGING

Goods need packaging to protect them from damage and to keep the contents in a saleable condition. It can also be needed to display ingredients, weight and cooking instructions on food packaging.

However, packaging can do much more than just protect the goods. It is part of the company's image, it gives instant recognition to the company. It can create an image of basic good-value goods, such as Sainsbury's Price Check range of goods, or sheer luxury such as Chanel perfumes. Packaging can be what makes a customer pick up the goods off the shelf rather than a competitor's product, because it looks so attractive or so different.

KEY POINTS

- Products can be promoted by:
  – packaging
  – advertising
  – sales promotion
  – sponsorship
  – public relations.

- Packaging promotion can present an image and make goods look more attractive.

UNIT 3 SALES AND MARKETING

TOPIC 2 Advertising

Advertising is the most common form of promotion. We see it and hear it all day. It is used to **inform** and **persuade** as many customers as possible to buy a company's product.

Its purpose is to catch the attention of customers enough for them to want to buy the product. Companies can use a variety of different media to get their advertising message across. Cinema, newspaper, magazines, radio, television, billboards, even the sides of buses are used for advertising. The choice of media is often dictated by the amount of money the company has to spend on advertising. Small businesses are likely to use such methods as:

- word of mouth
- Yellow Pages
- local newspapers
- public transport
- leaflets
- catalogues

whereas large companies are more likely to use such methods as:

- radio
- specialist trade magazines
- television
- trade fairs
- national press
- billboards.

The cost of advertising on television is very high. Also, it varies immensely depending on the time of day when the advertisement is to be shown. The peak time of between 6.00 pm and 10.00 pm is the most expensive. Only large companies can afford television advertising.

PURPOSE OF ADVERTISING

Advertising is used by companies to promote their product to the public and try to encourage them to buy it. There are two main types of advertising:

- informative
- persuasive.

INFORMATIVE ADVERTISING

The purpose of **informative** advertising, as it suggests, is to give out information. The government uses informative advertising more than any business

COURSEWORK ACTIVITY

1 Choose a current advert in a magazine. Analyse its contents, i.e. what component parts go together to make it:
- company name
- product description
- pictures
- slogan.

Then try to decide who it is aimed at:

- Who is the target market?
- What will attract them to the advert – is it funny, sexy, does it offer lots of factual information?
- Do you think the advert is successful?

Give reasons for your answers. Make a note of your findings.

2 Choose an everyday product e.g. a canned drink and produce an advert for it, on the computer. Take into account the target market, company image and impact of the design when producing your advert.

3 Select the most appropriate medium for placing the advert. Choose from a magazine, newspaper, billboard, or radio. Give reasons for your choice of advertising media.

organisation. It is not used to promote a product or service, but instead to inform the public about a particular issue. For example, the drink-driving campaign at Christmas or health warnings about smoking. Both are used to inform the public of the dangers and implications involved, they are not used to **promote** a product.

PERSUASIVE ADVERTISING

The purpose of persuasive advertising goes further than just giving out information. The advertisements are designed to persuade the public to buy the product or service. A whole range of methods are used when designing advertisements:

- television, film and sports personalities are used, such as Gary Lineker in the Walkers crisps advertisements
- adverts are written around an appealing story, such as the Gold Blend advertisements
- sex appeal is used, as in the Levi Jeans and Peugeot car advertisements
- children and animals are used because they appeal to the public, for example, the children in the Safeway advertisements and the Labrador puppy on the Andrex toilet tissue advertisements.

ADVERTISING AGENCIES

Some large companies employ their own advertising team, but many companies contract in advertising agencies to do the work for them.

The agency will take on an account with a company and they will plan the complete advertising campaign. This includes carrying out the market research for the product. This information is then used to develop the advertising campaign. Graphic designers and artists are employed to draw up the advertisements, including the graphics and the text to be used. Once the ideas for the advertisements have been developed, the agency then has the advertisements produced, either in printed format or as film footage for a television advertisement. Finally, they buy the space in the newspapers or magazines or the time slot on the television.

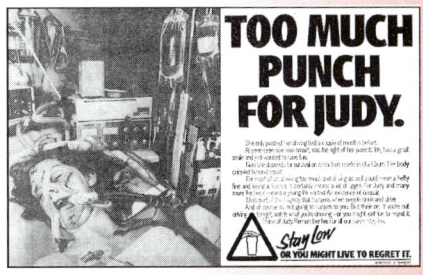

KEY POINTS

- Advertising can be:
  - informative – used to just give out information
  - persuasive – used to persuade the public to buy a product.

- Advertising agencies hired by a company will:
  - do market research
  - develop an advertising campaign
  - create the advertisement, e.g. a poster design
  - buy advertising space.

UNIT 3 SALES AND MARKETING

TOPIC 3: Sales promotion

Sales promotion is a method of boosting sales or trying to persuade the customer to try the product for the first time, at its launch. The most obvious way that companies use is to produce eye-catching point-of-sale displays and place them in prominent places, such as at the entrance to the outlets, where they sell their goods. Sales promotion can take a variety of forms:

TYPES OF SALES PROMOTION

Special offers

Customers are encouraged to buy the product by the company reducing the price on the first purchase. Buy one and get one free is another type of special offer, and selling in larger quantities at the same price, e.g. 25% extra free.

Free gifts

Some companies offer free gifts as an enticement to buy the product, such as some of the fast-food restaurants which give free gifts with their meals. Sometimes cosmetics companies offer a free lipstick if you buy a bottle of perfume or a moisturiser, and so are also trying to get you to try a different product.

Special offers

Some companies offer goods like clothing at a reduced price, or even free, if you collect enough tokens or vouchers. For example, a cola company might offer a free music tape for 30 ring-pulls.

Competitions

Some companies run competitions, for example being automatically entered into a draw for a prize such as a holiday or a new car.

Money off

Customers are encouraged to buy the product by getting a reduced price for buying in large quantities.

Sam and Harri need to know about sales promotion

INTEREST FREE CREDIT ON ITEMS OVER £300

BUY NOW – PAY NEXT JANUARY

20% DISCOUNT VOUCHER if you introduce a friend

Loyalty cards

Loyalty cards are a more recent type of sales promotion. Many supermarkets and retail outlets give their customers loyalty cards so that every time they use the store they gain points or rewards. These are added up and can be handed in either for cash or for products.

KEY POINTS

- Sales promotions are used to:
  – boost sales
  – help the launch of a new product.
- Sales promotions include:
  – special offers
  – free gifts
  – bonus packs
  – competitions
  – money off
  – loyalty cards
  – trade promotions.

Trade promotions

Trade promotions or trade fairs are held regularly in large cities, all around the world. They are fairs or exhibitions where businesses selling similar products or services join together under one roof to promote their goods to their customers. These customers are often retailers and not the general public, although some of the large trade fairs such as the Clothes Show Live, the Motor Show, and the Ideal Home Exhibition, are also open to the public to visit. At trade fairs both large and small companies can rent floor space for a stand, side by side, at the exhibition. It is a shop window on the particular trade and companies can promote, advertise and demonstrate their products.

UNIT 3 SALES AND MARKETING

TOPIC 4 — Sponsorship and public relations

SPONSORSHIPS

Companies offer sponsorship to draw people's attention to the company's product, such as Sharp sponsoring Manchester United, or the Midlands Bank sponsoring ITV programmes. Sponsorship can also be used at a local level for events such as sports meetings or concerts.

PUBLIC RELATIONS

Many organisations use public relations as a way of promoting an image of the business as a whole rather than just one product. Public relations is a long-term activity as it takes a long time to build up positive images of a whole company. This can be achieved through publicity in newspapers and magazines or by being involved with local or even national communities, for example by providing equipment for schools.

Sam and Harri need to understand sponsorship and public relations

REVIEW QUESTIONS

1. List three different ways of promoting goods, other than sales promotions.
2. Describe or do a sketch to show some of the information that must by law be included on a carton of yoghurt.
3. Explain how you might choose to promote:
   a) a new blockbuster film
   b) a technically advanced compressor for fridges
   c) your own car cleaning/valeting service
   d) a washing-up liquid
   e) a health drink.

SUPER REVIEW QUESTIONS

4. State three examples of different methods of sales promotion that companies have used, to encourage the customer to buy their product.
5. Explain why businesses use trade fairs and exhibitions to promote their goods or services.

PROMOTION SECTION 6

KEY POINTS

- Sponsorship, e.g.
  – sport
  – the arts.
- Companies use public relations to promote the image of their organisation.

CASE STUDY

You are the Marketing Manager of a large retail chemist. You have been asked to produce a report for the Managing Director on the effects of sales promotions on goods currently being sold in the store.

1. Look around a similar store or supermarket in your local area. Make a list of all the different methods that companies are using, at present, to promote their goods or services in the store such as special offers, free gifts or competitions.
2. Choose an everyday item such as a bar of chocolate or a bottle of shampoo that has a sales promotion on. Survey your friends to see if they are aware of the promotion, and how much it could influence them to buy the product.
3. Include the results from your survey in your report. Draw your own conclusions, from the results of your survey on the effect sales promotions might have on the sale of the goods. For example:
   - Are the public influenced by special offers?
   - Do they go looking for special offers?
   - Do they always use the same brand and ignore any sales promotions?
   - Are the sales promotions worth having?
   - Do the sales promotions involve the public in buying the product in order to get the special offer?
4. Make recommendations to the Managing Director on:
   - The sales promotions you found to be most effective. For example:
     - it was in a prominent position in the store
     - a salesperson was demonstrating it
     - it was attractively presented
     - it offered value for money.
   - The value of using sales promotions in the store in the future, particularly for own brand products – will the sales promotion attract new customers to the product and the store, or simply persuade the same customers to buy the promotion product instead of their usual brand?
   - Add any alternatives you think might be more appropriate to help increase sales, such as an advertising campaign.

UNIT 3 SALES AND MARKETING

❓❓❓❓❓❓❓❓❓❓❓❓❓❓❓❓❓❓
QUESTION TIME

Marketing is all about:

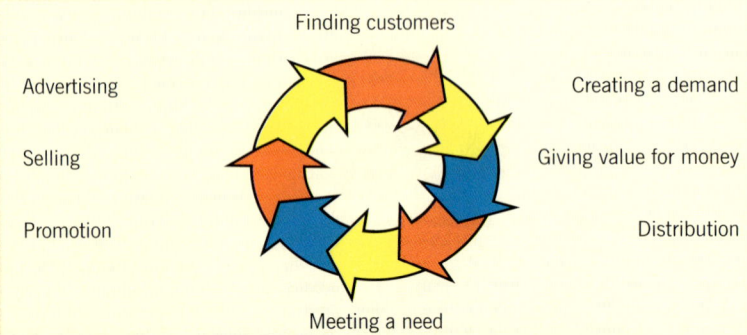

Draw this diagram on the computer to illustrate the processes involved in marketing. Now answer the following questions to help you understand what marketing is about.

1. Imagine that at the moment you **need** a new pair of trainers. Use the title **Meeting a need.** Draw up a list of all the different brands you can think of for this product, e.g.
    - Nike
    - Reebok
    - Umbro
    - Hi-tec.

   Put them in the order you would buy them, favourite down to least favourite. The top company is best **meeting your need** for a pair of trainers.

2. Use the title **Giving value for money**. Write down what attracts you about your favourite brand. What is it that makes them **good value for money** for you?

3. Use the title **Creating a demand**. Explain how if you bought this particular pair of trainers you would be **creating a demand**.

4. Use the title **Advertising**. Write down all the different media that this company uses to **advertise** their trainers, e.g. television, posters. Write down the techniques they use to **advertise** them, e.g. a famous athlete, sport sponsorship.

5. Use the title **Finding customers**. Produce a questionnaire on the computer. Carry out some market research to see how many other people of your age buy the same brand. What features attract them, how often do they buy them, what prompts them to buy a new pair, do they consider buying other makes, and if so, why? Add any other questions you think might be relevant. Record and analyse your findings. What percentage of the people questioned used the same make of trainers as you? This information would help a company to **find customers** for the product.

6. Use the title **Promotion**. Your research was among people of your own age group. Make a list of other age ranges you think also buy this brand. This will show you the target market. This information will help the company decide on an appropriate **promotion campaign** for their trainers.

7. Use the title **Selling**. Having identified its target market, the company now needs to decide where to **sell** the trainers. Make a list of all the different outlets where you

PROMOTION **SECTION 6**

can buy trainers, e.g. sports shops, shoe shops. Having decided on the most appropriate retail outlets, the company has to ensure the goods are **distributed** on time. Which methods of distribution are available to the company?

By answering these questions, you have shown how important marketing is to the company, and that the purpose of marketing is: through market research, to find the right product and sell it at the right price, in the right place and at the right time.

EXTENSION TASKS

8 Having shown the importance of marketing to a product, evaluate the importance of the consumer to the product. Explain the features of this brand that attract consumers more than other brands. How does this create demand?

9 What events could change the demand? For example, a competitor bringing a new design on to the market. Draw up a list of events with their possible effects.

10 In your research you identified how often people buy trainers and why they buy new ones. Plot a graph showing the frequency of consumer buying against age range and draw conclusions. From your questionnaire, analyse what the consumer wants from a pair of trainers.

11 In your questionnaire you asked how many people considered buying other makes, and why. Analyse their reasons, e.g. more money to spend, changes in their needs, or an advertisement for a different brand.

12 If marketing is about 'getting the right product at the right price, in the right place at the right time and encouraging the consumer to buy', analyse the importance of the customer to the company. Consider: survival of the business, contribution to profits and importance of attracting repeat business.

COURSEWORK ASSIGNMENTS

You work for an advertising agency. You have been asked to produce a marketing campaign for a particular product. The product is aimed at the teenage market, so your campaign should be geared to their interests. Below is some desk research that has been gathered about the teenage market to help you plan your campaign:

- ◆ Teenagers have different interests and so react differently to advertising.
- ◆ Teenagers prefer brand names to own-brand products.
- ◆ Teenagers are attracted by colour, music, humour and catchy jingles.
- ◆ The average teenager gets £5 per week pocket money.

1 Make a list of hobbies, interests, music and television tastes that are popular with teenagers.

2 Choose a product for your marketing campaign from the following list:
  - ◆ a can of diet cola
  - ◆ a popular deodorant
  - ◆ a savoury snack
  - ◆ a computer game.

Choose a make that has been on the market for a while and is well known. Imagine that sales are falling and the product needs a marketing campaign to give it a boost.

UNIT 3 SALES AND MARKETING

3. Identify the target market. Choose the age range from a narrow band e.g. 14/15-year-olds.
4. If your product was being targeted at the adult population, their socio-economic groupings would be taken into consideration as well as the age range. Describe the different socio-economic groupings, and state which groupings your product would be aimed at.
5. Draw up a questionnaire to find out consumer feeling on the product. Include:
   - gender
   - age
   - does the person buy the product?
   - what is their favourite brand?
   - how often do they buy it?
   - how much do they spend on it?
   - what other brands do they buy?
   - what are their interests and hobbies?
   - what current adverts do they remember most, and why?
   - any other questions you think may be relevant.
6. Using all the information you have available, your field research and the desk research you were given, plan an advertising campaign. Answer these questions to help you plan it:
   - What particular feature of the product do you intend to emphasise in the advert, e.g. the type of people who drink diet coke, the power of the perfume in a deodorant.
   - What sort of theme do you want to use, e.g. fast action, colourful and bright, funny, zany?
   - What are the most popular films, television programmes, music at the moment and how can you use their popularity?
   - Think of a jingle for the advert.
   - Which media do you intend to use to advertise the product?
7. Having decided on the advertising media to be used draw up the first draft. Draw a rough sketch of the advert if it is to go in a newspaper, magazine or poster. Draw a storyboard including graphics and text if it is to be a television advert. Write the text and choose the musical background if it is to be a radio advert.
8. Remember an advert should be 'legal, decent, honest and truthful'. Check that your advert meets these criteria.
9. Produce the advertising campaign. Identify the media to be used and the timings and frequency of the advertisement.
10. The company uses market-orientated pricing for its products. Explain the term **market-orientated**, and how it applies to your product.
11. Identify the most appropriate retail outlets for selling the product and give reasons.
12. State and explain the legislation that would apply to your product, e.g. the Trade Descriptions Act, the Weights and Measures Act.
13. Now that the product is about to be launched, identify the methods of sales promotion you would use. Give reasons for your choices.
14. Produce a predicted product life cycle for your product. Explain each stage of the cycle.

UNIT 4

Accounting and Finance

Section 1 Financial planning

LEARNING OBJECTIVES

By the end of this section you should have learnt:
- the function of the Finance department in the business
- why businesses need financial forecasting
- how to draw up and interpret a cash flow forecast
- how to draw up and interpret a budget statement
- fixed and variable costs and revenue
- what a break even chart is and what it is used for
- assets and liabilities
- why a business needs working capital.

UNIT 4 ACCOUNTING AND FINANCE

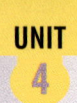

TOPIC 1 — Functions of business finance

Every business needs finance:
- to start up the business
- for the day-to-day running of the business
- for business growth.

FINANCIAL PLANNING

Good financial planning is at the heart of any successful business – without it the business will fail. Financial decisions have to be made in every section of the business. For example:
- Human Resources have to make financial decisions on the pay costs: how many staff does the company need and how much can it afford to pay them?
- The marketing budget dictates the type of marketing campaign the company can afford.
- In the Production department, it is the amount of finance that is available that will dictate whether the business can invest in new technology, or expand, or relocate to a new site.

All of these are major financial decisions that need to be taken by the managers and owners of the business and need a great deal of forward planning.

Sam and Harri need to understand the functions of finance

MAIN AREAS OF FINANCE

There are five main areas of finance that any business has to deal with. They are:

Cash flow forecasting – planning the cash flowing in and out of the business to make sure that there is always enough money in the business to pay the bills.

Budget planning – where the financial budgets for the company and for the individual departments are set.

Raising finance – when the Finance department has to analyse and select the most appropriate sources of finance for a particular project.

Management accounting – identifying methods of controlling costs to make the business more efficient and so increase profits. It also provides managers with information on performance and efficiency.

Financial accounting – drawing up and interpreting the financial records of the business and producing an analysis and evaluation of the company's finances for internal or external use.

KEY POINTS
The five main areas of finance are:
- cash flow forecasting
- budget planning
- raising finance
- management accounting
- financial accounting.

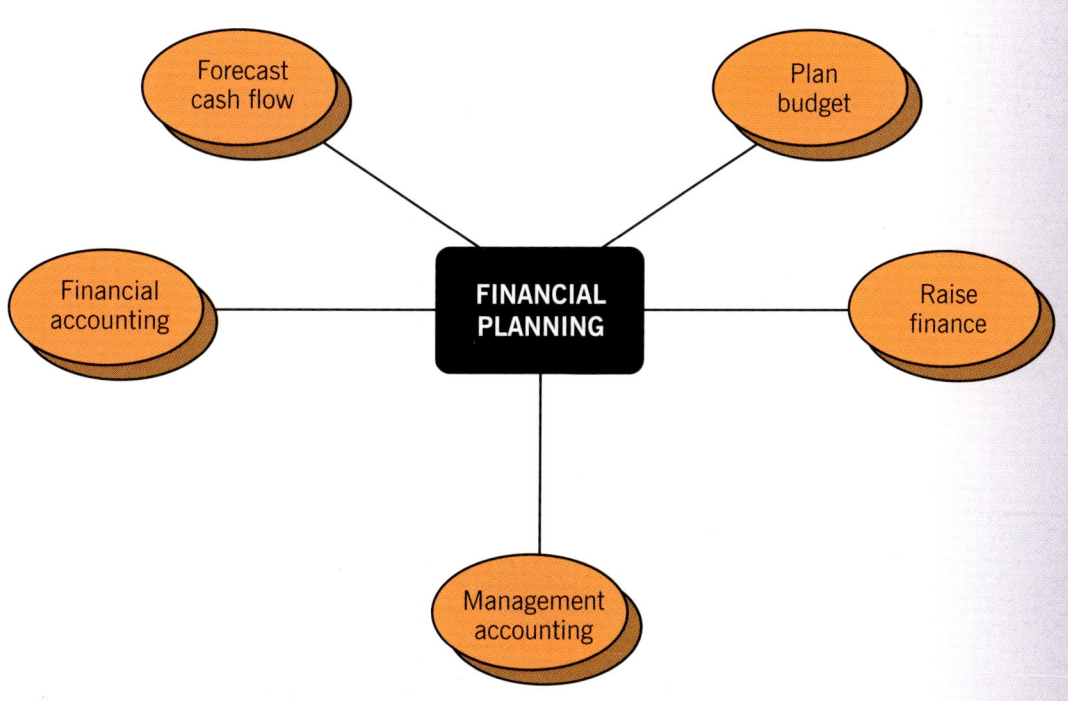

UNIT 4 ACCOUNTING AND FINANCE

TOPIC 2: Financial forecasting

WHY DO COMPANIES NEED FINANCIAL FORECASTING?

Financial forecasting has a wide range of uses. It is used by the company:
- to help in decision-making
- as a management tool to aid control
- to assess the profitability of the business
- to plan strategies
- to control resources
- to measure the efficiency of the business
- to forecast possible future trends.

Sam and Harri need to understand financial forecasting

Before a business can plan how it is going to use its finances, it needs to try to forecast what is likely to happen in the future and what will be needed by the business, during a set period of time, such as the next six months, year or five years. To work this out, the Finance department will collect information on what has happened in the past, as well as try to predict what is likely to happen in the future.

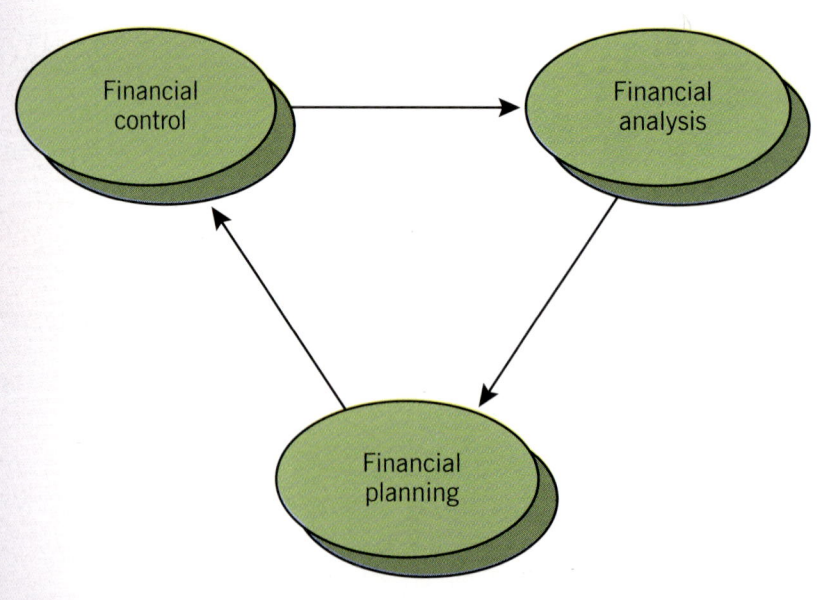

The management accounting process

FINANCIAL PLANNING **SECTION 1**

CASH FLOW

Cash flow forecasting is a very important part of a business's financial forecasting. It is a prediction of the cash flowing in to the business (the receipts) and the cash flowing out of the business (the payments). From the cash flow forecast the managers will hope to foresee any possible cash flow problems and assess when overdrafts might be needed.

KEY POINTS
- Financial forecasting is necessary to predict what is likely to happen in the future.

Cash flow of a clothes manufacturer.

CASE STUDY

Below is the cash flow forecast for The Picture House Ltd. The Picture House is a multiplex cinema with five screens.

The Picture House Ltd: Cash flow forecast 20X1

	July	August	September	October	November	December
Receipts (Cash inflow)	42 000	34 000	40 000	44 000	48 000	50 000
Payments (Cash inflow)	37 000	38 000	40 000	38 000	38 000	40 000
TOTAL (=/–)	5 000	–4 000	0	6 000	10 000	10 000
Opening bank balance	100 000	105 000	101 000	101 000	107 000	117 000
Closing bank balance	105 000	101 000	101 000	107 000	117 000	127 000

It is normal for businesses to have some months when they pay out more than they take in. The important thing is to know that this will happen and to budget accordingly. If the Finance Director knows that a large sum of money will be spent on, for example, buying new equipment he or she can budget accordingly. In the case study The Picture House has a large sum in the bank already. If it did not, then the Finance Director would have had to arrange an overdraft for August. Forecasting would help him know this and arrange the overdraft well in advance.

The cash flow forecast is set after the business's master budget statement has been calculated for the next financial year.

The budget is a statement of the financial targets set for each department and the business as a whole, for every month of the next financial year.

These targets can then be checked against the actual results in each department, month on month, and if a department does not meet its targets it can be investigated immediately and a course of action put into place to correct it to make sure the budget and the forecasts are more accurate in the future.

Computers are now used in financial forecasting, so the Finance department can use spreadsheets to ask 'What will happen if ...' questions.

The Picture House could use such a model to give them an idea of what might happen if, for example, they increase prices by 10 per cent and then lose 5 per cent of their ticket sales as a result; or what would happen if the staff are given a 2 per cent pay rise instead of 3 per cent?

Financial forecasts are, however, only an indication. They are not totally reliable, as unforeseen events can take place, such as a new blockbuster movie that has had rave reviews in the USA proves not to appeal to a UK audience, and flops.

Opposite is a possible format that could be used for a budget statement:

FINANCIAL PLANNING SECTION 1

The Picture House Ltd: Budget Statement for period ..July–Sept.......... 20X0 ....

	Budget	Actual	Budget	Actual	Budget	Actual
Receipts	28	29	20	27	35	
Cash sales	8	8	6	7	10	
From debtors	1.5	1	1	1	1.5	
Other revenue sources	2.5	2.5	4	5	2	
1 – TOTAL RECEIPTS – CR	40	40.5	31	40	48.5	
Payments	6	6	6	6	6	
Cash purchases	1	1	1	2	1.5	
To creditors	4	4	1	1	1	
Wages/salaries PAYE	12	11	12	11	12	
Rent/rates/insurance	1.5	1.5	1.5	1.5	1.5	
Light/heat/power	1.5	1.5	1.5	1.5	1.5	
Telephone/postage/stationery	1	2	0.5	1	1	
Repairs/renewals	1	2	10	9.5	1	
VAT	0	0	0	0	14	
HP payments/ leasing charges	0	0	0	0	0	
Bank/finance charges and interest	3	3	3	3	3	
Loan repayments	3	3	3	3	3	
Other taxes	0	0	0	0	0	
Sundry expenses	2	1	1	0.5	2	
2 – TOTAL PAYMENTS – DR	36	36	40.5	40	47.5	
3 – Net Cash flow (1–2) CR (+) DR (–)	+4	4.5	–9.5	0	+1	
4 – Opening Bank Balance CR (+) /Balance brought forward DR (–)	50	50	54	54.5	44.5	
5 – Closing Bank Balance CR (+) (3 +/–) DR (–)	54	54.5	44.5	54.5	46.5	

The budget figures are worked out by looking at the previous years' figures, as well as predicting what is likely to happen in the future, for the same time slot.

Any exceptional circumstances, such as a new housing estate that is being built near to the cinema, or a new bowling alley, are all taken into account and the budget figures are set, for each department and for the whole business.

The actual figures are then recorded and an analysis is carried out. Any differences between budget and actual figures are questioned. A course of action is then put into place to try to prevent these differences occurring again.

UNIT 4 ACCOUNTING AND FINANCE

TOPIC 3 Costs and revenue

Every business wants to make a profit. The simple calculation for profit is:

Profit = sales revenue – costs.

The costs of the business are divided into two main categories:
- fixed costs
- variable costs.

FIXED COSTS

Fixed costs are payment for such things as:
- rent or mortgage payments
- uniform business rate
- maintenance and repairs
- interest charges
- administration
- insurance.

These are costs which stay the same, whatever level of output the business is producing and selling over a period of time. They are also known as overheads. Because fixed costs do not change as output or sales change, the more sales the business makes, the easier the business will find it to pay the fixed costs. If sales fall, the business might find itself making a loss because it will still have to pay these fixed costs.

Sam and Harri need to know about costs and revenues

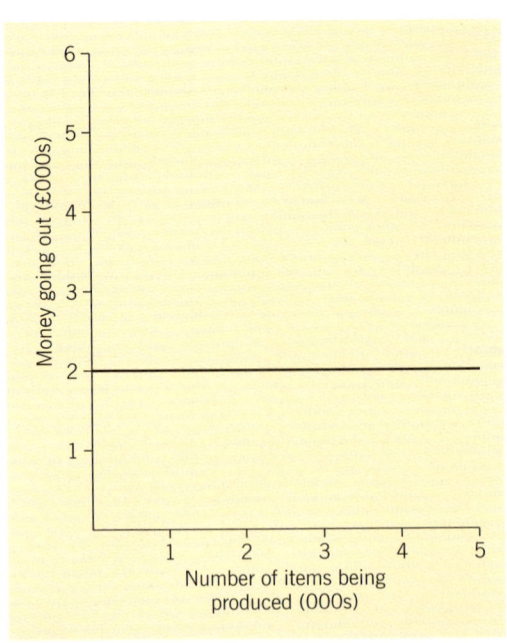

Fixed costs

VARIABLE COSTS

Variable costs are payment for such things as:
- labour
- raw materials
- fuel.

These are costs that vary according to the amount of work being done (the **output**) of the business. These costs vary because the more goods the business produces the more staff they will need to do the work, the more raw materials they will need to make the goods and the more fuel they will need for such things as distribution. These costs are directly related to the production of the goods.

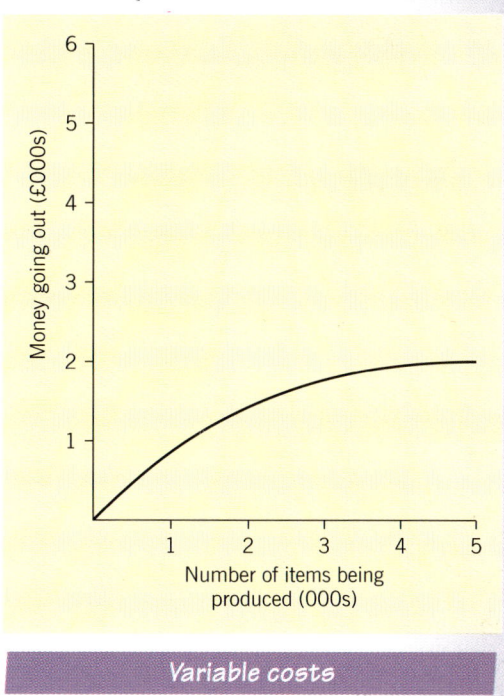

Variable costs

SALES REVENUE

Revenue or **sales turnover** is the value of the sales of the business. It is the income the business receives from selling its products or services. It is calculated by:

Sales revenue = price × quantity sold.

The sales revenue can change if the business:
- increases the price of its products
- increases the number of sales.

An increase in price does not automatically mean an increase in profit because, as we saw in Unit 1, if the increase in price is not linked to an increase in demand, the price increase can lead to a reduction in the numbers sold and therefore a decrease in profits.

Other factors that can affect the sales revenue include:
- a new marketing campaign
- changes in competitors' products
- the economic climate.

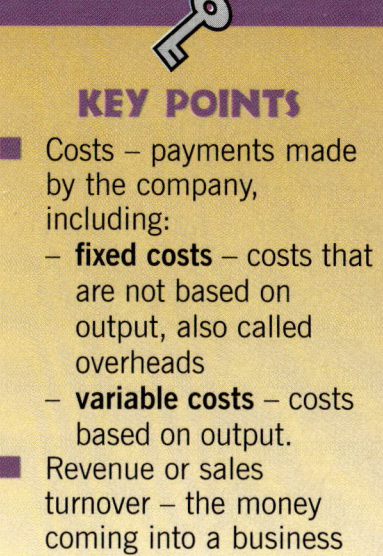

KEY POINTS

- Costs – payments made by the company, including:
  - **fixed costs** – costs that are not based on output, also called overheads
  - **variable costs** – costs based on output.
- Revenue or sales turnover – the money coming into a business from sales.

UNIT 4 ACCOUNTING AND FINANCE

TOPIC 4 Breaking even

BREAK EVEN CHART

All the information about costs and revenue is needed by the business to produce a **break even chart**. A break even chart is a graph which shows the business the level of sales needed if its total revenue is going to be equal to its total costs. Knowing the 'break even' will help managers decide if they should invest in a new product. If they don't think they can achieve the sales to break even then perhaps they should not develop, make and sell the new item. The break even point is where:

Total revenue = total costs

or

Selling price × number of units sold
    = fixed costs + variable costs

Sam and Harri need to understand break even

For example, Shoot Enterprises Ltd make sweatshirts for various sports. Their sweatshirt sells for £12.

The variable costs are:

£4 labour per unit

£4 materials and notions (pins, thread, etc) per unit

The fixed costs of the company are £120 000.

The total variable costs for each sweatshirt are £8. Therefore the gross profit on each shirt is £(12−8) or £4.

To calculate break even we need to know how many sweatshirts must be sold to cover the £120 000 fixed costs. We already know each sweatshirt makes a gross profit (or **contribution**) of £4. How many sweatshirts will be needed to make £120 000?

$$\frac{£120\,000}{£4} = 30\,000$$

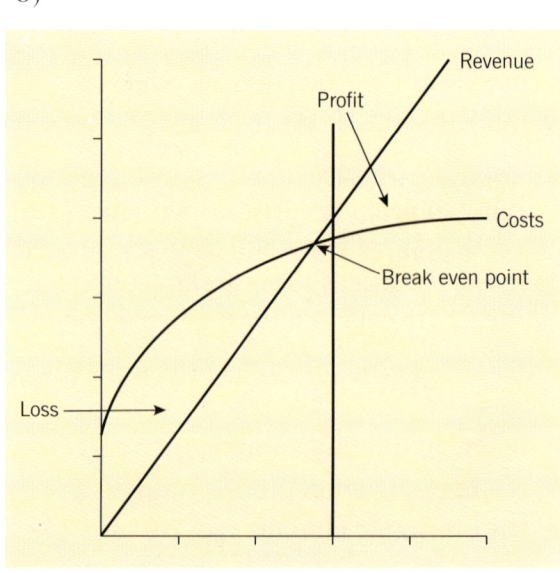

Break even

FINANCIAL PLANNING — SECTION 1

IMPORTANCE OF THE BREAK EVEN CHART

The break even chart is important to the business as it can be used to make decisions on prices and to forecast profit. It can also be used by financial institutions if the business is applying for a loan. Below is an example of how a break even chart could be produced for Shoot Enterprises Ltd.
It is helpful to draw up a table of the relevant figures before trying to plot the graph.

KEY POINTS

- **Break even** – the point where the costs are equal to the revenue.
- Break even graphs are used to:
  - decide prices
  - predict profit
  - determine financial needs.

Sweatshirt sales	Total revenue (12 x no. of sweatshirts sold)	Total fixed cost	Total variable cost £8 x number of sweatshirts sold	Total cost (Total fixed cost + Total variable cost)
	£	£	£	£
5 000	60 000	120 000	40 000	160 000
10 000	120 000	120 000	80 000	200 000
15 000	180 000	120 000	120 000	240 000
20 000	240 000	120 000	160 000	280 000
25 000	300 000	120 000	200 000	320 000
30 000	360 000	120 000	240 000	360 000
35 000	420 000	120 000	280 000	400 000

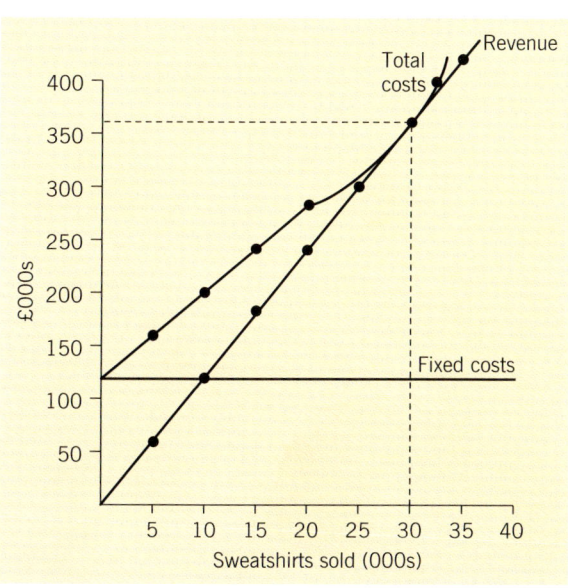

Break even chart for Shoot Enterprises

UNIT 4 — ACCOUNTING AND FINANCE

REVIEW QUESTION

1 The Picture House needs to produce a break even chart. Below are the figures it will use:

Revenue
Average ticket sales are £4

Fixed costs
£400 000 per year

Variable costs
For every ticket sold 25 per cent of the ticket price has to be paid to the film distributors, i.e. £1 off every ticket.
You may find it easier to draw up a table of the figures before trying to plot the graph.

Ticket sales	Total revenue	Total fixed cost	Total variable cost	Total cost (Total fixed cost + Total variable cost)
	£	£	£	£
10 000	40 000	400 000	10 000	410 000
20 000				
30 000				
40 000				
50 000				
60 000				

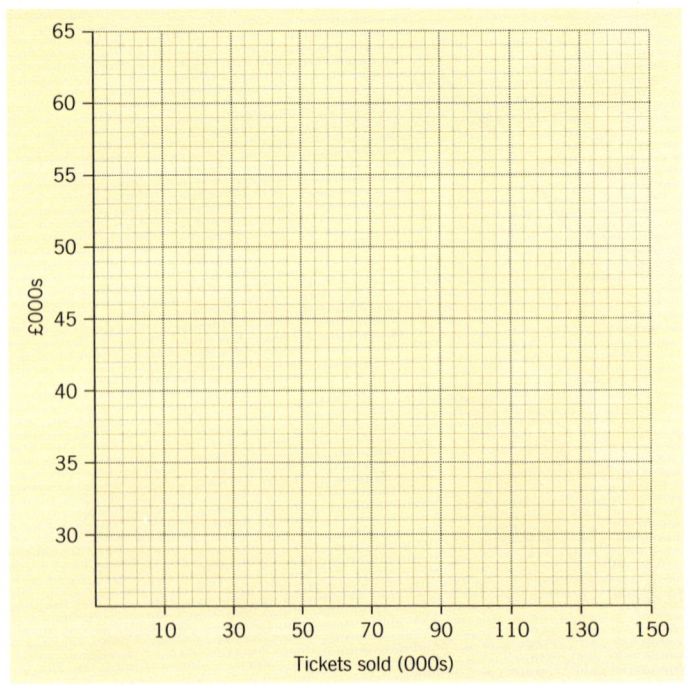

SUPER REVIEW QUESTIONS

2 The fixed cost line is always drawn as a straight horizontal line. Explain why.
3 State how much profit a business makes at its break even point.
4 Explain why a business needs to calculate its break even point.
5 Complete the cash flow forecast for The Picture House for the next three months from January to March 1998.

The Picture House Ltd: Cash flow forecast 1997

	January	February	March
Receipts (Cash inflow)			
Payments (Cash outflow)			
TOTAL (+/−)			
Opening bank balance			
Closing bank balance			

Months	Receipts	Payments
January	52 000	40 000
February	54 000	41 000
March	48 000	42 000

Opening bank balance in January £101 000

TOPIC 5: Assets and liabilities

Limited companies, both private and public, are obliged by law to produce an audited balance sheet each year (you can find out more about balance sheets in Unit 4 Section 3). The balance sheet is a record of the assets and liabilities of the company. It is an indicator of the value of the business. Every business has assets and liabilities.

ASSETS

Assets are what the company owns. Assets can include buildings, plant and equipment, stock and cash in the bank. Assets can also include money owed to the company by other businesses. Assets are classed as **fixed** and **current**.

Fixed assets: e.g. buildings, machinery and equipment, computers or vehicles. These are all things that you can 'see and touch' and so are **tangible assets**. Fixed assets are also items that are likely to stay in the company for a reasonable length of time, i.e. more than a year. Other assets e.g. investments or goodwill, are known as **intangible assets**. Goodwill is the loyalty customers have to a particular company. If they are happy with the product or service they return again and again. Goodwill is difficult to calculate but it has a value to the company.

Current assets: e.g. stock, debtors (people who owe money to the business) and cash. These may all change in value from day to day. Like the variable costs on the break even graph, current assets can change as output changes. Current assets can also be easily changed into money and are called **liquid assets**. There are three main categories of current assets:

Stock, which is:
- **raw materials** bought to make the goods
- **work in progress** – goods whilst they are being made
- **finished goods** ready for sale.

Debtors, who are:
- outside businesses and people that owe the company money. Most businesses allow other businesses to buy from them on credit, giving a period of time for payment after delivery.

Cash, which is:
- money in the bank, petty cash within the company, or other cash the company has in hand.

LIABILITIES

Liabilities are what the company owes to others. **Current liabilities** are the amounts of money that will have to be paid back within the next 12 months. The most common current liabilities are:
- **trade creditors** – outside businesses that the company owes money to
- bank overdrafts
- dividends for shareholders.

Long-term liabilities are amounts of money that will have to be paid back in more than 12 months' time. The most common long-term liabilities are:
- long-term loans
- mortgages
- taxes owed.

FINANCIAL PLANNING **SECTION 1**

WORKING CAPITAL

Every business needs working capital. This is the money the company has readily available, or expects to have soon, to pay for day-to-day costs. The working capital is also called the **net current assets**. It is calculated by:

Working capital = current assets − current liabilities

If the business is running efficiently it will normally have current assets of between 1 and 2 times the value of its current liabilities. With this level of coverage the company should have enough capital to deal with most unforeseen problems. If the company increases output it must also increase working capital, otherwise it may have cash flow problems later on and this could threaten the future of the company.

Any business needs a strong financial base. This means having a working knowledge of:

◆ the value of the business – its assets and liabilities
◆ the costs and revenue of the business
◆ the break even level of sales
◆ the cash flow around the business
◆ target setting for the budget.

REVIEW QUESTIONS

1. Explain the difference between assets and liabilities.
2. Give two examples of current assets and two examples of current liabilities.
3. Explain what is meant by the term **working capital**.

SUPER REVIEW QUESTIONS

4. Explain why a business needs working capital.
5. Distinguish between debtors and creditors.

KEY POINTS

- **Assets** – what the company owns such as:
  - buildings
  - plants
  - equipment
  - stock
  - money in the bank
  - debts owed by others to the company.
- Assets can be:
  - **fixed** – assets that are likely to retain the same value
  - **current** – assets that change value often
  - **tangible** – assets that can be touched and seen
  - **intangible** – assets that that have no physical form
  - **liquid** – assets that can be easily turned into money.
- **Liabilities** – what the company owes.
- Liabilities can be:
  - **current** – debts that must be paid within 12 months
  - **long term** – debts paid back over more than 12 months.
- **Working capital** or **net current assets** – the value of current assets minus current liabilities.
- Working capital is used to pay for day-to-day costs.

Section 2 Sources of finance

 **LEARNING OBJECTIVES**

By the end of this section you should have learnt:
- the different ways there are of raising finance for the business
- the internal sources of finance available to businesses
- the external sources of finance available to businesses
- the criteria that will influence a company when choosing the most appropriate source of finance
- the main sections of a business plan.

UNIT 4 ACCOUNTING AND FINANCE

TOPIC 1 Raising finance

As we saw in Section 1 of this unit every business needs finance:
- to **start up** the business,
- for the **day-to-day running** of the business
- for business **growth**.

The money needed to set up the business and buy fixed assets such as land, buildings, vehicles, plant and equipment is called **capital expenditure**. The money that is spent on the day-to-day running of the business is called **revenue expenditure**. This is the money spent on such things as mortgage, rates and wages.

Sam and Harri need to know about raising finance

CAPITAL EXPENDITURE

SOURCES OF FINANCE SECTION 2

CAPITAL EXPENDITURE

Capital expenditure can be financed either by using *internal* sources of finance such as company profits, or *external* sources such as bank loans. Some items of capital expenditure such as land and buildings will need long-term borrowing to finance them. Internal sources of finance would not be sufficient on their own, so the company will need to look at external sources such as a bank loan.

The advantage of using an internal source of finance is that the money does not have to be repaid and there are no interest charges to be added on.

KEY POINTS

- **Revenue expenditure** – money used for the day-to-day running of the business, paid for by working capital.
- **Capital expenditure** – money used to start the business and to make large purchases such as new machinery.
- Capital expenditure is raised either internally or externally.

Joey raises finance from his dad

UNIT 4 ACCOUNTING AND FINANCE

TOPIC 2 — Internal sources of finance

The number of sources of finance available to different types of businesses varies greatly. For the sole trader the **internal sources** are limited to:

- the owner's money which he or she has in the bank, for example, redundancy money or savings may be used to start up the business;
- the owner may sell personal assets such as a car or house to help finance the business;
- the profits from the business can be reinvested into the business;
- some of the profit from the business may have been invested in a bank deposit account, for any emergencies that might happen.

Larger companies have access to many more internal sources of finance.

Sam and Harri need to know about internal sources of finance

SHARES

Private limited companies can raise capital by selling more shares to the family, friends or colleagues involved in the business. The only problem with this is that the shareholders may want a bigger say in the running of the business.

A **rights issue** of new shares is the most common internal source of finance used by public limited companies. The rights issue gives current shareholders the right to buy more shares, in proportion to the number they own already. This way the balance of control in the business is not changed. However, the issue of the shares is usually underwritten by one of the financial institutions, so that if any shareholders do not want to take up the offer, the financial institutions guarantee to buy the shares. For example, Eurotunnel went back to its shareholders on several occasions to try to raise more capital as the cost of building the Channel Tunnel went up.

There are two main types available. **Ordinary shares** are the largest single form of long-term capital used by companies. The ordinary shareholder may receive a share of the profits in the form of a **dividend**. The dividend can vary according to the amount of profit made by the company and the amount the directors keep back for **reinvestment** in the company, which is called **retained profits**.

Preference shares also give the shareholder part ownership in the company. However, the preference shareholder is paid a **fixed** dividend and has priority over the ordinary shareholder when the profits are shared out. The return in dividends may be less than that to an ordinary shareholder in a good year, because they are taking less risk.

PROFITS

Retained profits are the profits kept back by the directors to pay for such things as new plant and equipment and to put towards any expansion plans.

ASSETS

Selling assets is another way of raising finance. A sole trader may sell off a large van and buy a smaller one.

A medium-sized company may sell off factory space or land that it is not using. Large companies may sell subsidiary companies to raise money.

SALE AND LEASEBACK

Sale and leaseback is a further internal source of finance. The company may sell one of its main buildings to a financial institution such as a pension fund company and then lease it back from them. The company then has to pay rent to the financial institution but has raised a large amount of capital from the sale of the property. This source of finance is commonly used by public limited companies but may also be used by private limited companies and sole traders.

KEY POINTS

- Internal sources include:
  - investing savings
  - selling assets
  - reinvesting profits
  - selling shares
  - sale and leaseback.

- Different types of business have different ways of raising money – sole traders are limited but public limited companies have many more options.

- **Rights issue** – offering more shares to existing shareholders.

- **Ordinary shares** or **equities** – the shareholder receives a share of the profits.

- **Preference shares** – the shareholder receives a fixed sum and has part ownership of the company.

UNIT 4 ACCOUNTING AND FINANCE

TOPIC 3 — External sources of finance

For some items of capital expenditure, internal sources of finance on their own are not enough and the business will need to look **outside** the business to raise the finance.

SMALLER COMPANIES

For small businesses the **external sources** are somewhat limited.

A **loan from relatives and friends** is one option. The problem with this is that they might then want a say in the running of the business.

The government sponsors a number of schemes to help small businesses set up:

The Training and Enterprise Council (TEC) may give an enterprise allowance to long-term unemployed people who want to set up a business.

Development agency loans are available in specific areas identified by the government as needing assistance, for example, some inner city areas.

The Small Firms Loan Guarantee scheme, available from the banks, has government-backed guarantees to support small-business owners who do not have enough money to obtain conventional loans for their business. It applies to new and existing small businesses in the manufacturing, construction and service industries. The banks offer **start-up loans** for small businesses. The owners choose the length of time to be taken to pay back the loan and whether to take out the loan with a fixed rate, or variable rate of interest. The bank will need some security as guarantee for the loan, such as the owner's house.

When capital expenditure is needed for such physical items as vehicles, computers, plant and equipment, there are several methods that can be used to obtain these assets:

Sam and Harri need to know about external sources of finance

Starting a Business
- Borrowing
- Insurance
- Further Information

- **Borrowing**

Overdraft
This is short-term borrowing, available to cover cash-flow problems. It is paid back within a number of months.

Loan
This is medium-term borrowing, available for the purchase of such things as equipment. It is paid back over a few years.

Mortgage
This is long-term borrowing, available for the purchase of business premises and other large assets. It is paid back over a number of years – between 10 and 50.

- **Insurance**

You are required to take out insurance when you agree to any borrowing.

The Bank provides an excellent policy through our partners **The Insurance Company** (see leaflet INSX2).

You may, of course, go elsewhere for your insurance. However, it is essential that you provide us with proof that you are covered.

Hire purchase which means the goods are the property of the hire purchase company until the last payment has been made. A deposit has to be paid at the beginning of the agreement and regular payment is then made by instalments (usually monthly). The payments include a rate of interest for use of the hire purchase scheme.

Leasing is paid by fixed instalments over a period of time, usually one to three years. During the lease period the sole trader never owns the items but at the end of the lease there is the option to buy. Leasing is most useful for items such as computers and cars where models are regularly upgraded and this is a way of keeping up with the latest technology.

Contract hire is paid by a rental for a fixed period of time. Contract hire is often used for vehicles or plant and equipment, and a maintenance contract can be taken out with the hire. The items are not the property of the business hiring them, they are just being rented.

BORROWING FROM RELATIVES.

LARGER COMPANIES

In addition to the external sources highlighted above, larger companies has further options available:

The company can go public. A private limited company may decide to become a public limited company and invite the general public to buy shares in the company. The company needs the approval of the Stock Exchange Council before it can be floated on the Stock Exchange (see Unit 1 Section 2, pages 32–35).

Financial institutions such as banks, insurance companies and pension funds may provide mortgage loans for buying land and buildings.

Venture capitalists are risk-takers who invest in companies (usually small companies), and make a return on their investment. They help to build up the company and, in return, they may want a seat on the Board of Directors, shares in the company or interest on their investment.

The European Union, central government and local government all have schemes which provide loans or grants to help businesses.

Mortgages and overdrafts

VERY LARGE COMPANIES

Further external sources available to very large and multinational companies are:

Foreign bank loans are often used by multinational companies. They may borrow money from the foreign countries where they trade, if the interest rates are lower than in this country.

Unsecured bank loans. We saw how sole traders have to offer such items as their own house as security when taking out a bank loan, so that if the sole trader cannot pay back the loan the house can be possessed by the bank and sold to pay off the loan. Companies with high credit ratings find it much easier to obtain loans as they are not seen as such a risk because of the value of their business. As a result they are not asked to put up security when taking out a loan.

Debentures are long-term loans with a fixed rate of interest and an agreed repayment date. Unlike a share, a debenture is not permanent and the debenture holder receives interest in payment for the loan. The debenture holder is not a part owner of the business.

SOURCES OF FINANCE **SECTION 2**

REVENUE EXPENDITURE

All of the above sources of finance are used for capital expenditure items. Businesses may also need loans to cover day-to-day running costs (revenue expenditure). You will see, in the last section, how even profitable businesses can have cash flow problems. Sources of finance that can be used for revenue expenditure, or the day-to-day running of the business include:

An **overdraft** – this is frequently used by businesses to provide finance for working capital. The overdraft is often used as a short-term solution to cash flow problems, e.g.

- a need for short-term cash
- to handle a time delay between purchasing goods and payment for them
- unexpected but limited expenditure items.

Trade credit is useful as it allows the business to buy goods or services on credit, and not pay for them until they have used them. Payment is delayed for a set period of time, usually a month. No interest is paid during this time, but the business may lose the chance of cash discounts if the payment is not made on time.

Factoring. If a business has run up a large amount of trade debts it can ask a factoring company to pay part of its debt off. The business then pays the money back to the factoring company in instalments. This helps the cash flow of the business, but the cost of using a factoring company is that it charges interest and an administrative fee for its services.

REVIEW QUESTION

1. Draw up a table for small, medium and large companies and make notes on the different internal and external sources of finance available to each of them.

SUPER REVIEW QUESTION

2. Explain why some of these internal sources and external sources of finance are not available to a sole trader or a private limited company.

KEY POINTS

- External sources of finance available to sole traders include:
  - loans from relatives or friends
  - government schemes
  - small-business bank loans
  - hire purchase
  - leasing
  - contract hire.

- Larger businesses can also raise finance externally through:
  - financial institutions
  - venture capitalists
  - government schemes.

- Large and very large businesses can also:
  - borrow money from foreign banks
  - take unsecured bank loans.

- A private limited company can raise finance by becoming a public limited company.

- Public limited companies can raise finance through debentures.

UNIT 4 — ACCOUNTING AND FINANCE

TOPIC 4 Choosing sources of finance

If a company needs to raise finance there are a number of issues it needs to take into account:
- the cost to the company of raising the finance
- what the company intends to use the funds for
- the current trading position of the business
- balance between the need for the capital against the desire not to get in debt.

Sam and Harri must understand how to choose sources of finance

COSTS

When a company wants to borrow money there are several costs involved:
- the interest rate to be paid back if a loan is taken out
- the legal costs and fees paid to the broker if shares are being issued
- the extra dividends paid out to new shareholders
- the administrative fees charged by factoring companies
- the seat on the Board or shares acquired by the venture capitalist
- the charges paid to hire purchase, leasing and contract hire companies.

All of these costs have to be balanced against each other, when deciding on the best way to raise finance. If interest rates are low the alternatives to loans become less attractive as they have extra costs such as administrative costs, or legal fees. If interest rates are high the alternatives become much more attractive. All the costs have to be weighed against each other when making a decision.

> Credit is only available to those aged over 18 and whose application is suitable.
>
> Mortgages loans are available from The Bank, High St, NEWTOWN, NW2 2HP.
>
> For a written quotation please write to Customer Services, The Bank, High St, NEWTOWN, NW2 2HP or ask at one of our branches.
>
> You are obliged to provide security and arrange insurance for mortgage loans.
>
> **YOUR HOME IS AT RISK IF YOU DO NOT KEEP UP THE REPAYMENTS ON A MORTGAGE OR OTHER LOAN SECURED ON IT.**

Long-term investment

USE OF FUNDS

If the capital is needed for a long-term investment such as the purchase of land or buildings, the company will need to consider long-term methods of raising finance such as mortgage loans, venture capital, or share issues in order to make the source of finance acceptable.

If the capital is needed for medium-term investment such as vehicles, plant and equipment, medium-term methods of raising finance such as debentures, retained profits, hire purchase, leasing, contract hire

> Cash price £1000 including VAT & delivery. Pay nil deposit and nothing for 12 months. After 12 months pay the total amount (£1000) interest free. APR 0% only if loan is repaid after 12 months. Finance also available over a longer period of 3 years at APR 26.6%. No deposit, no payments for 12 months then 24 payments of £65.79. Total price £1579.00.

Medium-term investment

should all be considered, as all offer different facilities to the company, for example, no repayments with retained profits, no maintenance costs with contract hire.

If the capital is needed for short-term finance such as cash flow problems, or buying raw materials, short-term methods of raising finance such as trade credit, or overdraft facilities should be considered, as these offer low interest rates or no interest to be paid at all.

THE TRADING POSITION OF THE BUSINESS

The timing of raising finance is important. Limited companies have to produce Annual Accounts and so financial institutions are aware of the financial state of the business. If the company is showing good profits it will find it much easier to borrow money. If the company is looking less profitable it may have to look to people like venture capitalists to raise finance as they are more likely to take a risk.

THE BALANCE BETWEEN DEBT AND CAPITAL

This is called **gearing**. It is the balance between the amount of money a company has raised through long-term loans (its debts) and the amount of money it has raised through issuing extra shares (its capital). The company must make sure the ratio of debt to capital is not too high.

KEY POINTS
Factors which influence the source of finance include:
- the costs of raising the finance
- the duration of any finance deals
- what the finance will be used for
- the current trading position of the company
- the balance between debt and capital.

REVIEW QUESTIONS

1. State the difference between revenue expenditure and capital expenditure.
2. List and explain two internal sources of finance available to a sole trader.
3. List and explain two external sources of finance available to a large company, that are not available to a sole trader.
4. Describe two different sources of finance that could be used to help a company with cash flow problems.
5. Explain the difference between ordinary shares and preference shares.

SUPER REVIEW QUESTIONS

6. Identify the criteria a company may take into consideration when trying to raise finance for four new company cars.
7. Select the source of finance you consider most appropriate for this capital expenditure and justify your answer.

UNIT 4 ACCOUNTING AND FINANCE

TOPIC 5: Business plan

WHY DO COMPANIES NEED A BUSINESS PLAN?

Every business needs to produce a business plan if it is to succeed. Every business has objectives or targets it wants to achieve. If a company is planning expansion, it will need to finance it. If the business is hoping to raise this money by borrowing from a financial institution or other possible investors, it will want to see the business plan, which outlines how the expansion is to be undertaken.

Business plans are important as they show potential investors that the ideas for the business have been well thought out. For any business starting out or considering expansion, a business plan must be prepared.

Companies also need a business plan to show to other people involved in the business, such as partners or managers, what they want to do, where they want to go and how they intend to get there.

Sam and Harri must understand the need for a business plan

Business plans should include certain details, such as:
- company objectives
- management details
- a description of the company product/service
- production plans
- marketing proposals
- financial requirements
- company assets.

Opposite is an example of a structure that could be used for a business plan:

Discussing the business plan

BUSINESS PLAN

Summary

(The purpose of the summary is to grab the attention of the reader. It should not be more than one page long, and should include details of: the business proposal, the main benefits of the proposal and the support needed from outside agencies. The summary should not be written until everything else in the business plan is finished, as it should highlight the key points from the plan.)

The background

(This gives details of the history of the business, e.g.
What does the business do?
Type of ownership
Does it have key suppliers, customers?
How big is the business – turnover, profits, staff.
How many outlets or factories do they own?
The business address
Does it sell a product or a service?

The personnel

(Details of the key personnel – names, qualifications, job titles, ages, length of service, previous experience. An organisation chart of the business could be included here.)

Outline of the business

(Gives an explanation of the product or service, how it is different from other products on the market, distribution methods, location of business.)

The market

(Outlines the market for the product/service, identifies competitors, and explains how the business competes.)

Trading summary

(Contains details of the business's past performance and future expectations. It could include such details as turnover, gross profit, overheads and profit before interest and tax for the last three to five years. There is no set format for the trading summary, but it could include copies of the business's Trading Account, Profit and Loss Account, Balance Sheet (see Unit 4 Section 3, pages 262–3), cash flow forecast and a break even chart (see Unit 4 Section 1, pages 232–3).)

The proposal

(This states what the business needs, i.e. what help the business needs from the reader of the business plan. It should also include details of the amount of investment the business is putting into the proposal itself, and its assets.)

KEY POINTS

- A business plan is used:
  - to convince potential investors, to make the investment
  - by managers inside the company, to help them understand their jobs.

COURSEWORK ACTIVITY

You and a partner are to imagine that you are going to set up a small business, like Sam. For example, it could be a business making soft toys, making home-made cookies, making jewellery such as bead bracelets, or leather wrist bangles. You may have some better ideas of your own of the type of business you would like to set up.

1 Discuss your ideas with your partner. You need to consider the following:
    - the type of business you want to start
    - to begin with it might be cheaper to work from home
    - the costs of the materials you will use
    - the quantities of products you intend to make when you start
    - how you will advertise your products.

2 Use the details on the business plan shown, and draw up a business plan for your proposed new business to take to the local bank manager for discussion.

   Produce your business plan on the word processor.

Section 3 Accounting

LEARNING OBJECTIVES

By the end of this section you should be able to undertake the following tasks:

- draw up and interpret a trading account
- draw up and interpret a profit and loss account
- draw up and interpret a balance sheet
- measure business performance by calculating the return on net assets employed and the profit margin.

UNIT 4 ACCOUNTING AND FINANCE

TOPIC 1 Recording financial activities

All businesses, large and small, need to keep accurate records of every financial transaction in the business. These records are called the accounts. Large companies will employ an accountant, but sole traders have to record their financial transactions themselves or pay an accountant to keep their records.

All businesses need to know what is happening to their money on a day-by-day basis and be able to answer questions such as:

- how is the company performing?
- can the debts be paid?
- what taxes need to be paid?
- can the business expand?

Sam and Harri need to know how to record financial activities

ACCOUNTING

Accounting means the methods and procedures used to keep a record of financial activities within the business. This information is then used by managers, owners, employees and creditors to see how well the business is doing.

- The managers want to see the accounts to help them make decisions and plan the future of the business.
- The shareholders want to look at the accounts to see if the value of the money they have invested in the company has increased.

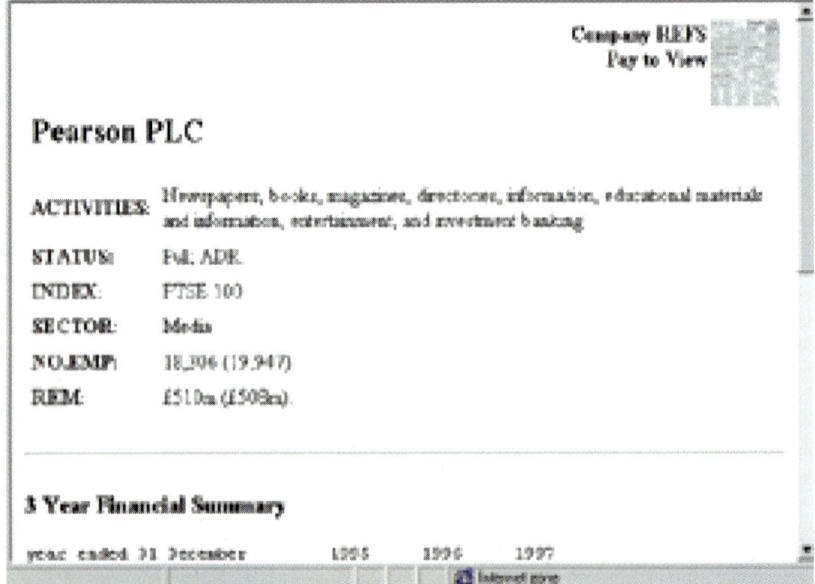

- Potential shareholders want to know if it is worth investing in the company.
- The employees want to look at the accounts to see how the company is performing and check that their jobs are secure.
- The creditors want to look at the accounts to see if it is safe to give the company credit in the future.
- The Inland Revenue want to see the accounts to make an accurate assessment of the taxes due.

There are rules about how financial transactions are recorded and the sort of information that is put in different accounts. Most of this information has to be made public. For example, limited companies must publish a Trading Account, a Profit and Loss Account and a Balance Sheet. These are all published in the company's audited **Annual Report and Accounts**. The Annual Accounts, or Final Accounts as they are sometimes called, are a summary financial statement drawn up at the end of the year's trading.

KEY POINTS

- **Accounting** – the way financial activity is recorded and used.
- The company's performance, as shown in the accounts, is used by:
  – managers
  – employees
  – creditors
  – the Inland Revenue.
- Registered companies must produce an audited financial report and make it public.
- An Annual Report has:
  – a trading, profit and loss account
  – a balance sheet
  – statements on the position of the company.

Business people need to keep accurate accounts which the tax inspector and VAT inspector can check

UNIT 4 ACCOUNTING AND FINANCE

TOPIC 2 Trading account

The **trading account** is the simplest of the accounts and is a record of the **gross profit** of the company.

To work out the gross profit, the accountant has to know the amount of money coming in from selling goods or services and how much it actually costs to produce or buy in the goods or services, for example, how much it costs The Picture House Ltd to buy the refreshments it sells in the cinema.

Below is the Trading Account for The Picture House Ltd. The Picture House is a small group of cinemas located on the outskirts of London.

Sam and Harri must know what is meant by a trading account

The Picture House Ltd
Trading Account for year ended 31 December 1996

		£	£
Sales	**(1)**		200 000
Opening Stock (refreshments)	**(2)**	60 000	
Purchases (refreshments)	**(3)**	25 000	
less Returns	**(4)**	5 000	(deduct this from Purchases)
Total Stock available	**(5)**	80 000	
less Closing Stock	**(6)**	40 000	
Cost of Sales	**(7)**	40 000	
Gross Profit	**(8)**		160 000

Key to The Picture House Trading Account

(1) Sales: the total amount of money taken by the cinema over the year from ticket sales, refreshments, etc.

(2) Opening Stock: the value of stock or goods left over from last year (the refreshments) that are available to sell at the beginning of the next year.

(3) Purchases: the value of the new stock (new refreshments) bought during the year.

(4) Returns: the amount of money lost from damaged goods such as crushed sweets or damaged cans, that could not be sold and had to be returned.

(5) Total stock available is calculated by:
Purchases – returns + opening stock = total stock

(6) Closing stock: the value of the stock (the refreshments) that have not been sold at the end of the year, that is 31 December, when the Trading Account is worked out. This will then become the Opening Stock when the Trading Account is started for the next year. This is deducted from the Total Stock available.

(7) The **cost of sales** is calculated by:
Total stock available – closing stock = cost of sales

(8) The **gross profit** is calculated by:
Sales – cost of sales = gross profit
(when calculated as a percentage of sales it is called the **gross profit margin**)

KEY POINTS
- **Gross profit** – profit before overheads and expenses are deducted.
- **Trading account** – a simple record of gross profit.

COURSEWORK ACTIVITY

1. Using the model shown for The Picture House Ltd for 20X1, draw up the Trading Account to calculate the gross profit for the company for 20X2, using the figures below:

Sales in 20X2 are	£240 000
Opening Stock is	£40 000
Purchases are	£45 000
Returns are	£5 000
Closing Stock is	£40 000

2. Calculate the Gross Profit for The Picture House for 20X2.
3. Calculate the gross profit margin (%) for 20X2.
   Gross profit margin (%)
   $= \dfrac{\text{Gross Profit}}{\text{Sales Revenue}} \times 100\%$ Sales

UNIT 4 ACCOUNTING AND FINANCE

TOPIC 3 Profit and loss account

The **profit and loss account** shows how much net profit – or loss – the company has made over the previous financial year. The **net profit** is the actual profit the company has made after all overheads such as rent, rates, heating and lighting and expenses such as office and vehicle expenses, have been paid. Net profit is calculated by deducting the overheads from the gross profit. When expressed as a percentage it is called the **net profit margin**.

For example, The Picture House Ltd made a gross profit of £160 000 in 20X1, but this was not the final profit, as the Trading Account had not taken into account all the bills they had to pay such as the mortgage, rent, rates and wages. Below is the Profit and Loss Account for The Picture House Ltd.

Sam and Harri need to understand Profit and Loss accounts

The Picture House Ltd
Profit and Loss Account year ending 31 December 20X1

	£	£
Turnover (sales)		200 000
Cost of sales		40 000
Gross profit		160 000
Wages	60 000	
Rates/Insurance	10 000	
Heating and lighting	3 000	
Advertising	7 000	
Depreciation*	7 000	
Administration	5 000	
Other expenses	8 000	100 000
Net profit		60 000

NB: This Profit and Loss Account is for a small business.

***Depreciation** is the amount by which the machinery and fixtures and fittings (e.g. projection equipment and seating) fall in value over a period of time as they become worn out. As these represent assets of the company their fall in value needs to be shown on the profit and loss account.

The profit and loss account for a public limited company would be worked out in a similar way, but the format would be slightly different. Profit and loss accounts for public limited companies will include the details of at least the previous year, so that the two years or more can be compared. There will be less detailed information on costs though this can vary

ACCOUNTING SECTION 3

from company to company. The profit and loss account is made up of three sections, each giving specific information about the company:

1. the **trading account** – this shows the gross profit of the company:
2. the **profit and loss account** – this is an extension of the trading account and shows the **net profit** of the company
3. the **appropriation** account – this gives details of how the profit has been used by the company

A typical format for a profit and loss account for Wilton Sports plc, a public limited company, is shown below:

	20X2 £('000)	20X1 £('000)
Turnover (sales)	2 000	1 500
Cost of sales	1 250	1 000
Gross profit	750	500
Less expenses		
Operating expenses	200	150
Administration	50	40
Distribution	30	25
Depreciation	10	5
Operating profit	460	280
Interest receivable (payable)	(10)	(5)
Net profit	450	275
(Profit before taxation)		
Tax on profits	100	75
Profit after tax	350	200
Dividends	200	100
Retained profit	150	100

COURSEWORK ACTIVITY

Using the model shown for The Picture House Ltd for 20X1, draw up the Profit and Loss Account for the company for 20X2, using the figures below:

	£	
Turnover (sales)	240 000	
Cost of sales		40 000
Gross profit		200 000
Annual wages bill	60 000	
Rates/Insurance	10 000	
Heating and lighting		4 000
Advertising		8 000
Depreciation		10 000
Administration		5 000
Other expenses		8 000
Tax on profits		0 (No dividend paid out this year)

See page 160, where you can find out more about the profit and loss account.

UNIT 4 — ACCOUNTING AND FINANCE

PART 1 – THE TRADING ACCOUNT

Turnover or sales: the value of the goods sold, such as the sportswear, throughout the year.
Cost of sales: the total stock available minus the closing stock.
Gross profit : the sales minus the cost of sales.

PART 2 – THE PROFIT AND LOSS ACCOUNT

This is the actual profit and loss account, and it shows the calculation of the net profit.
Operating expenses: the overheads or costs that are not directly related to production, such as advertising.
Administration: the managerial costs.
Distribution: the transport and warehousing costs.
Depreciation: a calculation of the fall in value of items such as cars or computers, over the period.
Operating profit: the profit before any interest payments are added or deducted and before taxation is deducted.
Interest receivable (payable): is calculated by deducting the amount of interest **paid to the company** from bank deposits or other deposits that are earning them interest from the amount of interest **the company has to pay** on such things as bank loans, hire purchase, leasing. This means that if the company receives more interest than it pays, then the net amount is added to its operating profit. Usually companies pay out more interest than they receive, and this amount is taken off the operating profit. To show the money is being taken off it is shown in brackets on the profit and oss account.
Net profit shows the profit before any taxation is paid.

ACCOUNTING SECTION 3

PART 3 – THE APPROPRIATION ACCOUNT

This section shows how the net profit has been used by the company.

Tax on profits: how much tax the company pays to the government.

Profit after tax: the profit that is left once the taxes have been paid.

Dividends: the amount that is paid to the shareholders in dividends on their shares.

Retained profit: the amount of money kept by the company to use for investment, expansion or deciding to pay off debts.

REVIEW QUESTIONS

Using the Profit and Loss Account for Wilton Sports plc for 20X1:

1. State the Gross Profit and Net Profit for the company
2. State the total Overheads for the year.
3. Calculate the Net Profit margin for 20X1.

$$\text{net profit margin (\%)} = \frac{\text{net profit}}{\text{sales}} \times 100\%$$

SUPER REVIEW QUESTION

4. Explain the information the profit and loss accounts tell you about the business in 20X1 and 20X0, such as how the company has performed over the two years – compare sales, overheads, gross profit and net profit margins.

KEY POINTS

- **Profit and loss account** – a detailed account showing net profit or loss over a period of time.
- **Net profit** – profit after overheads and expenses have been deducted.
- Profit and loss account is divided into three sections
  – trading account
  – profit and loss account
  – appropriation account.
- **Appropriation account** shows how the profit has been used by the company.

ADMINISTRATION   OPERATING EXPENSES   DIVIDENDS
OVERHEADS   DISTRIBUTION
DEPRECIATION
OPERATING PROFIT   INTEREST RECEIVABLE   TAX   NET PROFIT

UNIT 4 ACCOUNTING AND FINANCE

TOPIC 4 Balance sheet

The **balance sheet** gives details of the financial state of the business at a particular time. It shows what the business owns, or is owed (assets) and what it owes (liabilities).

The balance sheet must balance because the assets that the business buys must be paid for from the money it borrows, or from the business's own capital. The balance sheet can be used to calculate the business's **liquidity** (whether or not it can pay its debts). The balance sheet and profit and loss accounts can also be used together to see how efficiently the business is performing. For this a calculation is worked out on the **return on capital employed**. This shows how efficiently the business is using its capital to make profit.

Below is the Balance Sheet for The Picture House Ltd.

Sam and Harri must understand balance sheets

The Picture House Ltd :
Balance Sheet as at 31 December 20X2

	£ ('000)
Fixed assets	
Tangible assets	500
Investments	20
	520
Current assets	
Stocks	60
Debtors	20
Cash	100
	180
Current liabilities	
Creditors: amounts falling due within one year	(100)
Net current assets (Current assets – current liabilities)	80
Total assets less current liabilities	600
Long-term liabilities	
Creditors: amounts falling due after one year	(150)
Net assets	450
Capital and reserves	
Called up share capital	300
Share premium account	30
Other reserves	20
Profit and loss account	100
Capital employed	450

NB: This balance sheet has been simplified to make it easier to understand.

In order to understand the Balance Sheet for The Picture House Ltd, we also need to know what the following terms mean.

CAPITAL AND RESERVES

Called-up share capital: the value of the shares sold by the company when it started.

Share premium account: the value of the shares issued later on, at a higher value, possibly to finance new technology or expansion.

Other reserves: other money in the company – it may be that the company owns the property and it has increased in value over the years.

Profit and loss account: the total amount of profit that has been kept by the company over the years instead of paying it in dividends to the shareholders. This amount is 'transferred' from the profit and loss account.

The final line of the balance sheet shows the **total capital** of the company and this must balance with the **net assets**.

KEY POINTS

- **Balance sheet** – shows the financial state of the company as:
  – assets
  – liabilities
  – liquidity
  – return on capital employed.

INTERPRETING THE ACCOUNTS

The profit and loss account and balance sheet must be included in the Annual Report and Accounts of any company with private investors.

REVIEW QUESTIONS

Using the Balance Sheet for The Picture House Ltd for 20X1, answer the following:
1. State the total fixed assets and current assets.
2. Give one example of a fixed asset and one example of a current asset.
3. State the amount of money owed to The Picture House Ltd by its debtors.

SUPER REVIEW QUESTIONS

4. Explain why the current liabilities and long-term liabilities are in brackets.
5. Explain why a balance sheet must balance. Use the figures in the Balance Sheet for The Picture House Ltd to illustrate your answer.

UNIT 4 ACCOUNTING AND FINANCE

TOPIC 5 — Efficiency of capital use

The profit and loss account and the balance sheet are used to calculate such things as the company's liquidity (its ability to pay its debts), and how efficiently it is using its capital. Below are some of the formulae that are used for these calculations.

CURRENT RATIO

The **current ratio** shows people interested in the company's accounts how easily it is able to pay its current liabilities out of its current assets – in other words how easily it can pay its debts.

$$\text{Current ratio} = \frac{\text{current assets}}{\text{current liabilities}}$$

Current ratios should be between 1.5 and 2.0 for a healthy company.

e.g. The Picture House Ltd's current ratio is:

$$= \frac{180}{100} = 1.8$$

which means The Picture House Ltd has 1.8 times the amount of current assets to current liabilities if it needed to pay off the liabilities. This tells people looking at the balance sheet that the company is in a healthy position.

ACID TEST

The **acid test ratio** is another test of the company's ability to pay off its current liabilities. With acid tests, stocks are not included in the calculation, as these may not always be sold within the current year.

$$\text{Acid test ratio} = \frac{\text{current assets} - \text{stocks}}{\text{capital employed}}$$

The Picture House Ltd's acid test ratio is:

$$= \frac{180 - 60}{100} = \frac{120}{100} = 1.2$$

Acid test ratios should be over 1.0.
This again shows that The Picture House Ltd is able to pay its current liabilities, straight away, from its current assets.

Sam and Harri need to understand how to use capital efficiently

To find the figures for current assets, liabilities, stocks, capital employed and operating profit, a company needs to look back at its balance sheet.

RETURN ON CAPITAL EMPLOYED (ROCE)

The **return on capital employed** formula shows how efficiently the company is using its capital to make a profit. This uses data from the profit and loss account and the balance sheet.

Return on capital employed = $\dfrac{\text{operating profit}}{\text{capital employed}}$

The Picture House Ltd's return on capital employed is:

$$= \dfrac{100}{450} \times 100 = 22.2\%$$

In simple terms this means that for every £100 invested in the company you would receive £122.20 back, making £22.50 profit.

KEY POINTS

- **Current ratio** – how easily a company can pay its debts.
- **Acid test** – how well a company can pay its debts without including sales of stock.
- **Return on capital employed** – how well a company is using capital to make profit.

REVIEW QUESTIONS

1. Using the Balance Sheet produced for the Picture House Ltd, state the total assets of the company.
2. State the difference between fixed assets and current assets.
3. Give three examples of current assets.

SUPER REVIEW QUESTIONS

4. Calculate the current ratio and acid test ratio for the company.
5. Use these ratios to interpret the balance sheet and to explain the financial state of the cinema at the end of 20X2. Does the company have enough money to pay its debts? Do the finances look healthy?

UNIT 4 ACCOUNTING AND FINANCE

❓❓❓❓❓❓❓❓❓❓❓❓❓❓❓
QUESTION TIME

The Picture House Ltd owns five small cinemas in towns on the outskirts of London. The seating in each cinema is as follows: The revenue for each cinema comes from ticket sales, advertising and refreshments.

Cinema	number of seats
1	200
2	140
3	120
4	130
5	110

Revenue
Ticket sales are £4 per customer (this is the average ticket price calculated from the adult/child/OAP prices combined). An extra £1 per customer is raised from advertising and sales of refreshments.

Fixed costs
Rates, repairs, bank charges, etc. total £400 000 per year for the five cinemas.

Variable costs
For every ticket sold, 25 per cent of the ticket price has to be paid to the film distributors, i.e. £1 from every ticket.

1. Produce a break even graph for the company.
2. Calculate the break even point on the graph.
3. Explain the terms **revenue**, **fixed costs** and **total costs** on the break even graph.

Below is data showing the predicted flow of money in and out the business for a six-month period.

	Cash in £	Cash out £
July	40 000	35 000
August	30 000	34 000
September	31 000	36 000
October	44 000	36 000
November	47 000	38 000
December	50 000	38 000

The opening balance in July is £130 000.

4. Produce the cash flow forecast for The Picture House Ltd for these six months.
5. It is likely that the company will have a negative cash flow in August and September. Give reasons why this may happen.
6. The Picture House Ltd wants to raise £50 000 to replace some of the damaged seats in the cinemas. State which internal sources and/or external sources of finance the company could use to pay for this. Give reasons for your choices.
7. Explain the purpose of the following financial records:
   A trading account
   A profit and loss account
   A balance sheet.
8. State which of these financial records must be included in the Annual Report and Accounts of a company.
9. State the three parts that make up a profit and loss account for a public limited company.
10. Explain the following terms:
    assets   liabilities   net assets   working capital

EXTENSION TASKS

11. Using the break even graph produced in Question 1, work out approximately how long it will take for the company to break even, if the average attendance for the week, for the five cinemas, is 2500 customers.
12. Analyse the cash flow of The Picture House Ltd over the six-month period shown on the cash flow forecast. Recommend a course of action to deal with any areas of concern.
13. Using the Trading Account provided for The Picture House Ltd for 20X0, calculate the gross profit margin for the company for that year.
14. Compare the Trading Accounts for 20X0 and 20X1. State your findings after this comparison.
15. Using the Profit and Loss Account and Balance Sheet for The Picture House Ltd, calculate the current ratio and the acid test ratio for the company. Give your opinions on the liquidity of the company based on these calculations.

COURSEWORK ASSIGNMENT WORK

The Picture House Ltd is a limited company now owned by 15 shareholders. Each has an equal share in the business. The business is made up of five small cinemas located in towns on the outskirts of London. Since cinemas have grown in popularity two new multiplex cinemas have been built in the local area.

The films shown at the cinemas are rented from the big film rental companies:

UIP (Paramount, Universal, MGM)	20th Century Fox
Columbia Tristar	Warner Brothers
Buena Vista (Disney)	The Rank Group

The cinemas sell refreshments, which are mainly soft drinks and popcorn, as they bring in the highest return.

It is the end of the financial year and you have to produce the Annual Report.
Obtain a copy of an Annual Report, either for a local company or one of the large high-street companies. Discuss the Annual Report with your teacher. Look at the content, the format and the presentation of the Report.

1. Make notes on the different sections that need to be included e.g.
   ◆ a statement from the directors about the business and its financial performance over the last year.
   ◆ a profit and loss account
   ◆ a balance sheet.
2. From the information you have just collected from the Annual Report, and using the word processor and a spreadsheet, produce the Annual Report for The Picture House Ltd for 20X2, using the figures provided below:

Trading Account 20X2	
Sales	£250 000
Opening Stock	£50 000
Purchases	£25 000
Returns	£5000
Closing Stock	£40 000

3 Calculate the gross profit margin for the company.
4 Using the figures provided below, produce the Profit and Loss Account. Take the turnover, cost of sales and gross profit from the Trading Account.

Wages	£65 000
Rates/Insurance	£12 000
Lighting and heating	£3 000
Advertising	£5 000
Depreciation	£10 000
Administration	£5 000
Other expenses	£5 000

5 Using the figures below, produce the Balance Sheet.

	Fixed assets		Current assets
Tangible assets	£550 000	Stocks	£40 000
Investments	£30 000	Debtors	£20 000
Cash	£100 000		
Current liabilities	(£100 000)		
Long-term liabilities	(150 000)		
Capital and reserves			
Called-up share capital	300 000		
Share premium account	80 000		
Other reserves	30 000		
Profit and Loss account	120 000		

6 Calculate the current ratio and the acid test ratio for the company. Include these details in the Annual Report, and include comments on any changes in the company's profitability and liquidity over the last two years.
7 Explain why the mortgage on the properties is a long-term liability for the business.
8 Explain why the share capital is a liability to the company.
9 The shareholders decide that they need to expand to compete with the new multiplex cinemas in the area. They decide to sell off three of the least profitable cinemas and to expand the remaining two into multiplex cinemas with five screens in each. The shareholders need to raise a large amount of money for the expansion.
10 Describe the options that the owners might consider as sources of finance for the expansion. Which would be the most appropriate, and why?
11 Consider all the internal and external sources of finance the owners could use. Identify the ones you think might be most appropriate for the following tasks:
   ◆ to extend the buildings to accommodate the new screens
   ◆ the purchase of the new screens
   ◆ to pay for furniture and fittings for the cinemas
   ◆ to purchase and install a computer system for ticket sales and bookings.
   Give reasons for each of your choices.

UNIT 5

Production

Section 1 Production objectives

LEARNING OBJECTIVE

By the end of this section you should have learnt:
- the **objectives** of the Production department in any large company.

UNIT 5 PRODUCTION

TOPIC 1 — Product, quantity and price

Production or **operations** is about the methods and procedures used to turn raw materials into an end product that can then be distributed to the consumer to meet their needs or wants. For example, what a clothing manufacturer does to turn cotton fabric into T-shirts and sweatshirts.

The main objectives of any Production department are to produce:
- the right product
- in the correct quantities
- at the right price
- using the most efficient methods
- and guarantee a quality product.

These factors have already been dealt with in the Marketing unit (Unit 3). No single part of business operates on its own – all departments must work together to make the business successful.

Sam and Harri need to know how to decide on the quantity and price of products

QUANTITY

QUALITY

PRODUCT

PRICE

METHOD

THE RIGHT PRODUCT

Production is the process of using resources and adding value to them, to make a product that the consumer will want to buy. Marketing will already have provided information on the consumer's needs and wants that will be necessary to do this.

THE CORRECT QUANTITIES

Another objective of the Production department is to produce quality goods in the right quantities. Producing too many goods, known as **over-production**, can lead to saturation of the market. As we saw in Unit 1 on Supply and Demand, this will mean that there are more goods than the consumer wants, and this will lead to goods staying on the shelves unsold. This will lead to the company having capital tied up in unsold stock, and with perishable goods this may lead to stock being written off altogether. Equally, if supply does not meet demand, the company may lose customers to its rivals.

PRODUCTION OBJECTIVES **SECTION 1**

AT THE RIGHT PRICE

The company must decide the best price for its goods and this must be a price that consumers are able and prepared to pay and which gives the company a profit. We saw this in Unit 3 when looking at cost plus pricing and market-orientated pricing. There is no point in a company developing the best-quality football shirt in the world if it is going to cost a ridiculously high price to make, because no one will buy it just because it has high production values.

KEY POINTS

- **Production** – turning raw materials into end products.
- The main objectives of the Production department are:
  – right product
  – correct quantity
  – right price
  – efficient methods
  – product quality.

An example of T-shirt production

First the material is laid out, then the patterns are placed on the material. An automated cutting machine then cuts out the T-shirt shapes. Next, the designs are printed onto the fronts of the T-shirts. Then a machinist sews the T-shirts together and finally the T-shirts are placed into boxes ready for delivery.

UNIT 5 PRODUCTION

TOPIC 2 — Methods and quality

THE MOST EFFICIENT METHODS

The manager in the Production department has most of the responsibility for deciding how the products are produced, that is, choosing the most efficient method of production according to the product being made. This is important, because if the method of production used by one company is very **labour intensive**, while its competitors use the latest technology to produce their goods, its productivity levels will be lower than its competitor's productivity levels.

An example of the difference in productivity levels because of different methods of production is the Morgan sports car. The company still uses traditional methods for building cars. Each car is hand built and people wanting to buy a new Morgan have a six-year wait. By contrast, Ford builds its cars on an automated production line using all the latest technology, and customers could order a new car and probably take delivery of it within a few weeks.

If the Production department does not meet its objectives there will be implications for the company as a whole. It will lose customers and profit through not being able to produce sufficient quantities to meet consumer demand.

Sam and Harri need to know about production methods and quality

Morgan body shop

PRODUCTION OBJECTIVES **SECTION 1**

A QUALITY PRODUCT

Companies are always trying to produce a high quality product. Most companies have some form of **quality control system** in place. (See Section 6 for more details on systems of quality control.)

Outside agencies such as the British Standards Institute (BSI) also check the standard of some goods, before giving them their BSI Kitemark of approval. The BSI Kitemark is recognised as a sign of high quality by the consumer, and so businesses are very keen to have their goods BSI approved.

The two parts of the production process over which the department has most control are efficient methods and quality control. Production managers strive to be efficient. This means knowing about job enrichment and team working (see pages 122–123) in order to keep operators interested and motivated. It means keeping up-to-date with the very latest technological advances in CAD/CAM and CNC engineering.

If the company's products are of poor quality, or fail altogether (e.g. sweatshirts that shrink in the wash, permed hair that falls out in handfuls), then customers will not seek out this company's products or services. These days consumers are less and less likely to put up with shoddy goods – they demand high quality – and it is the Production department that must produce it.

KEY POINTS

- Businesses should use the most efficient method of production
- Businesses should also use some form of quality control

Safety marks

Section 2 Methods of production

LEARNING OBJECTIVES

By the end of this section you should have learnt:
- the main methods of production
- how new technology has changed manufacturing processes
- the effects and benefits of introducing new technology.

UNIT 5 PRODUCTION

TOPIC 1 — Different methods of production

Manufacturing managers have to decide the best methods to use to produce their goods. There are three main methods:
- to produce each item individually (**job production**)
- to produce the items continuously (**flow production**)
- to produce the items in batches (**batch production**).

In making this decision, the company will consider:
- the **cost of production** with each method
- which method produces the **best-quality** product
- **how many** products they want to make.

Sam and Harri need to know about different methods of production

JOB PRODUCTION

This is when each product is made individually to meet each customer's specific order. Every order is likely to be different and so batch or flow methods are not suitable. **Job production** often involves skilled labour or craftspeople. It is a very **labour-intensive** method, which means it relies heavily on labour rather than machinery and heavy capital costs. The emphasis is quality, not quantity. Products made by job production are often very expensive, as there are few economies of scale.

This method of production is suitable for such items as made-to-measure clothing. This does not apply just to small items, large products can also be individually made. For example, boat building, where clients will want their boat fitted out to their own individual requirements.

Job production

FLOW PRODUCTION

This is where the production process is based on a continuous flow of production. It is used for making large quantities of similar products at high speed, e.g. circuit boards for computers. It is also used for many primary business activities, e.g., production of oil in a refinery. There are great economies of scale to be made with this method. It is used in the manufacture

Flow production

Batch production

of such products as cars and electrical goods. The Rover Group uses **flow production** for the manufacture of its cars. This method of production is usually **capital intensive**, which means the number of people employed (labour costs) are low compared with the amount of money used (capital employed), for the machinery.

BATCH PRODUCTION

This is a common method of production, where products are not made individually, but where a range of different products are made, and so cannot be made by flow production. The products are made in batches, e.g. cake manufacturers make one range of cakes, then change production to another range, e.g. mince pies at Christmas, then jam tarts, then apple pies. Clothes manufacturers also use batch production, e.g. winter-weight trousers are made for a number of weeks and then summer-weight trousers for so many weeks. Thornton's is a company that uses **batch production** in the manufacture of their chocolates. Many of the workers involved in batch production are skilled workers.

Both flow and batch production use **division of labour**, which means each worker specialises in one job on the production line. This makes the jobs very repetitive and boring. However, many of these jobs have been replaced by machinery. This has caused mass unemployment for unskilled workers. It is more common now for workers to be multi-skilled and do different jobs, or work in teams.

KEY POINTS

- The three main methods of producing goods are:
  - **job** – making products individually to order
  - **batch** – making sets of different products
  - **flow** – making products continuously on a production line.

- Using job production:
  - needs skilled workforce
  - is labour intensive
  - makes products expensive to make.

- Using batch or flow production means:
  - large quantities can be made
  - economies of scale – to make products cheaper
  - capital is needed for machinery.

- **Division of labour** – workers are responsible for one small job.

REVIEW QUESTION

1. What is the most appropriate method of production for each of the following:
   - a bakery making a range of breads and cakes
   - manufacturing soft drinks
   - a made-to-measure wedding dress
   - building a new road
   - an oil rig extracting oil
   - a computer manufacturer?

SUPER REVIEW QUESTION

2. Explain what factors will be taken into consideration when deciding which is the most appropriate method of production for a product.

UNIT 5 PRODUCTION

TOPIC 2 — New technology

As we saw in Section 1, in recent years computers have been introduced into the manufacturing industries and these have changed production techniques significantly. Computers are used in manufacturing for:

Sam and Harri need to know about new technology

COMPUTER AIDED MANUFACTURE (CAM)

Computers are used to control machines during the manufacturing process. For example, in the fashion industry the cutting machines can be computer controlled. They are also used in the medical profession, to control lasers during surgery.

COMPUTER NUMERICALLY CONTROLLED (CNC)

Computers are used with other machines such as lathes, to cut out very intricate shapes in a variety of materials. The item can be designed on the computer and then the machine set from the computer to follow the design. For example, a component part for an aircraft can be made using a CNC machine. The machine can be easily reset if the design changes and so would give the greater flexibility during the production process.

CNC

COMPUTER AIDED DESIGN (CAD)

The products are designed on a computer. The designer is easily able to change the design, improve it, change the specification altogether or change details such as colour and pattern. The computer stores a large amount of technical data and this can be accessed to help solve technical problems. The computer can also be programmed to show how the product will react to a variety of conditions. For example, garden designs are now often produced for the client on a computer, and it has the facility to show them:

- how the garden will look with different colours and sizes of shrubs and plants
- how it will look in the different seasons
- how it will look when first planted
- then in 12 months' time
- then in 5 years' time
- it can show the client views of the garden from different angles.

COMPUTER INTEGRATED MANUFACTURING (CIM)

Computers control large parts of the production process. Robots are used to replace humans doing the repetitive tasks, and humans are employed to control the computers. CIM is used extensively in the car industry for such jobs as paint spraying and spot welding.

Automation has led to more and more manual workers being replaced by machines, and the workers then supervise the running of the machines. Computers are now also controlling machines and again replacing the people who used to operate machinery. The workers are needed only to program the computers and maintain the equipment. This has led to a big reduction in employment for unskilled workers, but an increase in jobs for skilled workers.

Many industries now expect their employees to be multi-skilled, that is trained to do a variety of jobs, as this makes the workforce more flexible and they can be used more efficiently to carry out any tasks required. The demand for skilled workers will continue to increase to keep up with the technological changes taking place.

KEY POINTS

- **CAM (Computer aided manufacture)** – computers used to control machines.
- **CNC (Computer numerically controlled)** – computers used to control machines cutting intricate shapes.
- **CAD (Computer aided design)** – computers used to help design a product.
- **CIM (Computer integrated manufacturing)** – computers used to control extensive parts of the production process.
- Automation has meant:
  - more jobs done by machines
  - increase in need for skilled workers and multi-skilled workers
  - decrease in need for unskilled workers.

CIM

UNIT 5 PRODUCTION

TOPIC 3 — Benefits and effects of new technology

The benefits to be gained from the introduction of new technology include:
- increased productivity and therefore reduction in manufacturing costs
- increased quality standards
- wider choice of products.

Sam and Harri need to understand the benefits and effects of new technology

INCREASED PRODUCTIVITY

Companies are now able to produce more goods, because the computer and machines together are taking over the repetitive jobs. They can do the jobs more quickly because they can work continuously, and they do not need to stop for lunch breaks or go on holiday. This has meant an increase in levels of productivity.

INCREASED QUALITY

The quality of goods can also be improved. Humans make errors but technological equipment can make the same quality of goods at the same rate continuously. The only time this goes wrong is if the computer develops a fault or the operator inputs wrong instructions.

METHODS OF PRODUCTION SECTION 2

A WIDER CHOICE AND NUMBER OF GOODS

Companies have to **compete** with their rivals, and so are always looking for ways to make their product slightly different, or cheaper, or more attractive than that of their competitors, in order to encourage the consumer to buy their product. When cars were first mass-produced the only colour you could have was black. These days, as a car passes along the production line, the various robots can be programmed to add the particular extras that a purchaser has ordered and then spray the car in the chosen colour of paint.

Even Levi will make a pair of jeans to suit your particular measurements.

KEY POINTS

Benefits of using new technology include:
- increased productivity
- reduction in production costs
- better quality
- wider range of products.

UNIT 5 PRODUCTION

CASE STUDY

Cherry Pie Ltd designs and makes its own T-shirts and sweatshirts. The designers use a CAD package when creating their designs to put on the T-shirts and sweatshirts. The company uses CAM in many of its manufacturing processes.

The designer produces a portfolio of sketches of the designs to be printed on the shirts. The company selects the designs they like, sometimes suggesting changes in fabrics or colours. These changes are then made by the designer on the computer.

Another computer program (called a computer lay program) is used to find the best fit for the pattern pieces on the material, to avoid wastage or for matching patterns. A graphics plotter is used to print out the pattern layouts.

The roll of fabric is automatically unrolled and placed layer on layer on the cutting table. The garment pieces are cut out by a machine which is programmed to follow the shape of the pattern pieces from the computer program.

The garment pieces are sorted into the order in which they will be sewn. The T-shirts are then made up by the machinists. The chief printer works out the printing of the designs on the shirts. The screens or stencils are made.

The computer controlled carousel printers are set up. The designs are printed on the shirts.

The garments are then pressed and packed ready for despatch to the wholesalers or retail outlets.

1. List the different jobs where computers are used by Cherry Pie Ltd in the design and manufacture of its T-shirts and sweatshirts. Produce the list in the form of a flow chart.
2. State which type of new technology is used for each of these jobs.
3. State and explain the method of production used by Cherry Pie Ltd.
4. Evaluate the benefits to Cherry Pie Ltd of its investment in new technology.
5. Discuss the effects of the introduction of this new technology on the workforce at Cherry Pie Ltd.

Section 3 Calculating the costs of production

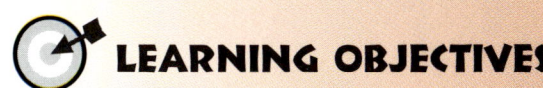# LEARNING OBJECTIVES

By the end of this section you should have learnt:
- how fixed, variable and total costs are calculated
- the difference between standard costs and unit costs
- what overheads are
- what depreciation is and how is it calculated.

UNIT 5 PRODUCTION

TOPIC 1 Costs

FIXED, VARIABLE AND TOTAL COSTS

When calculating the costs of production a variety of factors has to be taken into consideration. The costs of the business are divided into two main categories:

- fixed costs
- variable costs.

As we saw in Unit 4 (pages 223–268), the **fixed costs** are the costs which stay the same at whatever level of output the business is producing and selling over a period of time. The **variable costs** are the costs that vary according to the amount of work being done (the output of the business).

Total cost = fixed costs + variable costs

Sam and Harri need to understand the different costs of production

Looking back at our sweatshirt company from Unit 4 on Finance: Shoot Enterprises Ltd make sweatshirts for various sports. Their sweatshirt sells for £12. The variable costs are:
£4 labour per unit
£4 materials and notions (pins, thread, etc) per unit
Variable costs of £8 per unit (sweatshirt)
The fixed costs of the company are £120 000 per year. We calculated earlier that Shoot Enterprises Ltd would need to sell 30 000 sweatshirts to break even and cover these fixed and variable costs. This means they would need to sell more than 30 000 sweatshirts if they are to make a profit.

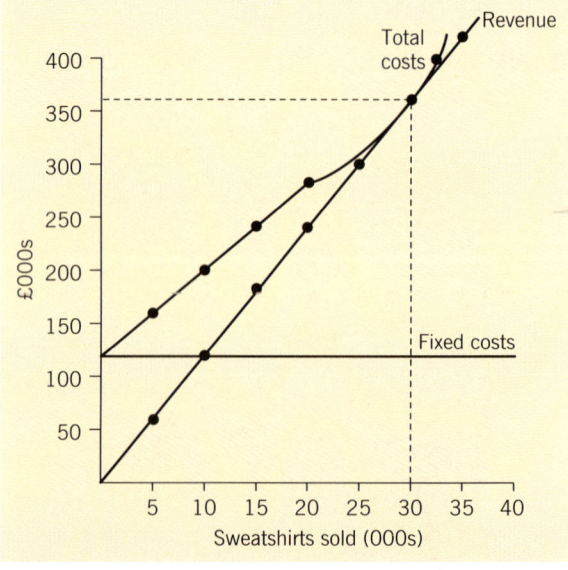

Break even chart for Shoot Enterprises

CALCULATING THE COSTS OF PRODUCTION — SECTION 3

STANDARD COSTS AND UNIT COSTS

The fixed and variable costs are used to calculate the **standard cost** of producing one unit (one sweatshirt). This standard cost is calculated before the products are made and is used to set the target for the cost of producing one unit. This calculation is also needed to make sure that when the selling price is calculated all the costs of production have been taken into account. Once the product has been made the **unit cost** can be calculated. This is the *actual* cost of producing one item. The difference between the standard cost and the unit cost is called the **variance**.

A JOB FOR PRODUCTION OR ACCOUNTS!

In this book we have looked at costing as part of the job of the Production department. In many organisations costing is carried out by management accountants who may work either in the Production department or the Finance department. So sometimes you will see this treated as an Accounts role.

KEY POINTS

- **Standard cost** – the estimated average cost of producing one unit.
- **Unit cost** – the actual average cost of producing one unit.
- **Variance** – the difference between the standard cost and the unit cost.

UNIT 5 PRODUCTION

TOPIC 2 Depreciation

Depreciation is the reduction in value of items such as machinery, vehicles or computers owned by the company. As this equipment is used it deteriorates through age, use, wear and tear or even because it becomes out of date as new technology comes on to the market. A typical example of this is the computer, which is always being upgraded, improved and so quickly depreciates in value. The depreciation of any machinery, vehicles, computers owned by the company has to be included in the costs of the business. It is a fixed cost to the business.

Sam and Harri need to understand depreciation

There are two main methods of calculating the cost of depreciation to the business:

The **straight line method** which reduces the value of the item by an equal amount each year. The formula that is used is:

$$\text{Annual depreciation} = \frac{\text{Cost of item} - \text{its scrap value}}{\text{estimated life of item}}$$

e.g. the printer used by Cherry Pie Ltd to print the designs on the shirts is valued at £100 000. It is expected to last for ten years. It has a residual value of £10 000.

The depreciation would be:

$$\frac{£100\,000 - £10\,000}{10} = £9\,000 \text{ each year}$$

The other method is called the **reducing balance method**. This reduces the value of the item by a set percentage every year of its life. With this method the depreciation is greater when the item is new and reduces year on year.

If the printer were to be depreciated by 10% per year the calculations would be:

$$£100\,000 \times \frac{10}{100}$$

= £10 000 depreciation in first year.

The value of the item would then be £90 000, so

$$£90\,000 \times \frac{10}{100}$$

= £9000 depreciation in second year.

The value of the item would then be £81 000 and so on.

CALCULATING THE COSTS OF PRODUCTION SECTION 3

REVIEW QUESTIONS
1. Explain the difference between standard costs and unit costs. State the purpose of standard costs.
2. Explain and give examples of overheads at Cherry Pie Ltd.

SUPER REVIEW QUESTIONS
3. Cherry Pie Ltd also had to buy a gas-fired drier for drying the designs quickly once they are printed on the shirts. The drier cost £30 000 to buy and has an estimated life of ten years. It has a residual value of £3000. Calculate the depreciation on the drier using both the straight line method and the reducing balance method.
4. What kind of cost is the depreciation to the business.

KEY POINTS
- **Depreciation** – the reduction in value of items over time.
- Depreciation is added to the costs of a business after being calculated by:
  – straight line method
  – reducing balance method.

Computers are an example of products that change rapidly. Depreciation needs to be taken into consideration.

Section 4 Stock control systems

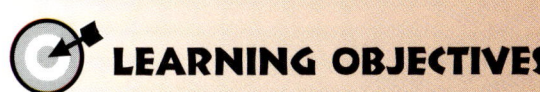 **LEARNING OBJECTIVES**

By the end of this section you should have learnt :
- how stock control procedures work
- the advantages and disadvantages of a just-in-time system.

UNIT 5 PRODUCTION

TOPIC 1 — Stock control procedures

Stock control is an important part of the production process. It is the process of trying to decide the right amount of stock items, such as raw materials and component parts, that will be needed to make the products, without ever running out of stock.

OVERSTOCKING

The business has to think about the cost of holding large stocks of items (overstocking) and the implications that has for:
- storing the goods
- the shelf life of the goods
- insuring the goods
- the amount of money tied up in the stock.

Sam and Harri need to understand stock control procedures

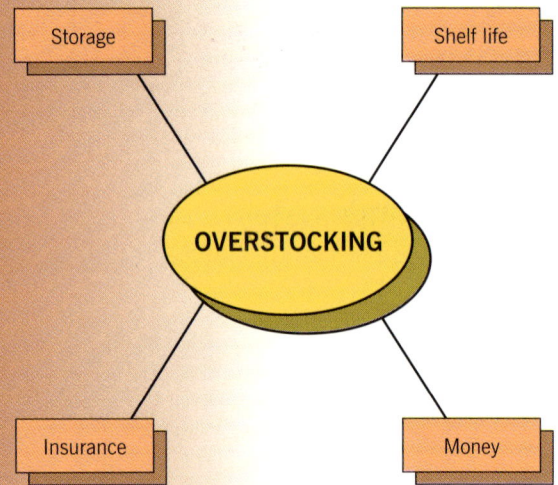

UNDERSTOCKING

All of this has to be balanced against the cost of running out of stock (understocking) and possibly losing production. The **stock controller** has four main functions:

- to decide the **minimum** level of stock the company needs to hold
- to decide the **maximum** level of stock the company should hold
- to decide the **re-order** level for stock (this is the level of stock at which an order is placed, to make sure the company never runs out of stock)
- to decide the **quantities** to be ordered to keep the stock above the minimum level and below the maximum level.

When deciding on the re-order level the stock controller has to take into account how often the stock item is used, and also the **lead time** (how long it takes from the order being placed to it arriving). A company does not hold the same amount of different stock items that it uses – it varies a great deal. Some items may be used only once a year whereas other items may be used every day, or in larger quantities. For example, if the business uses, on average, only one widget curler per year and the delivery time is four days, then there is little point having ten in stock. But printer cartridges would be different – there could be 20 or more in stock. So stock levels have to be decided for each individual item stocked by the company.

KEY POINTS

- **Overstock** – when a company has too much of an item.
- **Understock** – when a company has too little of an item.
- A stock controller should decide:
  - the minimum level of stock
  - the maximum level of stock
  - when to re-order stock
  - how much stock to re-order.

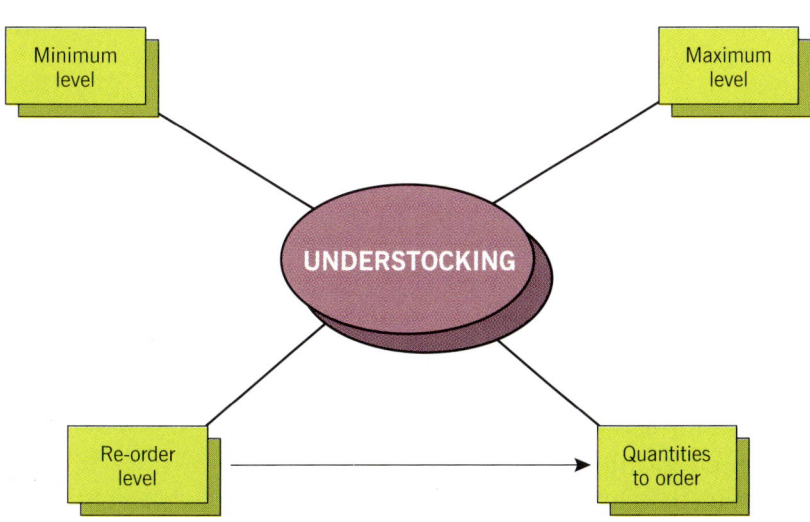

UNIT 5 PRODUCTION

TOPIC 2: Just-in-time system (JIT)

Japanese companies have for many years dominated trade in items such as electrical goods, motorcycles and, increasingly, in the motor industry.

They have aimed to reduce to the minimum their production costs. This has meant new technology on the production lines to reduce workers, and reducing their use of raw materials and factory space to the minimum. This method of production is known as **lean production**. Part of the reduction in factory floor space is achieved by reducing the amount of stock they carry. They have introduced a **just-in-time** system of stock control.

The amount of stock held is kept to a minimum. They have an agreement with their suppliers that they will provide regular deliveries. Suppliers have been known to move to premises next to the factory to cut down delivery times and costs. Stocks are not stored on the premises, they are delivered straight to the production line ready for use.

Sam and Harri need to understand the just-in-time system of production

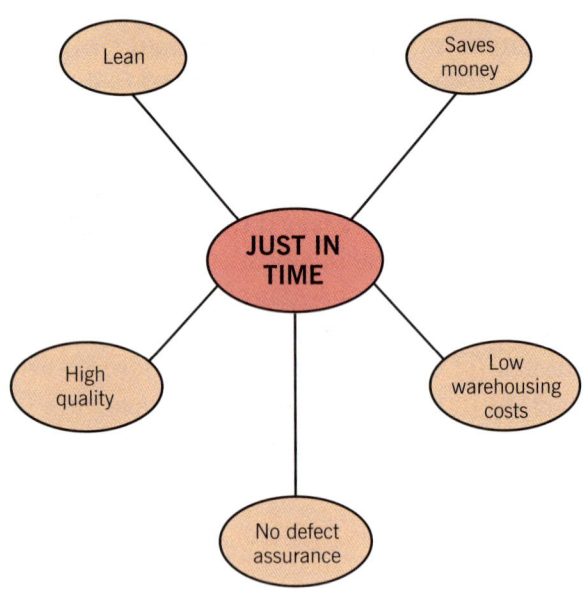

ADVANTAGES

There are a number of advantages from this method of stock control:

- The company saves money by not having to buy stock in such large quantities.
- Warehousing costs are reduced.
- The suppliers give an assurance that their products have no defects, saving the manufacturer the time normally spent checking the components before they go on to the production line. A penalty is incurred for any products coming from the supplier that are found to have a defect.
- This in turn improves the quality of the goods as quality control can concentrate on the quality of the work in progress, instead of checking the quality of the component parts as they arrive.

STOCK CONTROL SYSTEMS SECTION 4

DISADVANTAGES

The disadvantages of this method of stock control are:

- if the supplier fails to deliver, the production line may stop as it could run out of stock items
- it needs a skilled workforce as they need to be multi-skilled and able to move from area to area on the production line, wherever they are needed
- the success of the system depends partly on the quality standards of its suppliers, which can leave the company vulnerable, as it is not totally in control of its own production.

For the system to work, suppliers need to see themselves as part of the production team – stakeholders in the enterprise. It is important that the purchasing organisation treats its suppliers well so that they will cooperate.

Many companies worldwide have now adopted these lean production and just-in-time systems. JIT is now used in other types of production, not just manufacturing. Most large superstores, such as Sainsbury and Tesco have no storage space in their stores and are totally dependent on JIT deliveries to keep their stores stocked up.

KEY POINTS

- **Just-in-time** – keeping the amount of stock to a minimum.
- Advantages:
  – saves money
  – improves quality.
- Disadvantages:
  – can mean relying on supplier
  – needs skilled workforce.

REVIEW QUESTION

1. Describe the role of the stock controller in the Production department.

SUPER REVIEW QUESTIONS

2. Explain how lean production and just-in-time systems can reduce costs for the company.
3. State and explain the advantages and disadvantages to Cherry Pie Ltd of using a just-in-time system of stock control.

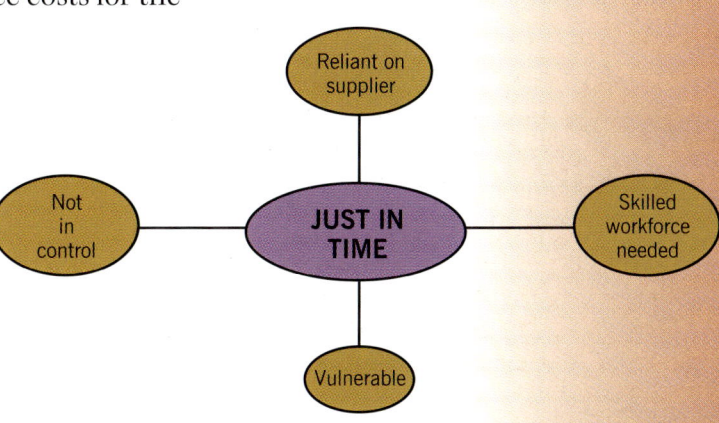

293

Section 5 Business location

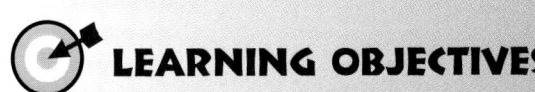
LEARNING OBJECTIVES

By the end of this section you should have learnt:
- the main factors to take into consideration when choosing a location for the business
- the possible economic costs and benefits of selecting a particular location
- the social costs and benefits of selecting a particular location
- the environmental responsibilities a business has when choosing a location.

UNIT 5 PRODUCTION

TOPIC 1 — Economies of choosing a location

When choosing a location for a business there are a number of factors that need to be taken into consideration:
- availability of land and premises
- transport costs
- nearness to market/raw materials
- the local environment – i.e. utilities, government incentives, telecommunications
- labour – availability and cost.

Sam and Harri need to understand the economics of choosing a location

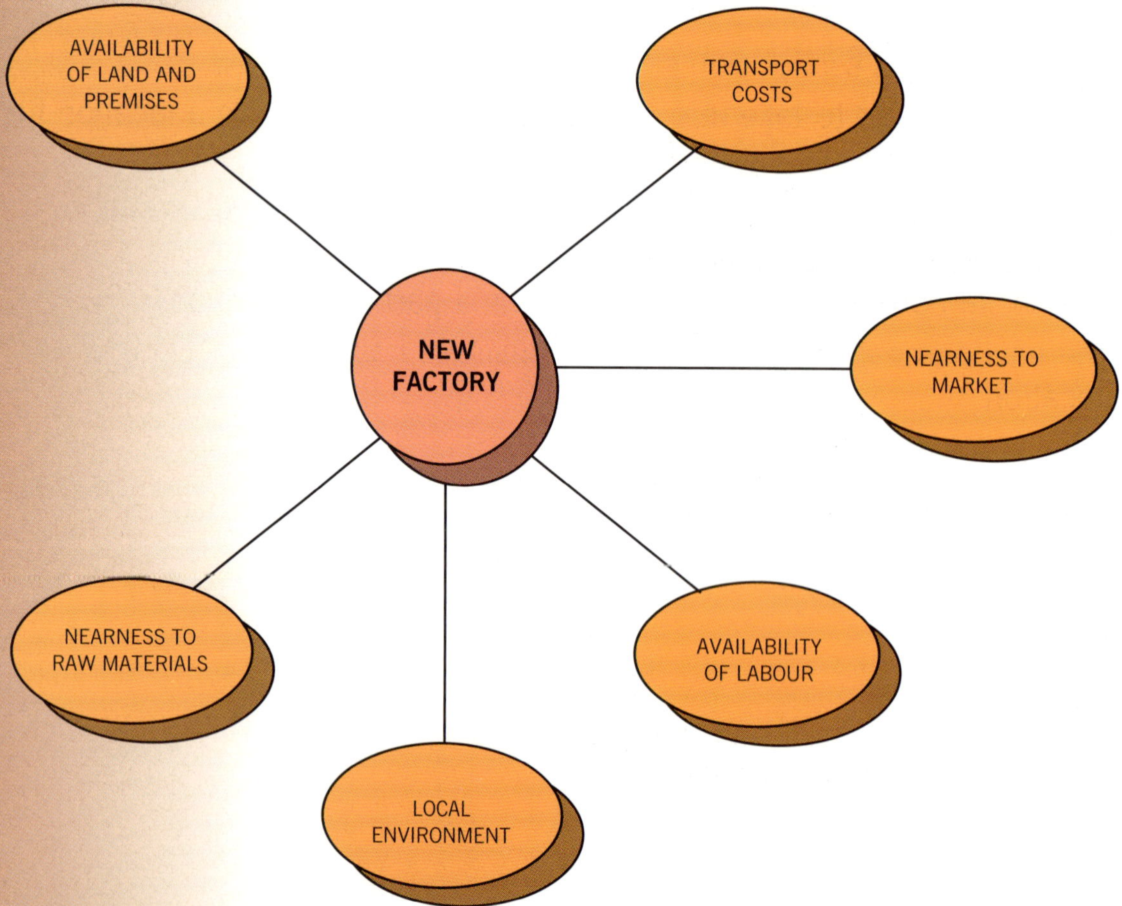

LAND AND PREMISES

The price of land and premises varies from area to area. Businesses will have to pay a much higher price for premises in the main high street than out in a rural area. This has led to moves by many of the large retail organisations such as Currys, Halfords, Sainsbury's and Tesco from the town centres into the rural areas, and the development of out-of-town shopping areas. Councils are now increasingly worried about the effects this is having on many town centres: taking customers away from traditional high-street shopping, and causing smaller retailers to suffer.

The condition of the premises also has to be taken into account, because although a new property may be more expensive initially, older premises may need a lot of money spent to bring them up to an acceptable state to work in, or to convert them to a different use. Checks should also be made that there are no structural problems with the premises or the site, so surveys need to be carried out. Manufacturing industries and offices are now often located on **industrial estates** or greenfield sites. Industrial estates are located in towns and cities and they are new sites which have all the infrastructure provided, such as roads and the public utilities of water, gas and electricity. **Greenfield sites** are located on the outskirts of towns and cities and are sites that have never been developed before. Business rates vary according to location and they are another consideration. Companies need to decide whether to buy the freehold of the premises or rent the premises on a lease. If buying the premises, it will mean borrowing a large amount of money, but commercial property usually increases in value, whereas renting the property adds no value to the business.

However, more companies are now moving to leasing their premises rather than buying, because their needs may change. For example, they may need to relocate to a larger or smaller site; trends change from regional distribution centres to local distribution centres and back again, and owning the land and property can be a disadvantage in these circumstances.

UNIT 5 PRODUCTION

TRANSPORT COSTS

For manufacturing industries, the transportation process (the movement of raw materials and goods to the factory, and of finished goods from the factory to wholesalers and retailers) needs good transport links near the chosen location. It is preferable that the site is located close to a motorway but other transport links are essential. The premises and land should be large enough to provide parking for staff, customers and deliveries.

If the business is located in the city, it is also important that there are good public transport links for staff and customers to use. Delivery access to sites is also important. The growth in out-of-town shopping centres in recent years has put a strain on local transport links and infrastructures, as well as taking trade from the city centres.

NEARNESS TO MARKET

Service industries – e.g. retailers, banks, leisure services – need to be near their customers. Manufacturing industries need to decide whether it is more cost-effective to be near their suppliers or near their markets. For example, an oil refinery needs to be located near a seaport as the majority of our oil supplies are imported by sea in oil tankers. If the finished goods are bulky or heavy, it is probably better to be close to the market. Manufacturers that produce finished goods that are more expensive to transport than the raw materials are known as **bulk-increasing industries**.

THE LOCAL ENVIRONMENT

The local environment is important when choosing a location; it helps the business to attract staff and customers. Businesses look for an environment that offers a wide range of facilities – e.g. good housing, education, shopping, entertainment and local transport. Many people now want to live in the countryside. This has led to problems in many rural areas due to the increase in the rural population. The local councils want the government instead to encourage more development in **brownfield sites** – derelict or unused land in towns and cities.

BUSINESS LOCATION SECTION 5

LABOUR

A ready supply of suitably skilled workers is important. If the right type of workers are not available in the local area, the company may need to relocate employees or train new ones – all of which costs money. The Prudential Insurance Company has recently decided to relocate to Derby as its research has shown that the city has a ready supply of the type of skilled workforce it needs for its new telephone banking service. This will bring 1 500 new jobs to the city. The difference in wages from region to region is also a factor to consider.

There are other factors that can affect choice of location, e.g.

- Planning permission from the local planning authority is needed when building new premises, or changing the use of existing premises.
- Certain parts of the country are given regional aid by the government to attract businesses to the area. These areas are called **assisted areas**. Businesses in assisted areas are given grants to create new jobs.
- The government has set up **enterprise zones** to attract businesses to certain areas of the country. The aim of enterprise zones is to give the area a better infrastructure – e.g improved roads and land clearance. Enterprise zones last for ten years and the businesses in the area are given a capital allowance to build premises. A further attraction is that the companies do not have to pay any business rates during this period.
- The European Union also provides financial help for schemes to create new jobs, train employees, or improve the infrastructure of the area.

The economic costs and benefits – or private costs and benefits – are those related to the business when choosing the best location for the business.

KEY POINTS

Business location depends on:
- availability of land and premises
- cost of transport
- nearness to market
- local environment
- availability of labour.

UNIT 5 PRODUCTION

TOPIC 2 — Social aspects of choosing a location

When a large business locates to a new area, it will affect the people living there and their environment. Sometimes these effects are negative (bad); sometimes they are positive (good). These effects are known as the **social costs and benefits**.

SOCIAL COSTS

The **social costs**, to the local area, of starting up a new business might be:
- damage to the local flora and fauna on the land where the business is located
- strains on the local infrastructure – e.g. schools and hospitals – if lots of new employees are brought in
- increased congestion on roads near the location
- increased pollution from the increase in traffic
- noise pollution.

SOCIAL BENEFITS

The **social benefits** of a business deciding to locate in a particular area might be:
- creating jobs for local people
- creating more jobs for the company's suppliers
- creating more jobs for other local businesses and services – e.g. local shops, restaurants, schools, doctor's surgeries.

It will also have national effects – the business has to pay corporation tax, and the employees have to pay income tax and national insurance, all of which contribute to the national economy.

ENVIRONMENTAL ISSUES

Environmental issues are often a concern for local people when some businesses try to locate to their area. The siting of businesses such as chemical factories, abattoirs, landfill sites and major road schemes are often strongly opposed by local – and

Sam and Harri need to understand the social aspects of choosing a location

sometimes national – pressure groups trying to protect the local environment. These days, the public is very aware of the impact of industrial pollution which can take many forms:

◆ Water pollution can be caused by businesses disposing of waste liquids in rivers or the sea near its premises.
◆ Air pollution can be caused by the emission of gases, ash, dust, or smoke from factory chimneys into the atmosphere.
◆ Noise pollution can be caused by heavy machinery, noise from aircraft at airports or large amounts of traffic on the roads.

REVIEW QUESTIONS

1. Explain the difference between an industrial estate and a greenfield site.
2. List four different types of business that need to be near their market.

SUPER REVIEW QUESTION

3. State and explain the economic costs and benefits and the social costs and benefits of a new superstore – selling computers – locating to your local area.

KEY POINTS

■ **Social costs** – the negative effects a business has on the community, e.g.
  – environmental damage
  – increased strain on local amenities
  – increased road congestion.

■ **Social benefits** – the positive effects a business has on the community, e.g.
  – creation of jobs with the business
  – creation of jobs with other local businesses
  – contribution to national economy.

■ Environmental issues can affect the building of new businesses.

■ Companies can create pollution which harms the local environment, e.g.
  – water pollution
  – air pollution
  – noise pollution.

Section 6 Quality control and quality assurance

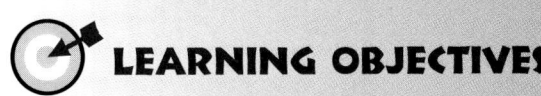**LEARNING OBJECTIVES**

By the end of this section you should have learnt:
- the methods used for quality control
- about quality circles
- the importance of quality assurance.

UNIT 5 PRODUCTION

TOPIC 1 — Quality control

METHODS OF QUALITY CONTROL

Businesses realise the importance of meeting their customers' needs and wants by providing them with a quality product. Quality control is the method used by a business to make sure the product will meet the standard expected by the customer.

There are three main methods of checking the quality of goods:
- quality control
- quality assurance
- total quality management.

Sam and Harri need to know about quality control

STEPS OF QUALITY CONTROL

With **quality control** the goods may be tested at different stages of the production process.

The first step is to check the raw materials or components coming from the suppliers. If a just-in-time system is in place (see pages 292–293), the supplier is expected to test the products and guarantee they are free from defects before delivering them. The next step is to check the work in progress. This means taking random samples of the products at various stages of the production process and checking the quality of the work and of the product. The final step is to check the finished product. Any faulty goods are taken out and scrapped.

QUALITY CONTROL AND QUALITY ASSURANCE **SECTION 6**

Quality control can be expensive, as there can be a lot of waste if a batch of products is found to be faulty. Errors can occur from:
- workers not paying attention
- workers making mistakes
- machinery breaking down
- design faults going through to production undetected.

External methods of quality control are put in place by official bodies such as the British Standards Institute (BSI). They regularly check the quality of a range of goods and if they meet their standards they are awarded the BSI Kitemark symbol which is displayed on the products.

KEY POINTS
- **Quality control** – raw materials, production and finished product checked at each stage

UNIT 5 PRODUCTION

TOPIC 2 — Quality assurance

This takes place during and after the product is made and involves the whole process of production, not just the goods being made. During production the emphasis is put on the workers checking their own work rather than inspectors doing random checks. The idea of workers being responsible for their own quality checks was first introduced by Japanese companies.

Quality assurance after the product is made can be in the form of **guarantees** to the customer on the quality of the product. Any product found by the customer to be below standard can be returned to the manufacturer. **After sales service** is also a form of quality assurance, where the product – e.g. a car or electrical goods – is sold with a warranty for a period of time (usually a year) where any replacement parts and labour costs are paid for by the manufacturer.

Sam and Harri need to understand quality assurance

QUALITY CONTROL AND QUALITY ASSURANCE **SECTION 6**

TOTAL QUALITY MANAGEMENT (TQM)

Total quality management is about encouraging everyone in the business to think about quality – not only the production teams, but also all the other employees in the business – and encouraging them to make suggestions for improving the standard of their work. Linked to quality circles, total quality management encourages all the employees to get the job right and get it right the first time. When used successfully this form of management can cut costs and wastage, and ensure customer satisfaction.

QUALITY CIRCLES

Quality circles are small groups of workers who meet regularly to discuss their work problems and provide solutions. A quality circle may be set up to solve a particular problem and the members of the group would be specially chosen. Other quality circles meet regularly and focus on general issues. The purpose of quality circles is to motivate the workers and improve efficiency; the workers are likely to be more responsive if they are involved in quality control.

KEY POINTS

- **Quality assurance** – workers checking the quality of their own work
- **Quality circles** – groups of workers discussing how to improve their work.
- **Guarantees** after the product is finished give quality assurance to the customer.
- **Total quality management** – making all employees consider the quality of a product.

UNIT 5 PRODUCTION

QUESTION TIME

1. List the three main methods of production.
2. Give an example of a product that could be made using each method of production.
3. State three different ways that new technology is used by manufacturing industries – either in the design or the making of a product.

A computer aided design package could be used in the design of a garden.

4. Explain the advantages of using a computer package in the design work.
5. Explain the facilities on the garden design package that might be useful to the client, when making decisions on the final design.
6. State which costs have to be taken into consideration when calculating the costs of production.
7. State three different methods used for checking the quality of goods.
8. Explain the importance of quality assurance to the business.

EXTENSION TASKS

9. Explain what kind of cost depreciation is, and why it has to be included in the cost of production.
10. Evaluate the benefits to Cherry Pie Ltd of introducing new technology to the design and manufacture of its shirts.
11. State and explain the objectives of the Production department within a business.
12. Choose a product that you use regularly – e.g. a CD player, a pair of trainers, a bar of chocolate,. Make a list of the different tests that could be carried out on the product during manufacture to make sure it reaches you in a good condition.
13. Carry out research on the guarantees found on some everyday products. Make a note of the types of things that are guaranteed.
14. Write out a guarantee for the product that you chose in question 12.

COURSEWORK ASSIGNMENT WORK

The Business Studies department at your school uses a variety of different stationery and equipment – e.g. paper, pens and pencils, staplers, computers, printers and computer supplies.

1. Make a list of ten different items that are used.
2. Set up a stock control system for these ten items. Produce stock control cards and decide on the minimum and maximum stock levels, re-order levels, order quantities, and record some issues and receipts of goods.

You may wish to set up the system on the computer.
(Below is an example of a stock control card.)

STOCK RECORD CARD			
Item		Supplier:	
Max Stock level:	Min Stock level:		Re-order level:
Date	Goods in	Goods out	Balance
Balance brought forward			

3 Explain the purpose of the stock control system and the importance of the minimum, maximum and re-order levels.

A site in your local area has become available and all the following businesses want to buy it:

- ◆ The owners of the town's football team want to build a new football ground and a sports stadium.
- ◆ A group of local farmers wants to build a new abattoir.
- ◆ A leisure group wants to build a multiplex cinema and night-club with parking for 1000 cars.
- ◆ A construction company wants to build a by-pass that goes straight through the local countryside and village.
- ◆ A local inquiry is about to be held because of the strength of public opinion against the site being used.

4 Work in a group of four. **Choose one of the above proposals for the use of the site**. Two of the group should put together the arguments for the proposed building going ahead. Two of the group should put together the arguments against the proposed building going ahead.

5 Produce a series of overhead transparencies to accompany your arguments.

6 Hold the public inquiry in front of the rest of the class. After hearing your arguments, the class should take a vote on whether the proposal should go ahead or not.

Index

*Note: Entries in **bold** refer to sections of the book and entries in italics refer to topics in the book.*

4 Ps 162, 168, 169

A

ACAS (Advisory, Conciliation & Arbitration Service) 115
Account, trading 256–7
Accounting 253–268
 – Management 225
Acid test 264
Advertising 214–5
 – informative 215
 – job 133, 136–7
 – persuasive 215
 – product 212, 214
After-sales service 185, 306
Agencies
 – advertising 214
 – recruitment 137
Annual General Meeting (AGM) 14, 29, 30, 31, 33, 35
Annual Report and Accounts 255
Application
 – form 139
 – *process* 138–9
Applying for a job 138–9
Appraisal 124–5
Appropriation account 260, 261
Articles of Association 30–32, 35
Assets 82, 83, 236, 243
 – and liabilities 236–7
Audit 31
Autocratic leaders 62, 63

B

Balance
 – of Payments 96, 100
 – sheet 262–3
Batch production method 277
Benefits, social 300–1
Bonus payments 120
Boom 96, 99
Brand names 188–9
Breaking even 232

British Code of Advertising Practices 171
Budget planning 225
Business
 – **activity 1–16**
 – documents 70–73
 – **influences on 1–102**
 – letters 72
 – **location 295–301**
 – **objectives 75–90**
 – ownership **17–46**
 – *plan* 250–1

C

CAD/CAM 104, 105, 108, 273, 278–9
Capital 10, 14
 – expenditure 240–1
Cartels 89
Cash and carry warehouse 205
Cash flow forecasting 225, 227
Centralisation 60, 61
Centralisation and decentralisation 60
Certificate of Incorporation 30, 33
Certificate of Trading 33
Chain store 206
Channels of distribution 202–3
 – changes in 204–5
Charts, organisation 48–59
CIM 278
CNC 278
Collective bargaining 153
Command, chain of 49, 64
Communication 64–5
 – channels of 66–7
 – examples of 70–74
 – internal/external 64–5
 – methods of 68–9
Competition 100
Competition-based pricing 196, 197
Computers, use of 104–5
Conciliation and arbitration 155
Confederation of British Industries (CBI) 152
Conglomerates 87, 89
Consumer
 – Association 94, 173
 – Credit Act 171

 – durables 3
 – needs and wants 2, 3, 122
 – protection 170–1
 – Protection Act 170
Contract hire 245
Control, span of 49
Co-operative Society 40
Co-operatives 18, 38–40, 41
Corporation Tax 98
Cost, opportunity 2, 3
Cost-plus pricing 194, 195, 197
Costs
 – *and revenue* 230–1
 – *fixed, variable and total* 284–5
 – social 300–1
 – unit 285
 – variable 231, 284
Current
 – assets 236–7
 – ratio 264
Curriculum vitae 138
Customs duties 98, 104–5, 108, 198

D

Debentures 246
Decentralisation 61
Deed of partnership 25, 27
Demand and supply 4–5
Demerging 87, 89
Democratic leaders 63
Department store 206
Depreciation 258, 286–7
Desk research 177 8, 179
Destroyer pricing 197
Developments in telecommunications 106–7
Direct selling 204
Disabled Persons (Employment) Acts 127
Discount warehouse 207
Diseconomies of scale 80
Dismissal 147
Distribution 202–3
 – channels of 202–3
 – importance of 202
 – methods of 208–9
Diversification 85
Division of labour 277

INDEX

E

Economies
- *of choosing business location* 296–299
- *of scale* 77–9

Economy
- market 6–7
- mixed 7
- planned 7

EDI 105
Efficiency of capital use 264
EFTPOS 105
Electronic mail 70, 197
Employees 13, 132
Employer/employee relations 149–55
Employment
- Acts 127, 147, 155
- contract of 127, 133, 141
- laws 126
- protection 126, 147, 155
- termination of 146–7

Enterprise 10–11
Entrepreneur 10–11
Environment 92–3, 298
- *international* 100–1
- *local* 92, 298, 300

EPOS 105
Equal
- opportunities 126
- pay 126

Equilibrium point 5
Ethical constraints 172–3
European Union 101, 246, 299
Excess supply/demand 5
Exchange rate 199
Excise duties 98, 198
Expansion
- external 84
- internal 84–5
- methods of 84–5

Exports 100, 101

F

Factoring 247
Factors of production 10–11
Fax 107
Field research 177–9
Finance, raising 225, 240
Finance, sources of 239–52
- *choosing* 248–9
- *external* 244–7
- *internal* 242–3
- *raising* 240–1

Financial
- accounting 225
- forecasting 226
- **planning 223–238**

Fiscal 96
Fixed
- assets 236
- costs 230, 231, 284

Flat organisation 52–3
Flow production method 276–7
Food and Drugs Act 170
Food Safety Act 171
Franchises 18, 36–37, 41, 77
Fringe benefits 121
Functional
- organisation chart 54
- structure 55, 58, 59

Functions of business finance 224

G

Gearing 249
Goods and services 3
Government
- *central* 42, 43, 93, 96–99, 246, 299
- *legislation* 99
- *local* 93

H

Health and Safety at Work Act 127
Hierarchy 48, 49, 50, 51, 115
Hire purchase 245
Human resources
- *importance of* 128–9
- *objectives of* 132
- **role of 131–148**

Hypermarket 207

I

Imports 100–1
Income tax 98, 118, 119
Independent store 206
Induction training 142–3
Industrial
- *action* 154–5
- *relations* 150–3
- *tribunal* 147

Inflation 96, 97, 99
Influences on business (see Business, influences on)
Informative advertising 215

Integration, type o 87
Internal expansion 84–5
Interview 133, 140–1
Interview procedures 140–1

J

Job
- advertisements 133, 136–7
- *description/person specification* 133–5
- improvement 123
- production method 275, 276
- *satisfaction* 122–3

Just-in-time (JIT) 292–3

L

Labour 10–11
Laissez-faire 63
LAN 106, 107
Land 10–11
Lead time 291
Leaders, democratic 63
Leadership styles 62
Leaseback 245
Leasing 138
Letter of application 138
Liabilities 237
Liability, limited 25, 28, 31, 35
Liability, unlimited 18, 21
Limited company, private 13, 28–31, 41, 46, 77, 247
Limited liability 25, 28, 31, 35
Loans 246
Local
- environment 92, 298, 300
- government 42, 43, 93, 246

M

Mail order 203
Management accounting 225
Management structures and organisation charts 48
Management, structures & organisation of business 48–73
Managers 202
Manufacturer 56
Mark up 195
Market 206
- economy 6–7
- niche 167
- share 82–3
- price 5
- research 160, 176–7

INDEX

Market segments
- *and niche markets* 166–7
- *identifying* 164–5

Marketing 159–73
- *objectives of* 162–3
- *mix* 168
- *what is it?* 160–1

Maslow 70
Memorandum 70
- of Association 30–2, 35

Merger 84, 86–9
Mergers and takeovers 86–9
Methods and quality 272–3
Mixed economy 7
Mobile shop 206
Monopolies and Mergers Commission 88–9
Monopoly 88
Motivation (what motivates people to work) 114–5

N

National Insurance 118–9
Nationalised industries 44
Needs 2, 3, 122
Network marketing 204
Networks – LAN/WAN 106
New technology 278–9
- *benefits/effects of* 280–1

Niche market 167

O

Objectives, business (see Business Objectives)
Office of Fair Trading 173
On-the-job/off-the-job training 144–5
Opportunity cost 2, 3
Organisation
- chart, functional 54
- charts 48–59
- *Flat* 52–3
- *Functional, regional and product* 58–9
- *Manufacturing* 56–7
- *Retail* 54–5
- *Tall* 50–1

Overdraft 247
Overheads 78
Owners 12–13
Ownership, types of (see Business Ownership, types of)

P

Packaging 190–1, 212, 213
Partnership
- Act 25
- Deeds of 25–7

Partnerships 13, 18, 24–27, 36–7, 77
Pay
- conditions of 150
- performance-related 121
- rates of 120
- slips 118–9

Payment systems, types of 116–21
People in business 12–13, 113–130
Person specification 133, 135
Place 160, 169, 201–210
Planned economy 7
Planning permission 93, 299
Pre-sales service 185
Pressure groups 94–5
Price 5, 83, 160, 168, 194–200, **271**
- *factors that effect it* 198–9
- fixing 89

Pricing
- cost-plus 194, 195, 197
- destroyer 197
- *methods* 194–7

Private limited companies 13, 18, 28–31, 41, 46, 77, 247
Privatisation 44–5, 46
Product 183–92
- *life cycle* 186–7
- organisational structure 58, 9
- *quantity and price* 270–1
- **what makes one?** 184–5

Production
- primary 8–9

Production
- **calculating the costs of 283–8**
- *different methods of* 275–7
- *factors of* 10–11
- **methods of 275–82**
- **objectives 269–74**
- scale of 78
- secondary 8–9
- tertiary 8–9
- *types of* 8–9

Production method, flow 276, 7
Profit
- *and loss account* 258–9, 261, 263
- related pay 121
- sharing 121

Profits 82, 83, 195, 243
Promotion 160, 169, 211–9, **212, 216–7**
- *sales/trade* 216–7
- *what is it?* 212

Protecting the consumer 170–1
Ps, the 4 162, 168, 169
Public
- corporations 43, 46
- limited company 13, 18, 32–5, 41
- relations 212, 218

Purpose of business 2–3, 40
Purpose of business 2–3, 40

Q

Quality
- *assurance* 306–7
- circles 307
- *control* 109, 273, 304–5
- **control and assurance 303–7**

Questionnaires 181
Quota sampling 180
Quotas 101

R

Race Relations Act 127
Random sampling 180
Rates of pay 120
Recession 96, 99
Recording financial activities 254–5
Recruitment 133, 136–7
- agencies 137

Redundancy 146
Regional distribution centres 209
Regional organisational structure 58, 59
Registrar of Companies 29, 31, 32, 35
Reports 71
Research
- desk 178–9, 179
- field 177–9
- **market 175–182**
- *purposes and methods of* 176–7

Resignation 146
Responsibilities 11
Retail organisation 54–5
Retailers 202, 206–7

INDEX

Retirement 146
Return on capital employed (ROCE) 265
Revenue expenditure 240–1, 247
Roles 11
Roles of different people 14–15

S

Salary 117, 119, 121
Sale and leaseback 243
Sale of Goods Act 170
Sales
  – promotion 216
  – revenue 231
Sampling and questionnaires 180–1
Sampling
  – quota 180
  – random 180
Scale
  – diseconomies of 80–1
  – economies of 78–9
Selling, direct 204
Services 3
Sex Discrimination Acts 126
Shareholders 12–3, 28–30, 32–5
Shares
  – preference 243
  – private limited company 28–30, 242–3
  – public limited company 32–4, 243
  – rights issue/ordinary 242–3
Shopping mall 207
Sleeping partners 25
Social aspects of choosing business location 300–1

Sole trader 13, *18–23*, 41, 77, 246
Sources of finance (see Finance, sources of)
Span of control 49
Sponsorship 212, 218
Sponsorship and public relations 218
Stakeholder system 13
Stock control 289–294
  – *procedures* 290
Stock Exchange 28–9, 32, 246
Success, measuring 82–3
Supermarket 207
Supply 4, 5

T

Takeovers 84, 86–9
Tariffs 101
Taxes 98, 119
Technology 103–119
  – *effects of new* 108–9
Termination of employment 146–7
Total quality management (TQM) 50, 307
Trade
  – credit 247
  – Descriptions Act 170
  – promotion 217
  – unions 151, 153
Trading account 256–7, 260
Training
  – induction 142–3
  – on-/off-the-job 144–5
  – youth 137
Transport 298
Turnover 82
Types of economy 6–7

U

Unit costs 285
Unlimited liability 18, 21
Use of computers 104–5

V

Value Added Tax (VAT) 98, 198
Variable costs 231, 284
Vending machine 206
Venture capitalists 246
Video conferencing 107
Volume 83
Voluntary codes of practice 171

W

Wages 116, 119, 121
WAN 106, 107
Wants
  – consumer 3
  – worker 122
Warehouse
  – cash and carry 205
  – clubs 205
  – discount 207
Weight and Measures Act 170
Wholesaler 202, 203
Workers co-operative 38–41, 77
Working
  – capital 237
  – conditions 150

Y

Youth training 137